Understanding Juvenile Justice and Delinquency

Understanding Juvenile Justice and Delinquency

Marilyn D. McShane
and Michael Cavanaugh, Editors

 PRAEGER™

An Imprint of ABC-CLIO, LLC
Santa Barbara, California • Denver, Colorado

Library of Congress Cataloging-in-Publication Data

Names: McShane, Marilyn D., 1956– editor. | Cavanaugh, Michael R., 1981– editor.
Title: Understanding juvenile justice and delinquency / Marilyn D. McShane and Michael Cavanaugh, editors.
Description: Santa Barbara, California : Praeger, [2016] | Includes bibliographical references and index.
Identifiers: LCCN 2015026427 | ISBN 978-1-4408-3962-7 (hardback) | ISBN 978-1-4408-4359-4 (pbk) | ISBN 978-1-4408-3963-4 (ebk)
Subjects: LCSH: Juvenile justice, Administration of—United States. | Juvenile delinquency—United States. | Juvenile delinquents—Rehabilitation—United States. | Juvenile corrections—United States. | BISAC: LAW / Child Advocacy. | LAW / Criminal Law / Juvenile Offenders.
Classification: LCC HV9104 .U475 2016 | DDC 364.360973—dc23
LC record available at http://lccn.loc.gov/2015026427

ISBN: 978-1-4408-3962-7 (hardcover)
ISBN: 978-1-4408-4359-4 (paperback)
EISBN: 978-1-4408-3963-4

20 19 18 17 16   1 2 3 4 5

This book is also available on the World Wide Web as an eBook.
Visit www.abc-clio.com for details.

Praeger
An Imprint of ABC-CLIO, LLC

ABC-CLIO, LLC
130 Cremona Drive, P.O. Box 1911
Santa Barbara, California 93116-1911

This book is printed on acid-free paper ∞

Manufactured in the United States of America

In loving memory of James David Simonis (1985–2015)
—Aunt Marilyn

To Sarah, my loving wife
—Mike

Contents

Part I

The Changing Boundaries of Juvenile Justice Issues

PREFACE TO PART I: PERCEIVING IS BELIEVING

Tracing beliefs about the causes of delinquency over time, we find that theories ranged from demons and climate variations to glandular dysfunctions and a lack of wholesome recreational activities. Around the end of World War II, the editors of the *Saturday Evening Post* wrote that "sinister effects on the behavior and character of America's children constitute one of the greatest evils of this war. Statistics gathered from a number of places reveal a sharp nationwide increase in juvenile wrong-doing."[1] Despite the attraction of explaining delinquency based on contemporary and powerful social events, the problem of delinquency persists, as do some of its basic themes such as the influence of family and friends, and learning and economic pressures. In the Gluecks' treatise *Delinquents in the Making*, the authors state that "the riddle of crime is so puzzling that to arrive at adequate explanations calls for the collaboration of many sciences."[2] It is no surprise, then, that the science of criminology and criminal justice is as interdisciplinary as it is controversial.

Today's juvenile delinquency textbooks devote multiple chapters to theories of causation. Biological, sociobiological, psychological, and sociological approaches embrace the latest technologies, testing methods, data sets, and discoveries. The evolution of theories reflects the practice of theory integration, as better data collection and analysis methods allow us to carry forward the best predictors and the most accurate descriptors.

Above all, theorists today emphasize the complexity of delinquency that involves not only the overlap between victimization and offending but also the way the process of maturing over the life course impacts our associations and activities. Hopefully, this is something that you will take away from the chapters in this first part.

At this point it is also valuable to recognize that, despite the advances in theory and research, much of how we approach juvenile justice policy is based on personal beliefs about the causes of delinquency and anecdotal snippets of what might work for whom. Take a minute now to think about each of the factors listed in the following table that some consider to be related to delinquency. Do you think any of these are important as explanations of juvenile crime? As an exercise for approaching the chapters that will follow, take a few minutes to summarize how influential you think each factor is and explain how you think it plays a role in the development of juvenile delinquency, how that might be related to various types of crime, and how the process might work. A clear explanation might involve whether a factor is more influential under certain circumstances, more for some forms of crime, or for some types of people. After you fill in the grid, save a copy and compare it to how you view these factors at the end of the readings where we will visit this exercise again.

In this part's readings you will explore some of the most recent issues that shape the dynamic study of delinquency as well as the most contemporary explanations for them. We will look at how perceptions of offending and offenses are defined by the social context or the social reality of the current environment and how these might change over time as certain crime problems and their perceived priorities change.

Pre-test: Factors Possibly Related to Delinquency

Factors	Amount and Nature of Influence on Delinquency
Poverty	
Mental Illness	
Low Education Level	
Drug /Alcohol Abuse	
Family Problems (fighting, divorce, criminal history)	
Personality/Self-Esteem	
Anger or Revenge	
Peer Pressure	
Bad Neighborhoods	
Poor Parenting	
Low Self-Control	
Other	

Today, people receive information about crime from a variety of sources including personal experiences, family and friends, social and news media, and government data and agency reports. Many of these sources are colored by a political or economic agenda. In particular, this agenda allows them to create biased or filtered information in ways that support their cause or campaign. It can be argued, for example, that cyber-sexual exploitation has been sensationalized by the media in a way that often misrepresents what is, in fact, a relatively rare event. This form of bias occurs when incidents are reported in a way that suggests people are surprised that offenders have somehow adapted to and are exploiting a new and apparently successful means of committing offenses. Accounts seem to give one the impression that predatory behavior by sex offenders is increasing rather than the possibility that offenders are simply changing their modus operandi. This failure to clarify the context of crime, or compare incidence to the likelihood of other forms of victimization when weighted for frequency of use, suggests we have difficulty in seeing or understanding these new trends as a routine function of crime and as a function of lifestyle changes. Yet this is precisely how behaviors change and adapt to new situations; in other words, change and adaptation should be expected. Offenders have traditionally moved to newer and less easily detectable methods as potential victims alter the dynamics of interactions and become available and suitable as targets. Meanwhile law enforcement races to adjust to these changes and as it attempts to prevent further victimization. To criminologists this is a well-established and "normal" cycle of activity.

The following part is made up of three chapters. It starts with discussion of the linkage between juvenile victimization and offending. As Chapter 1 by Alida V. Merlo and Peter J. Benekos explains, the linkage between victimization and delinquency has been known in early criminological circles and continues today. The following two chapters (Chapter 2 by Ming Li Hsieh, Marilyn D. McShane, and Frank P. Williams III and Chapter 3 by Stephanie Fahy) discuss this linkage in a bit more detail, with Chapter 2 chronicling both the delinquency and victimization opportunities prevalent across the Internet and Chapter 3 explaining the change in classification of juveniles engaged in prostitution from delinquents to victims. As society continues to evolve, the juvenile justice system is increasingly viewing juvenile delinquency as a symptom of underlying problems, oftentimes victimization.

REFERENCES

"Are We Raising Another Lost Generation?" *Saturday Evening Post*, 216, April 29, 1944, 28.

Glueck, Sheldon, and Eleanor Glueck. *Delinquents in the Making: Paths to Prevention*. New York: Harper & Brothers Publishers, 1952.

Chapter 1

Maltreatment and Delinquency: Breaking the Cycle of Offending

Alida V. Merlo and Peter J. Benekos

The history of juvenile justice demonstrates opposing views on how to respond to youthful offenders and what the mission should be for the juvenile justice system. Social developments, economy, theory, and crime all have influenced the development of juvenile justice. During the 1980s, as rates of juvenile crime and violence began increasing, public policy for dealing with youthful offenders decidedly shifted to punishment, deterrence, and incapacitation. This get-tough response reflected classical and neoclassical assumptions about crime and underscored a more conservative, reactive approach to reducing crime. Legislative reforms were based on rational choice principles, which focused on individual decisions to commit crime and on using more severe sanctions to deter criminal behaviors. This punitive era of juvenile justice and the adultification of youth were consistent with Bernard and Kurlychek's cycle of juvenile justice, which described policy shifts from less punitive to more punitive sanctions to be followed by shifts back to less punitive responses.[3]

In the 2010s, the cycle to less punitive policies is demonstrated by efforts to raise the age of juvenile jurisdiction, to remove youth from the adult criminal justice system, to reduce the use of incarceration, to shorten periods of confinement, and to identify correlates of delinquent behavior.[4]

As a result of decreasing crime rates, increasing fiscal constraints, and expanding implementation of evidence-based programs, policymakers have supported efforts that reflect prevention, intervention, and treatment. The return to concerns about why youth commit crimes, what the effects of environment are on behaviors, and what can be done to prevent delinquency are compatible with the positivist perspective on crime and the emergence of rejuvenalization. An additional element of this shift to concerns about juveniles is attention to children and youth as victims as opposed to only perpetrators of crime and violence.[5]

CHILD VICTIMIZATION

In its report on child maltreatment, the U.S. Department of Health and Human Services reported that in the federal fiscal year of 2013 (runs from October 2012 to September 2013), there were 678,932 child victims of abuse and neglect (9.1 per 1,000 children in the population) compared to 693,484 victims in 2009 (9.3 per 1,000 children in the population).[6] This is a 3.8 percent decrease. The victimization rate for maltreatment was highest for children under one year of age: 23.1 per 1,000 children compared to 11.8 per 1,000 children over one year.[7] A 20-year comparison of maltreatment rates that was reported by Office of Juvenile Justice and

Figure 1.1
Maltreatment Victimization Rate per 1,000 Children Ages 0–17, 1990–2010[8]

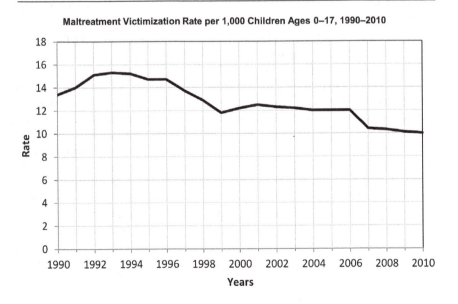

Delinquency Prevention (OJJDP) illustrates a declining trend in maltreatment from 13.4 per 1,000 children in 1990 to 10.0 per 1,000 children in 2010 (Figure 1.1).

Similarly, in its Fourth National Incidence Study of Child Abuse and Neglect report to Congress, the U.S. Department of Health and Human Services reported that the incidence of physical and sexual abuse and neglect had declined from 1993 to 2006.[9] The researchers also indicated that emotional neglect had increased since the last report; and it has been increasing since the 1990s. However, Sedlak et al. note in the 2010 report to Congress that the reported increase in emotional neglect could reflect a higher incidence or changes in policy and emphasis on such cases.[10] Specifically, children and youth who live in homes where there is domestic violence and/or alcohol or other drug abuse may be more likely to be included in this category due to greater collaboration with and sensitivity in child protective service agencies.[11]

In the case of child fatalities, the rates have decreased from 2.28 per 100,000 children in 2008 to 2.04 per 100,000 children in 2013 (Table 1.1). In 2013, of 1,315 child fatalities, 58.0 percent were boys and 41.7 percent were girls: 2.26 per 100,000 boys in the population compared to 1.77 per 100,000 girls in the population. Most child fatality victims were white (39.3%) compared to African American (33.0%) and Hispanic (14.5%).

Homicide is the third leading cause of death among youth between the ages of 10 and 24.[13] In addition to these data on child fatalities, the Federal Bureau of Investigation's (FBI) Supplementary Homicide Reports provide detailed demographic data on the victims of homicide. In 2013, the FBI reported that there were 1,027 victims under the age of 18 in the United States.[14] If victims under the age of 22 are included, there were 2,603 victims.[15] Although male youth are more likely to be victimized by homicide, it is the fourth leading cause of death for female youth between the ages of 10 and 24. Furthermore, the homicide rate of youth in the United States is considerably higher than that of countries with similar economic

Table 1.2
Child Fatality Rates per 100,000 Children, 2008–2013[12]

Reporting Year	National Rate per 100,000 Children
2008	2.28
2009	2.30
2010	2.08
2011	2.11
2012	2.19
2013	2.04

conditions. It is estimated that it ranges from 4 to 40 times higher than that of other comparable countries.[16]

TRAUMA AND CHILDREN EXPOSED TO VIOLENCE

In this context, Eric Holder, the U.S. attorney general, inaugurated a national commitment to address the effects of violence on children and youth. The Defending Childhood initiative, under the auspices of the U.S. Department of Justice, was unveiled in 2010 with the purpose of preventing children and youth from exposure to violence and mitigating the negative effects of exposure to violence on children and youth.[17] The Office of Justice Programs defines "exposure to violence" as "children's exposure to violence typically refers to children who witness or are victimized by violence. This includes physical assault, peer victimization, sexual victimization, child abuse and maltreatment, as well as witnessing (seeing or hearing) in the home, school, or community. Exposure to violence, particularly multiple exposures, can interfere with a child's physical, emotional, and intellectual development."[18]

The research that precipitated Holder's initiative identified that "children exposed to violence are more likely to abuse drugs and alcohol; suffer from depression, anxiety, and post-traumatic disorders; fail or have difficulty in school; and become delinquent and engage in criminal behavior."[19] The attorney general also convened a National Task Force on Children Exposed to Violence. That task force produced its final report and presented to Attorney General Holder in 2012. It included 56 recommendations and stressed the importance of identifying children and youth who are either victimized by violence or witness violence and offering them support and services.[20]

One of the major studies on child and youth victimization occurred in 2008. Between January and May 2008, the OJJDP collected data on childhood victimization with the National Survey of Children Exposed to Violence (NatSCEV).[21] The researchers gathered data on children and youth who were exposed to or victimized by violence in the prior year or earlier who were between the ages of one month to 17 years of age. Children and/or their caregivers responded to a series of questions regarding their current and prior victimization.

Finkelhor, Turner, Ormrod, Hamby, and Kracke[22] found that as many as 60 percent of children were exposed to violence, crime, or abuse, and as many as 40 percent were direct victims of two or more violent acts.[23] The findings of this government-funded study reinforced the conviction that children exposed to violence, as witnesses or victims, are at greater risk of committing crimes and acts of violence. In referring to this cycle of violence, Holder pledged federal resources and funding for prevention and intervention to break the cycle and to protect children from abuse and maltreatment.

Studies on youth victimization also include school violence. According to the Indicators of School Crime and Safety 2013 report, 749,200 students who ranged in age from 12 to 18 were the victims of violence at school. These data suggest that there are age differences associated with victimization rates at school. For those youth aged 12–14, the victimization rate was higher (65 per 1,000) than for youth aged 15–18 (41 per 1,000).[24] Male youth were more likely to be victimized than female youth, and urban and suburban residents had greater victimization rates than rural students. There were no significant differences in school victimization based on race or ethnicity among black, white, Hispanic, and Asian students. However, the data reflect a general trend that shows a decrease in youth victimization at school since 1992.[25]

In addition to studies on children and youth exposed to violence, crime, and abuse in school, research has been conducted on juvenile offenders. The Northwestern Juvenile Project study focused on 1,829 youth who were detained (pretrial) in Cook County, Illinois, in the 1990s. The results indicate that over 90 percent of the sample youth experienced one traumatic event, and approximately 57 percent had been exposed six or more times.[26] The most common trauma was witnessing violence; and 75 percent of the male youth and 63 percent of the female youth detained had such trauma. The researchers also found that one in 10 of the youth in the study had posttraumatic stress disorder (PTSD) in the year prior to the study.[27] The extent and consequences of youth victimization and trauma underscore the importance of prevention and intervention.

In her journalistic review of experiences of youth in custody, Bernstein reports on the abuse and mistreatment of adolescents confined in institutions, including excessive use of solitary confinement and physical and sexual abuse perpetrated by staff.[28] The youth and events that she describes reflect continuing concerns about the harmful effects of confining youth in detention centers and juvenile institutions. One example is solitary confinement for youth in custody. From the closing of juvenile facilities in Massachusetts[29] to the efforts in New York to reduce the number of youth sent to confinement,[30] there is clear evidence that children and youth who are placed in the care of juvenile justice professionals are often at risk for victimization and trauma.

Cycle of Violence

The cycle of violence hypothesis, that children exposed to abuse and neglect are at increased risk for criminal and violent behavior, is not new. In 1989, Widom reported findings on 908 substantiated cases of child abuse and the consequences of childhood victimization compared to a group of 667 nonofficially victimized children. Based on her cohort study, she concluded that childhood victimization was widespread and presented a "serious social problem that increases the likelihood of delinquency, adult criminality, and violent criminal behavior."[31] Abused or neglected children were more likely to have been arrested as delinquents (26% compared to 17%), as adults (29% compared to 21%) and for violent crime.[32] In disaggregating the types of abuse, she found that physical abuse resulted in the highest incidence of arrest for violent crimes (15.8%). Widom found higher rates of delinquency for children who were maltreated.

In an update of the study, Widom and Maxfield examined 1994 arrest data (compared to 1988 in the original study) and found similar outcomes.[33] Not only were physically abused children most likely to have been arrested for violent crime (21.1% compared to 20.2% for neglect only children and 13.9% for the control group), but victimized children were more likely to have been arrested as juveniles (27% compared to 17%), as adults (42% compared to 33%), and for violent crime (18% compared to 14%).[34] Widom and Maxfield also reported on additional detrimental consequences of childhood abuse including problems with mental health, education, occupation, and public health.[35] In discussing implications of their findings, the recommendations in 2001 were similar to those in 1992: intervene early, recognize the high risks of neglect and physical abuse, and reconsider out-of-home placement policies.[36]

While Widom and Widom and Maxfield examined the relationship of victimization and subsequent offending and violence, a broader question considers consequential behaviors of the exposure to violence. Cohen, Groves, and Kracke, for example, identify both direct and indirect exposure to violence in the home, school, and community, and describe the array of developmental problems that can result in children including depression, anxiety, aggression, conduct problems, and intellectual development.[37] While reactions to exposure to violence can be mitigated by social context, family dynamics, developmental stage, and other risk-protective factors, the researchers note that children who are chronically exposed to violence are at increased risk for "neurological changes" resulting from prolonged stress responses.[38] While childhood generally presents stressful experiences, Cohen, Groves, and Kracke discuss types of stress (e.g., positive, tolerable, and toxic) and consider how chronic and severe abuse and exposure to violence affect the stress management system.

Identifying children who have been abused and providing early intervention is significant in breaking the violence cycle. In efforts to assist law enforcement officers in recognizing abuse as opposed to injury, the OJJDP has released a fourth edition of its guide for investigating incidents of child injury.[39] The publication provides a checklist of conditions conducive to the risks for abuse as well as protocols for working with the medical community. In addition, the role of Children's Advocacy Centers (CAC) is acknowledged as integral to providing services and preparing medical evidence for prosecution.

The research presented by Cohen et al. essentially recognizes a distinction between exposure to traumatic events resulting in PTSD, and the effects of prolonged traumatic exposure identified as "developmental trauma disorder" (DTD), which is the diagnosis proposed by the National Child Traumatic Stress Network.[40] As distinguished from isolated traumatic incidents, "complex trauma" such as "chronic maltreatment or inevitable repeated traumatization . . . have a pervasive effects [*sic*] on the development of mind and brain."[41] In addition to problems of physical health, cognition, self-concept, and emotional responses, one of the common effects of prolonged trauma such as experienced by children exposed to violence is unstable or unpredictable attachments and relationships.[42] This results in problematic behaviors with authority figures such as teachers and police officers. Children exposed to violence in the home, school, and in the community are more likely to experience difficulty regulating their behaviors, developing a healthy worldview, and managing stressors.

In summary, victimized children and children exposed to violence are at greater risk for developing social dysfunctions and problematic behaviors, which are outcomes consistent with the dynamic relationship between victimization and delinquency.[43] Child abuse, neglect, and exposure to violence are traumatic experiences with detrimental consequences including victims who become offenders.[44] In their observation that "violence breeds violence," Weaver, Borkowski, and Whitman found that youth who experienced higher rates of victimization as children reported higher rates of violent behaviors in adolescence.[45]

CROSSOVER YOUTH

The recognition that children who come into contact with child protective services and child welfare agencies as victims may also be referred to juvenile justice systems as offenders presents challenges for responding to the population of dually-involved or crossover youth.[46] Goldstein reported that children receiving protective services, including residential placement, are at increased risk for engaging in delinquent and violent behaviors and for crossing over into juvenile justice systems.[47] Smith and Thornberry discussed the intergenerational transmission of violence and reported findings that supported the maltreatment-delinquency hypothesis.[48]

In describing this population of youth, Blakey, Campbell, and Bilchik distinguished among crossover youth, dually involved youth, and dually adjudicated youth, and focused on the importance of coordinated intervention with youth who experience maltreatment.[49] They presented information on the crossover youth practice model (CYPM), which provides for multiagency collaborative and comprehensive services and resulted in improved early identification of at-risk youth and decreased likelihood of receiving probation or correctional placement. Use of the informed practice model (CYPM) also reduced behavioral and mental health problems for post-model youth compared to pre-model youth.

Goldstein reported that the CYPM is used in 11 jurisdictions that are practicing more "coordinated case management and supervision" and fostering more effective partnerships and enhanced "stability and continuity of care."[50] Efforts to prevent and reduce the impact of exposure to violence recognize the importance of early identification and intervention.[51] With Department of Justice funding, eight communities were selected for demonstration projects to implement some of the strategies for preventing exposure to violence and mitigating harmful impact with early intervention. This includes use of evidence-based practices (EBP) and trauma-informed treatment.

TRAUMA-INFORMED CARE

From the perspective of staff working with youth in juvenile justice systems, delinquent and criminal youth have problem behaviors that are in need of treatment. While various interventions and EBPs can be effective, juvenile court and youth care professionals recognize obstacles to successful treatment including youth who are not motivated to change, who do not commit to treatment, who fail too easily, and who relapse too quickly.[52] In the context of traumatology, children who have been abused or exposed to violence, a trauma-informed approach to treatment presents a model that recognizes trauma as the "key to understanding treatment obstacles."[53] This model posits that the "problem behaviors" are coping behaviors or solutions that are used to protect the "sore spots" of trauma. In order to effectively treat the problem behaviors, the trauma must be addressed and resolved so youth can develop more stabilized behaviors and self-management skills.

The trauma-informed approach follows a series of steps that begins with providing a safe and structured environment in which sensitivity and success can be developed. As Bloom and Sreedhar explain, "Being trauma-informed means being sensitive to the reality of traumatic experiences."[54] In juvenile justice, as well as in child welfare organizations, this necessitates a different approach that includes a change in attitudes as well as culture.[55] It is an attempt to determine "what has happened to the youth" rather than "what is wrong with the youth." Researchers recommend screening all youth for trauma and assessing their needs when they enter the juvenile justice system.[56]

In a study of 74 youth aged 11–19 who were committed to state custody, Marrow, Knudsen, Olaf, and Bucher found that youth who received a special trauma focused intervention reported less depression and more optimism.[57] The youth were also involved in fewer threats of assaults on staff, and they were less likely to have to be restrained or placed in seclusion than the control group. Rather than just involving staff who are characterized as "treatment" staff, the intervention involved both treatment and "custody" staff and required them to work collaboratively in the facility. These data suggest that juvenile custodial facilities have the opportunity to intervene in the lives of youth who have been victimized successfully.

Research indicates that minority youth who live in inner-city neighborhoods experience significant trauma. Consistent with prior research, in their study of 65 youth (age 12–28) in Houston, Texas, Post, Hanten, Li, Schmidt, Avci, Wilde, and McCauley, found that over 80 percent of the sample reported two or more traumas.[58] The traumas were categorized as community, domestic, direct, and/or indirect. Although there were no differences in overall trauma among male and female participants, female participants were more likely to experience domestic trauma associated with forced or threatened forced sex and had higher PTSD scores than the male participants. The findings highlight the importance of gender responsive approaches to deal with the prevention and treatment of trauma.

Because of the trauma caused by violence, traditional approaches to treatment may actually exacerbate the problem behaviors. In contrast, the sanctuary model offers a trauma-informed, evidence-based approach that uses a psychoeducational model that changes both the organizational culture and the approach to working with troubled youth.[59]

In the Defending Childhood initiative, one of the goals is to "heal" youth who have been exposed to and traumatized by violence. The trauma-focused approach includes "trauma resolution" as a goal in reducing problem behaviors and traumatic symptoms.[60] As Bloom and Sreedhar explain, trauma-informed care can be used in a variety of settings to enable youth to confront unresolved traumas and to develop skills and behaviors to become "contributing and productive citizens."[61] As challenging as this may be for traumatized youth, it is also challenging for staff to learn, accept, and apply the assumptions and approaches predicated on this model. For example, Conners-Burrow et al. found that child welfare workers in an Arkansas study were successful in learning about trauma-informed practices but less consistent in implementing them.[62]

SIGNIFICANT CHANGES AND FUTURE CHALLENGES

In 2014, Robert Listenbee, the administrator of the OJJDP, testified before the Senate Judiciary Committee and identified the agency's goals in conjunction with the request for reauthorization of the Juvenile Justice and Delinquency Prevention Act (JJDPA).[63] In outlining OJJDP's initiatives, he stressed the importance of working with states to develop EBPs for prevention and intervention and noted that they should be "trauma informed" and relevant to the developmental needs of children and youth who are under the care or custody of the states.[64] His testimony reinforces the agency's continuing emphasis on these approaches and on programs that can prove their effectiveness.

In addition to federal efforts, states have made strides to address child and youth victimization and trauma. The state of Washington has developed a strategy to address adverse childhood experiences (ACE). In 2011, the legislature enacted reforms to address ACE.[65] Washington was the first state to acknowledge that ACE indicators like child abuse and neglect, observing domestic violence, and parental substance abuse can affect a child's ability to thrive at school, an adult's ability to succeed at work, to develop healthy relationships, and to be spared other behavior and physical health problems.[66] It is anticipated that other states will initiate programs and policies to reduce ACE among children and youth.

Researchers suggest that prevention and early intervention efforts can be initiated in high school as well as during prenatal care. These include making students and prospective parents aware of brain development and the effects of exposure to violence and trauma. Health care professionals can be trained to be more sensitive to victimization and traumatic experiences.[67] By referring children and their families for counseling or other services, professionals have the potential to deter further victimization and delinquent conduct. Historically, the system waited for a child to be referred to the juvenile justice system. The adoption of a more proactive and collaborative approach is an important step to address youth victimization and delinquency.

According to 2012 Washington State legislation (Final Bill Report E2SHB 2536, 2012), "Prevention and intervention services delivered to children and juveniles in the areas of mental health, child welfare, and juvenile justice be primarily evidence-based and research-based, and it is anticipated that such services will be provided in a manner that is culturally competent."[68] The legislators tasked two independent research groups with conducting the research and disseminating the results, the Washington State Institute for Public Policy (WSIPP) and the University of Washington Evidence-Based Practice Institute (UW).[69] Washington was the first state to mandate the collection and distribution of data and to commit to making policy and legislative decisions based on results.

In the area of juvenile justice, data on 18 different programs were published in 2013. The initiative documents what is working, how much it costs Washington taxpayers, and the odds of a positive net.[70] In terms of fiscal constraints, legislators now know the return on the state's investment and its success. Such policies will be expanded in the future and help guide approaches in juvenile justice and child welfare.

Recent changes also reflect the influence of technological advances. Technology facilitates the exchange of information on projects internationally and domestically. It also makes collaboration with other countries feasible. As Baum, Blakeslee, Lloyd, and Petrosino report, electronic publication makes it possible for research to be shared and disseminated easily around the world.[71] However, Baum et al. also stress the importance of communicating the information and research with practitioners and stakeholders using language that is clear and understandable.[72] They also discuss flexibility and sensitivity to local communities, their resources, and culture. In brief, prevention and intervention evidence based strategies are not "one size fits all" models.[73]

Finally, these collaborations, data, and prevention, intervention, and treatment strategies signify a change in attitudes toward youth victimization and youth offending. There is a greater understanding of youth development and the deleterious effects of child and youth exposure to violence. It is an opportune time to chart a new course guided by a more holistic focus for dealing with children and youth.

DISCUSSION QUESTIONS

1. What do we know about the rates of childhood victimization today?
2. What policies or changes in law could be developed to address the negative effects suffered by children exposed to violence?
3. Should we try to reduce the frequency with which we create "crossover youth" in trying to provide effective interventions? Why or why not?
4. If you were designing a program that is "trauma-informed" for working with youth, what specific elements would you include and why?

ADDITIONAL RESOURCES

Daglas, Rothanthi, Philippe Conus, Sue M. Cotton, Craig A. Macneil, Melissa K. Hasty, Linda Kader, Michael Berk, and Karen T. Hallam. "The Impact of Past Direct-Personal Traumatic Events on 12-Month Outcome in First Episode Psychotic Mania: Trauma and Early Psychotic Mania." *Australian and New Zealand Journal of Psychiatry* 48 (2014): 1017–1024.

Greeson, Johanna K. P., Ernestine C. Briggs, Christopher M. Layne, Harolyn M. E. Belcher, Sarah A. Ostrowski, Soeun Kim, Robert C. Lee, Rebecca L. Vivrette, Robert S. Pynoos, and John A. Fairbank. "Traumatic Childhood Experiences in the 21st Century: Broadening and Building on the ACE Studies with Data from the National Child Traumatic Stress Network." *Journal of Interpersonal Violence* 29, no. 3 (2013): 536–556.

Hanson, Rochelle F., and Jason Lang. "Special Focus Section: A Critical Look at Trauma Informed Care (TIC) among Agencies and Systems Serving Mal-treated Youth and Their Families." *Child Maltreatment* 19 (2014): 275–279.

Herz, Denise C., Joseph P. Ryan, and Shay Bilchik. "Challenges Facing Cross-Over Youth: An Examination of Juvenile-Justice Decision Making and Recidivism." *Family Court Review* 48, no. 2 (2010): 305–321.

Levenson, Jill S., Gwenda M. Willis, and David S. Prescott. "Adverse Childhood Experiences in the Lives of Female Sex Offenders." *Sexual Abuse: A Journal of Research and Treatment* 27, no. 3 (2014): 258–283.

Levenson, Jill S., Gwenda M. Willis, and David S. Prescott. "Adverse Childhood Experiences in the Lives of Male Sex Offenders: Implications for Trauma Informed Care." *Sexual Abuse: A Journal of Research and Treatment* (2014). doi: 1079063214535819.

RELATED WEBSITES

American Professional Society on the Abuse of Children (APSAC), http://www.apsac.org/

Center on Child Abuse and Neglect, http://www.oumedicine.com/pediatrics/department-sections/developmental-behavioral-pediatrics/center-on-child-abuse-and-neglect

Childhood Violent Trauma Center (CVTC), http://www.nccev.org/index.aspx

Juvenile Offenders and Victims: 2014 National Report, http://www.ojjdp.gov/ojstatbb/nr2014/downloads/NR2014.pdf

Program Profile: Adults and Children Together (ACT) Raising Safe Kids, https://www.crimesolutions.gov/ProgramDetails.aspx?ID=311

Sexually Assaulted Children: National Estimates and Characteristics, https://www.ncjrs.gov/pdffiles1/ojjdp/214383.pdf

SUPPORTING FILMS

An American Crime (2007)
Antwone Fisher (2002)
Sons of Perdition (2010)

NOTES

1. "Are We Raising Another Lost Generation." (1944), 28.
2. Glueck and Glueck (1952), 9.
3. Bernard and Kurlychek (2010).
4. Campaign for Youth Justice (2013).
5. Bernstein (2014).
6. U.S. Department of Health and Human Services (2010), 19.
7. Ibid., 22.
8. *OJJDP Statistical Briefing Book* (2012).
9. U.S. Department of Health and Human Services (2010).
10. Ibid.

11. Ibid., 20.
12. Ibid., 55.
13. Ibid.
14. "Crime in the United States 2013."
15. Ibid.
16. Centers for Disease Control and Prevention (2014).
17. U.S. Department of Justice (2009), 1.
18. "Juveniles: Children Exposed to Violence."
19. U.S. Department of Justice (2009), 1.
20. *The Juvenile Justice and Delinquency Prevention Act: Preserving Potential, Protecting Communities: Hearing before the Judiciary Committee, Senate,* 113th Congress, (2014). Statement of Robert Listenbee, Administrator with the Office of Juvenile Justice and Delinquency Prevention, 6.
21. Finkelhor, Ormrod, Turner, and Hamby (2012).
22. Ibid.
23. "Defending Childhood: Protect, Heal, Thrive."
24. U.S. Department of Justice (2014).
25. Ibid., iv.
26. Abram et al. (2013), 6.
27. Ibid., 7.
28. Bernstein (2014).
29. Miller (1998).
30. Papa (2011).
31. Widom (1992).
32. Ibid., 2.
33. Widom and Maxfield (2001).
34. Ibid., 3.
35. Ibid., 7.
36. Ibid.
37. U.S. Department of Justice (2009), 1.
38. Ibid., 2.
39. Office of Juvenile Justice and Delinquency Prevention (2014).
40. DeAngelis (2007); van der Kolk (2005).
41. van der Kolk (2005), 402.
42. Ibid.; National Child Traumatic Stress Network.
43. Cuevas, Finkelhor, Shattuck, Turner, and Hamby (2013); Widom (1989); Widom and Maxfield (2001).
44. Hodgdon, Kinniburgh, Gabowitz, Blaustein, and Spinazzola (2013).
45. Weaver, Borkowski and Whitman (2008), 108.
46. Blakey, Campbell, and Bilchik (2013); Goldstein (2012); Smith and Thornberry (1995).
47. Goldstein (2012), para. 2.
48. Smith and Thornberry (1995).
49. Blakey Campbell, and Bilchik (2013).

50. Goldstein (2012), para. 8.
51. Berson, Hernon, and Pearsall (2012), 270.
52. Greenwald (2009), 2.
53. Ibid., 3.
54. Bloom and Sreedhar (2008), 50.
55. Conners-Burrow et al. (2013); Bloom and Sreedhar (2008).
56. Baglivio et al. (2014), 13.
57. Marrow, Knudson, Olafson, and Butcher (2012).
58. Post et al. (2014).
59. "The Sanctuary Model: An Integrated Theory."
60. Greenwald (2009), 23.
61. Bloom and Sreedhar (2008), 52.
62. Conners-Burrow et al. (2013).
63. *The Juvenile Justice and Delinquency Prevention Act: Preserving Potential, Protecting Communities: Hearing before the Judiciary Committee, Senate,* 113th Congress, (2014). Statement of Robert Listenbee, Administrator with the Office of Juvenile Justice and Delinquency Prevention.
64. Ibid., 2.
65. "HB 1965-2011-2012: Concerning Adverse Childhood Experiences."
66. SHB 1965, C32, L11, E2, Sec.1, 2011, cited by Baglivio et al. (2014), 12.
67. Baglivio et al. (2014), 11.
68. Washington State Institute for Public Policy and University of Washington (2014).
69. Ibid.
70. Ibid.
71. Baum, Blakeslee, Lloyd, and Petrosino (2013).
72. Ibid.
73. Ibid., 6.

REFERENCES

Abram, Karen M., Linda A. Teplin, Devin C. King, Sandra L. Longworth, Kristen M. Emanuel, Erin G. Romero, Gary M. McClelland, Mina K. Dulcan, Jason J. Washburn, Leah J. Welty, and Nichole D. Olson. "PTSD, Trauma, and Comorbid Psychiatric Disorders in Detained Youth." *Juvenile Justice Bulletin.* Washington, DC: Office of Juvenile Justice and Delinquency Prevention, 2013.

Baglivio, Michael T., Nathan Epps, Kimberly Swartz, Mona Sayedul Huq, Amy Sheer, and Nancy S. Hardt. "The Prevalence of Adverse Childhood Experiences (ACE) in the Lives of Juvenile Offenders." *Journal of Juvenile Justice* 3, no. 2 (2014). 1–23.

Baum, Katrina, Katherine M. Blakeslee, Jacqueline Lloyd, and Anthony Petrosino. "Violence Prevention: Moving from Evidence to Implementation." Paper Discussion, Institute of Medicine, National Academy of Sciences, Washington, DC, October 15, 2013.

Bernard, Thomas J. and Kurlychek, Megan C. *The Cycle of Juvenile Justice,* 2nd edition. New York, NY: Oxford University Press, 2010.

Bernstein, Nell. *Burning Down the House: The End of Juvenile Prison*. New York: The New Press, 2014.

Berson, Sarah. B., Jolene Hernon, and Beth Pearsall. "Preventing Children's Exposure to Violence: The Defending Childhood Initiative." *National Institute of Justice Journal* 270, (2012): 26–29.

Blakey, Craig, Chad Campbell, and Shay Bilchik. "Improving Outcomes for Crossover Youth: Spreading Lessons Learned from Implementation of the Crossover Youth Practice Model." Lecture, Georgetown University Public Policy Institute, Center for Juvenile Justice Reform, Washington, DC, October 8, 2013. http://www.nga.org/files/live/sites/NGA/files/pdf/2013/1310HS PolicyInstituteJuvenileJustice.pdf.

Bloom, Sandra L., and Sarah Y Sreedhar. "The Sanctuary Model of Trauma-Informed Organizational Change." *Reclaiming Children and Youth: From Trauma to Trust* 17, no. 3 (2008): 48–53.

Campaign for Youth Justice. *State Trends: Legislative Victories from 2011–2013 Removing Youth from the Adult Criminal Justice System*. By Carmen Daugherty. Washington, DC: Campaign for Youth Justice, 2013.

Centers for Disease Control and Prevention. *Youth Violence: Opportunities for Action*. By Corinne David-Ferdon and Thomas R. Simon. Atlanta, GA: National Center for Injury Prevention and Control, Centers for Disease Control and Prevention, 2014.

Children's Bureau. *Child Maltreatment 2013*. Washington, DC: Children's Bureau, 2015. http://www.acf.hhs.gov/sites/default/files/cb/cm2013.pdf.

Conners-Burrow, Nicola A., Teresa L. Kramer, Benjamin A. Sigel, Kathy Helpenstill, Chad Sievers, and Lorraine McKelvey. "Trauma-Informed Care Training in a Child Welfare System: Moving it to the Front Line." *Children and Youth Services Review* 35, no. 11 (2013): 1830–1835.

"Crime in the United States, 2013." Federal Bureau of Investigation. http://www .fbi.gov/about-us/cjis/ucr/crime-in-the-u.s/2013/crime-in-the-u.s.-2013.

Cuevas, Carlos. A., David Finkelhor, Anne Shattuck, Heather Turner and Sherry Hamby. "Children's Exposure to Violence and the Intersection between Delinquency and Victimization." *Juvenile Justice Bulletin*. Washington, DC: Office of Juvenile Justice and Delinquency Prevention, 2013.

David-Ferdon, Corinne, and Thomas R. Simon. *Preventing Youth Violence: Opportunities for Action*. Atlanta, GA: National Center for Injury Prevention and Control, Centers for Disease Control and Prevention, 2014.

DeAngelis, Tori. "A New Diagnosis for Childhood Trauma? Some Push for a New DSM Category for Children Who Undergo Multiple, Complex Traumas." *Monitor on Psychology* 38, no. 3 (2007): 32.

"Defending Childhood: Protect, Heal, Thrive." U.S. Department of Justice. http:// www.justice.gov/ag/defendingchildhood/dc-factsheet.pdf.Federal Bureau of Investigation. "Supplementary Homicide Reports, 1980–2010." http:// ojjdp.gov/ojstatbb/ezashr/asp/off_selection.asp.

Finkelhor, David, Richard Ormrod, Heather Turner, and Sherry Hamby. "Child and Youth Victimization Known to Police, Schools, and Medical Authorities." *Juvenile Justice Bulletin*. Washington, DC: Office of Juvenile Justice and Delinquency Prevention, 2012.

Finkelhor, David, Richard Ormrod, Heather Turner, Sherry Hamby and Kristen Kracke. "Children's Exposure to Violence: A Comprehensive National

Survey." *Juvenile Justice Bulletin*. Washington, DC: Office of Juvenile Justice and Delinquency Prevention, 2009.

Goldstein, Brian. "'Crossover Youth': The Intersection of Child Welfare & Juvenile Justice." *Juvenile Justice Information Exchange*, November 15, 2012. http://jjie .org/crossover-youth-intersection-of-child-welfare-juvenile-justice/.

Greenwald, Ricky. *Treating Problem Behaviors: A Trauma-informed Approach*. New York: Routledge/Taylor & Francis, 2009.

Hodgdon, Hilary B., Kristine Kinniburgh, Dabowitz Gabowitz, Margaret E. Blaustein, and Joseph Spinazzola. "Development and Implantation of Trauma-Informed Programming in Youth Residential Treatment Centers Using the ARC Framework." *Journal of Family Violence* 28, no. 7 (2013): 679–692.

"HB 1965–2011–2012: Concerning Adverse Childhood Experiences." Washington State Legislature. http://apps.leg.wa.gov/billinfo/summary.aspx?year= 2011&bill=1965.

"Juveniles: Children Exposed to Violence." CrimeSolutions.gov. https://www .crimesolutions.gov/TopicDetails.aspx?ID=60#Overview.

Marrow, Monique T., Kraig J. Knudsen, Erna Olafson, and Sarah E. Bucher. "The Value of Implementing TARGET within a Trauma-Informed Juvenile Justice Setting." *Journal of Child & Adolescent Trauma* 5, no. 3 (2012): 257–270.

Miller, Joan G. *Last One Over the Wall: The Massachusetts Experiment in Closing Reform Schools*, 2nd edition. Columbus, OH: Ohio State University Press, 1998.

National Child Traumatic Stress Network. "Effects of Complex Trauma." http:// www.nctsn.org/trauma-types/complex-trauma/effects-of-complex-trauma.

Office of Juvenile Justice and Delinquency Prevention. *Recognizing When a Child's Injury or Illness Is Caused by Abuse: Portable Guide to Investigating Child Abuse*. By Robert Hugh Farley, Beoncia Loveless, Vincent J. Palusci, and Andrea Taroli. Washington, DC: Office of Juvenile Justice and Delinquency Prevention, 2014. http://www.ojjdp.gov/pubs/243908.pdf.

"*OJJDP Statistical Briefing Book, 2012*." Office of Juvenile Justice and Delinquency Prevention. http://www.ojjdp.gov/ojstatbb/default.asp.

Papa, Anthony. "Gov. Cuomo's Victory to Close Down Troubled Juvenile Detention Facilities." *The Huffington Post*, April 5, 2011. http://www.huffington post.com/anthony-papa/gov-cuomo-closes-juvenile-centers_b_844669 .html.

Post, Marina, Gerri Hanten, Xiaoqi Li, Adam T. Schmidt, Gunes Avci, Elizabeth A. Wilde and Stephen R. McCauley. "Dimensions of Trauma and Specific Symptoms of Complex Posttraumatic Stress Disorder in Inner-City Youth: A Preliminary Study." *Violence and Victims* 29, no. 2 (2014): 262–279.

"The Sanctuary Model: An Integrated Theory." The Sanctuary Model. http:// www.sanctuaryweb.com/sanctuary-model.php.

Smith, Carolyn, and Terence P. Thornberry. "The Relationship between Childhood Maltreatment and Adolescent Involvement in Delinquency." *Criminology* 33, no. 4 (1995): 451–481.

U.S. Department of Health and Human Services. *Fourth National Incidence Study of Child Abuse and Neglect (NIS–4): Report to Congress*. By Andrea J. Sedlak,

Jane Mettenburg, Monica Basena, Ian Petta, Karla McPherson, Angela Greene, and Spencer Li. Washington, DC: Administration for Children and Families, 2010.

U.S. Department of Justice. *Indicators of School Crime and Safety: 2013*. By Simone Robers, Jana Kemp, Amy Rathbun, and Rachel E. Morgan. Washington, DC: Office of Justice Programs, 2014.

U.S. Department of Justice. *Understanding Children's Exposure to Violence*. By Elena Cohen, Betsy McAlister Groves, and Kristen Kracke. North Bethesda, MD: Safe Start Center, Office of Juvenile Justice and Delinquency Prevention, 2009.

van der Kolk, Bessel A. "Developmental Trauma Disorder: Toward a Rational Diagnosis for Children with Complex Trauma Histories." *Psychiatric Annals* 33, no. 5 (2005): 401–408.

Washington State Institute for Public Policy. *Benefit–Cost Results*. Olympia, WA: Washington State Institute for Public Policy, 2014. http://www.wsipp.wa.gov/BenefitCost/WsippBenefitCost_AllPrograms.

Washington State Institute for Public Policy and University of Washington Evidence-Based Practice Institute. *Updated Inventory of Evidence-Based, Research-Based, and Promising Practices for Prevention and Intervention Services for Children and Juveniles in the Child Welfare, Juvenile Justice, and Mental Health Systems*. Olympia, WA: Washington State Institute for Public Policy, 2014. http://www.wsipp.wa.gov/ReportFile/1553/Wsipp_Updated-Inventory-of-Evidence-based-Research-based-and-Promising-Practices-for-Prevention-and-Intervention-Services-for-Children-and-Juveniles-in-the-Child-Welfare-Juvenile-Justice-and-Mental-Health-Systems_Full-Report.pdf.

Weaver, Chelsea M., John G. Borkowski, and Thomas L. Whitman. "Violence Breeds Violence: Childhood Exposure and Adolescent Conduct Problems." *Journal of Community Psychology* 36, no. 1 (2008): 96–112.

Weisler, Benjamin, and Michael Schwirtz. "U.S. Inquiry Finds a 'Culture of Violence' against Teenage Inmates at Rikers Island." *New York Times*, August 4, 2014. http://www.nytimes.com/2014/08/05/nyregion/us-attorneys-office-reveals-civil-rights-investigation-at-rikers-island.html?module=Search&mabReward=relbias:r,{"1":"RI:8"}

Widom, Cathy S. "The Cycle of Violence." *National Institute of Justice, Research in Brief*. Washington, DC: U.S. Department of Justice, National Institute of Justice, 1992.

Widom, Cathy S. "The Cycle of Violence." *Science* 244, no. 4901 (1989): 160–166.

Widom, Cathy S., and Michael G. Maxfield. "An Update on the 'Cycle of Violence.'" *National Institute of Justice, Research in Brief*. Washington, DC: U.S. Department of Justice, National Institute of Justice, 2001.

Chapter 2

Juveniles in Cyberspace: Issues in Enforcement and Parental Controls

Ming Li Hsieh, Marilyn D. McShane, and Frank P. Williams III

> It may seem like fun and games, and a lot of kids may think that they're too smart to fall for it. But that's not the case. . . . You can't be too careful. Very scary and serious things can happen.
> —Danielle Helms, mother of a 14-year-old girl who committed suicide after being sexually victimized by an older man she met online[1]

A recent White House report related that there are now "more than four billion digital wireless devices in the world" and that "a third of the world's population uses the Internet" as well as other forms of information and communication technology (ICT) in their daily life.[2] YouTube claims that its popularity amounts to more than 6 billion hours per month, 1 hour for every person on earth.[3] Once Facebook, iTunes, Instagram, and Twitter are added to the mix, teen use of these technologies easily surpasses the hours spent viewing any U.S. cable network. A recent study of 13- to 18-year-olds found that the "five most influential celebrities among the population are YouTube personalities."[4] The meaning of these facts could be interpreted through a generational lens, as has always been the case with the advent of new media forms. With each new genré of media, objections and criticisms are proffered by older generations who frequently see these new pastimes as a "cause" or contributing factor in delinquency. In some ways, these concerns may simply be a product of age-based conflicts with reflections of long-held generational disagreements concerning popular culture and taste. While, to some extent, contemporary news media play a role in inciting concern over the risk of these influences, the fact that research on, and knowledge of the, consequences of new genré media has been mixed and inconclusive has not helped either. Making matters even more equivocal is that modern Web-based information allows opinion on controversial matters to be misrepresented as solid research-based fact, thus creating public confusion about the real nature of risks involved. This confusion is not simply a matter of parents' overestimating threats to their children, but it also allows for the implementation of policies and laws that may appear to protect children against low-risk and worst-case scenarios as if they were common events.

Regulating access to perceived threats to the safety and well-being of children has long been recognized as a parental responsibility. The issue, however, lies in how one defines "responsibility." In fact, parents today face increasing pressure over a growing body of legal measures instituted to clarify social norms for raising children. The courts have, in many cases, found parents negligent and liable for failure to maintain and support their children according to rapidly evolving standards in a number of areas, including medical care, gang membership, vandalism, and debts accrued because of long-distance phone calls, credit cards, and cyber activities. Where the last of this is concerned, there is increased emphasis on proper supervision, parents being reported to child welfare services, and youngsters being harmed by Internet pornography. One product of this emphasis has been the spawning of a cottage industry of V-chips, Amber Alerts, fingerprint and DNA kits, and even home urinalysis testing, as well as sophisticated rating systems for video games, movies, and Internet sites. All of this justifies an examination of the nature, evidence, and assumptions behind the perceived high risk to children created by today's Internet.

THE HOME AND CHILD SAFETY: THE INTERNET AS A SOCIAL PROBLEM

An examination of the current sources of parental fears brings to mind the cultural and popular belief that views the home as a private sanctuary—a fact legally enshrined in the U.S. Constitution—creating a "safe-haven." In some cases, the image is so powerful that it causes difficulties in our embracing reality. Nowhere is this truer than in the perception that child sex offenders are strangers who lurk outside the home when most of them are, according to evidence from years of victimization studies,[5] relatives and friends. To raise concerns about events that take place within the home itself is to risk destroying the cherished notion of home sanctuary. Thus, parents are more comfortable with the notion that strangers are the real threat to their children, even in the context of the internet.

In situations that magnify the fears that are shared by members of a group, social scientists have identified a systematic set of events, otherwise known as the construction of a social problem (sometimes called "moral panics"). Social problems are based on a real or perceived threat to social order but are not tied to the actual prevalence of the threat. Instead the important factor is the degree of concern elicited by the threat, as brought to our attention by media and moral entrepreneurs (people or agencies who, for all good reasons, have a vested interest in the threat). Claims-making by the initial moral entrepreneurs are universally exaggerated, and the claimed facts are almost never checked in the beginning. When the threat involves members of society who are most protected, ideas and images that are most sacred, and/or "heinous" misdeeds, the claims are sensational and spread quickly through the media.

All of this results in multiple calls to "do something quickly." In the heat of the moment, other claimed instances of the threat surface, thus making it appear that the threat is growing. Action and social policy is, then, not far behind. History and a plethora of academic studies have demonstrated time and again that the threat or problem is rarely "worse" than at other times but our attention (and the attention of the moral entrepreneurs) simply makes it seem so. At some point in the future, the pubic usually loses interest or another problem catches our attention and the social problem dissipates.

Given this process, it would seem that a combination of nervousness about new forms of Internet technology, societal drives to protect children, and the concept of home, in conjunction with an already-existing social problem—sex offenders—would bring into play the elements most likely to precipitate a new version of a social problem. Indeed, it would be difficult to imagine an image of greater perceived threat than that of a child, playing in her own bedroom, being solicited by a stranger intent on sexual molestation. The fact is that this combination of ingredients is powerful enough to literally demand recognition as a social problem. And it did, spawning an industry of different technical methods of controlling access to Internet content and of assisting parents with recommended ways of supervising children when online. In support of the claims of online sex offenders preying on children, the Federal Bureau of Investigation (FBI) has taken an interest and reports that online predators are everywhere, adding that more than half-a-million pedophiles are online every day seeking a chance to find so-called easy victims, building emotional bonds and connections with teenagers and making "friends."[6] In an effort to reduce violent crimes against child, and the vulnerability of children to both in-person and cyber-sexual exploitation, threats, and abuse, the FBI has established an Endangered Child Alert Program (ECAP) to combat the sexual exploitation of children online and map safety guides[7] for parents and children.

Not all of the effects of our efforts and policies to protect children have been clearly desirable, however. We have already noted a steadily increasing governmental intrusion into parenting and new definitions of what it means to be a "responsible" parent. Other problems have resulted from hasty and sometimes overzealous policies promoted to protect children from cyber predators. There is little doubt that rapid advances in technology and consumer demands have created greater access to cyber communications, especially for younger generations. This access, as well as sometimes-oppressive approaches to controlling it, has opened debate about social control and reinterpretation of basic rights and freedoms vis-à-vis the risks of potential victimization and other forms of criminal behavior. Issues generating controversy range from free speech and expression to commerce between consenting adults and the possibility of civil rights violations in the promotion of practices that subjugate, discriminate, and oppress groups protected by age, race, gender, and religion. With a drive toward controlling or banning certain violent or sexually explicit materials on the Internet, or at least attempting to regulate or control them, these issues appear to be taking on the form of another social problem.

E-KIDS AND E-RISKS

In our contemporary cyber-society, children spend considerable amounts of time alone in an electronic environment with computers, tablets, phones, video games, and sophisticated music systems. "Teens" (often defined as the ages from 8 to 18) spend approximately 7 hours and 38 minutes per day on electronic devices and the duration of media exposure and media use has constantly grown longer over the past decades.[8] In 2003, according to the U.S. Census Bureau, approximately 47 million children (age 3 to 17) lived in a household with at least one computer, with over 90 percent of teens (age 15 to 17) accessing the Internet at home.[9] By 2011, about 52 million children were living in a home with at least one computer.[10] More importantly, however, some 60 percent of them were no longer limited to accessing the Internet at home.[11] Some 95 percent of those aged 12 to 17 are now estimated to be online every day, with about 74 percent of these as "mobile Internet users" who access the Internet with mobile devices, such as smart phones and tablets, anytime and anywhere.[12]

Although most of us were raised with exposure to the effects of a growing mass media, the vastness of the Internet and its capabilities are still disconcerting to older generations. For teens, though, the Internet is unquestionably an integral part of their everyday life and, in particular, their social life. And, because accessing the Internet is no longer limited to using computers at home or school, the younger generation's experience is much more likely to include mobile electronic devices such as smart-phones and tablets. As a result, for teens, much of their electronic activity takes place outside the home in unsupervised settings where conventional parental wisdom places both "danger" and "strangers." These outside cyber activities involve browsing the Web, texting, e-mailing, using social networking sites and chat rooms, sharing pictures and videos, making phone calls, and listening to music. Clearly, portable devices may also extend the potential risks of cyber-victimization for children if they can (or have permission to) use electronic devices (especially smartphones) whenever they want.

While home is still a common station of computer access, family income and parents' education are significantly and positively related to the proportion of children who use the Internet, and also *how* they use the Internet. Those from homes with higher incomes and parental educational levels are also more likely to involve in higher online activity, while being more immersed in social networking. The FBI reports that children are more at risk online when they connect to social networking sites, gaming forums, and chat rooms where predators often target children by specific activities, traits, or needs that they identify.[13]

This chapter explores a few of the most controversial areas of youthful offending and victimization related to exploration and activity using some of the more popular modern technologies. Many of these products and services have resulted in parental, as well as governmental, attempts to regulate children's behavior and access to these technologies. Many of these products have an ambiguous nature, particularly those of Internet "pornography," "violent" video games, texting, sexting, and personal websites. These activities and products are frequently interrelated and, in many ways, have been subject to scrutiny in earlier forms, such as television and movie violence, sexually oriented magazines, and the home video industry. We will also discuss some of the things parents can do and law enforcement has done more proactively to address Internet safety.

THE TECHNOLOGICAL REVOLUTION AND ITS EFFECTS

Even from the early days of public access to the Internet and personal computers, some were concerned over the fact that racist or hate groups, pedophiles, pornographers, and Satan worshippers all have access to videos, cable television channels, and computer bulletin boards. Trends have established, however, that online criminal operations are complex, are international, and increasingly involve children of younger ages.

A number of the more notorious hackers and spammers have been young people as news reports that a 15-year-old admitted hacking into National Aeronautical and Space Administration (NASA) computers, a 13-year-old hacked into his school testing system database and in China, a 12-year-old hacked into an Internet pricing system to reduce the cost of an item purchased from $400 to 16 cents. A network of hackers even sponsor a convention, DEF CON, each year, including a workshop for kids, where those aged 8–18 compete to find bugs in mobile apps, learn about digital forensics, and even teach classes and give talks.[14] The ability to work from home and in one's spare time has made some more illicit market activities attractive for the underaged compensation seeker. Others simply delight in the ability to crack into secure websites and to brag to online groups of colleagues about their technological skills. Downloading music, films, and videos illegally is also a common offense that worries business and criminal justice investigators. The pirating and illegal reproduction of copyrighted material amount to billions of dollars lost to the industry each year. This fact also worries delinquency experts who argue that the benefits and lack of sanctions at this level not only encourage criminal activity, but also may escalate into higher rates and more serious levels of offenses in the future.

Cyberbullying: An Extension of School Bullying

Years ago, the typical bully was a school-yard menace who physically intimidated children on the playground or engaged in verbal bullying by saying or writing hurtful taunts in schools. Now cyberbullying is an extensive array of new approaches including embarrassing photos that involve a much wider audience at the speed of instant messaging.

In school year 2010–11, there were 2,198,000 students (ages 12 to 18) who reported cyberbullying of various types such as receiving hurtful information on the Internet and being contacted through unwanted e-mail, texting, and instant messaging.[15] The nature of cyberbullying has considerable negative psychological effects and may impact all different age groups although in many cases, this event shares some similarities with more traditional school bullying. Slonje, Smith, and Frisén explain:

> Overall, cyberbullying and traditional bullying appear to have broadly similar negative impacts [such as feelings of anger, fright, depression and embarrassment]; but some features of cyberbullying, especially anonymity, lack of a safe haven, and embarrassment due to the potentially large breadth of audience, can make the impact of cyberbullying especially strong, for some young people and in some circumstances.[16]

The convenience of the Internet has extended cyberbullying to any-where and anytime as long as there is electronic access. For instance, Face-book is a platform for the potential extension of bullying from school to an adolescent's daily life.[17] Even though the percentage of school bullying is still higher than the percentage of cyberbullying, if bullying occurred, those adolescents who had been involved in school bullying were also involved with Facebook bullying.[18] Moreover, adolescents who had been victimized in school were more likely to be victimized on Facebook as well.[19] With the prevalence of social networks, adolescents have more opportunities to engage in bullying and become the victim of bullying. The possible harm, both mental and physical, has increased as well.

News reports claim that a 12-year-old girl in Florida committed sui-cide after being bullied online. Parents of a middle-school student who received violent and threatening sexually explicit e-mails, allegedly from a classmate, demanded that the school take punitive action. While stories like these are common in the media today, officials claim there is often lit-tle they can do. Aggressive antibullying measures in schools are difficult to enforce in communications sent and received outside of the classroom and over the weekend and holidays.[20] The difficulty in tracking and sub-stantiating specific users in anonymous communications further compli-cates attempts to address this issue with disciplinary measures.

Fortunately, the same advanced technology that increases the likeli-hood of children's risk of harm and victimization in a virtual world[21] also might offer solutions. Motivated by the distress of a bullied little sister, two tech-savvy students developed an app, named Bully Alert, that allows bullying victims to report the incident without being seen talk-ing to a teacher or principal. The advantage of Bully Alert is that "there's no need to know email addresses or phone numbers for text messages, and reports can be made confidentially from mobile devices and comput-ers."[22] The app also improves over previous reporting methods by allow-ing the incident to go directly to the school and not the regional or school district headquarters. The app is currently being piloted at schools in the Clark County Nevada area by its developers Marcos Ontiveros, Blaze Brooks, Evan Savar, and Sokoll.[23] Another app STOPit has also been used to allow student to anonymously report cyberbullying to both school offi-cials and legal authorities.[24]

Given the extension of bullying through the use of ICT, middle-school students and highschool students are more vulnerable as either bullies and victims or both in a cyberworld.[25] The prevalence of cyberbullying includes posting hurtful information and mean words and pictures, send-ing harassing messages and e-mails, and spreading rumors that cross gender, race/ethnicity, and grade-level boundaries. Consequently, youth who are victimized are more likely to manifest depression, which acts as a risk factor for suicide,[26] when poorly dealing with peer aggression.

Cyberbullying has also been found to enhance the likelihood of suicidal thoughts and behaviors more than traditional bullying.[27] Researchers have demonstrated a correlation between depression, cyberbullying, and suicide for youth as the following findings indicate[28]:

- Depression is a considerable risk factor for suicide attempt for both genders.
- Male cyberbullies are more likely to be directly associated with suicide attempts.
- Female cyber-victims are more likely to have suicidal behaviors resulting from depression.

Children who have their own profile on any kind of social network sites and currently use them are at twice the risk of being bullied on the Internet than those who do not have an active profile on social network sites.[29] Cyberbullying has escalated that scenario on a global scale, causing teens considerable embarrassment and emotional trauma.[30] Today, 37 percent of children report an experience of cyberbullying that engaged mean, cruel, and threatening behavior and other forms of online harassment.[31] Children who experienced cyberbullying were more likely to report being a victim of any crime at school as well.[32] There is also some indication that children may try to stay home and avoid school because of fears related to this form of intimidation.

Access to Pornography Online

Another concern for parents is the fact that erotica is not hidden on the Internet. The initial moral panic over the availability of Internet pornography was primarily a computer bulletin boards (CBB) issue and availability was scarce, even for adults. Since that time, the growth of the graphics-based Internet, the World Wide Web (WWW), has made the technical abilities required to access materials rather moot. The focus of the WWW is a transparent use of the Internet, even for those who have no knowledge of the technology behind it. Thus browsers require no knowledge of downloading and compiling techniques; no identification of the types of file formats; and no specialized software to access graphics, texts, and blogs for any social media sites (e.g., Facebook, Instagram, Twitter, Pinterest) or other websites. Everyone can easily "stock" any child pornography-related images, text, and videos on personal computers and can either downloaded for free or subscribed for a fee that varied by degree of "customer needs."

Further, the growth and sophistication of search engines such as Google and Yahoo! make expertise in locating information moot, as well. Rarity of an item or type of material is no longer a bar to locating it. A simple search term and a click of the mouse are all that is necessary to bring up virtually any subject, text, or graphic on today's browsers.[33] Today's children, just like adults, have unparalleled access to information, including erotic content. Research shows that 96 percent of adolescents had Internet access and 55.4 percent of those had visited sexually explicit websites (SEWs) (i.e., X-rated or pornographic websites).[34] Adolescents are exposed to SEWs were more likely to have sexually permissive attitudes and with a higher propensity to engage in high-risk sexual behaviors[35] along with other risks of victimization.

In the early 1990s, the Justice Department's Child Exploitation and Obscenity Section established "Operation Long Arm" to track and prosecute child pornography transmitted from personal computers to network bulletin boards. They focused on paid subscribers who downloaded pornographic text, images, and computer games through various child pornography electronic bulletins.[36] Officials in Mexico and the United States claimed to have broken a child pornography ring run through e-mail with a $250 subscription and other additional fees. The investigation involved sites in New Jersey, California, Chicago, and Tijuana and included 2,000 subscribers of hard-core pornography.[37] State agents also shut down and seized the equipment from bulletin boards suspected of transmitting obscene photos and selling pornographic documents. A couple from California was charged and convicted of 11 counts of distributing pornography via interstate phone lines that depicted, among other things, bestiality. In that case, the materials were on a members-only bulletin board and downloaded by a postal inspector in Memphis.[38] Recently, a teacher in California was arrested on child pornography allegations even though he was not accused of creating it. The local police found that he had at least 1,000 video images of child pornography (ages 4 to 9) saved on his home computer and federal charges are pending.[39]

While sexual predators and potential kidnappers seem to represent the major thrust of media coverage, access to pornography is a much more common experience and, according to some surveys, a greater parental concern. According to a Pew Research Center (PRC) survey, parents feared that their children's privacy might be violated and their behavior could be monitored by others.[40] The parent concerns were meeting and interacting with strangers (72%), accessing undesirable information and advertisers (81%), and impacting children's reputations (69%).[41] The pedophile or pornography-producing entrepreneur has developed a more sophisticated operation over the years from the use of the Polaroid to the home video, from watching the CD/DVD at home to watching live streaming video online, and from use of hard-line paid telephones for phone sex to using visual chat rooms on the Internet. These advances have allowed better quality production while still affording privacy and the appearance of common household technology. Pornography businesses have also adapted various mainstream sale and distribution techniques that allow consumers's convenience and anonymity.

In fact, most pornography businesses do not deny "young" populations access to their material. Even though SEWs ask whether viewers are of legal age, only 3 percent of these websites would verify and require proof of age.[42] In other words, a 12-year-old adolescent could access most SEWs by simply entering "I am age 21" or clicking on the "I am an adult" box if the homepages have viewer "age restrictions." A majority of minors (grades 7 to 11) reported in a Canadian survey that they never looked for pornography online, yet that "majority" of nonviewers is misleading because of gender differences.[43] Eighty-eight percent of boys reported have visited sites containing pornography or have looked at pornography at least once a month or more; girls are less likely to do so but did report looking for online pornography once a year.[44] The trend among minors of seeking out pornography online has continually increased in the past years.[45]

Online Sexual Predators and Victimization through Social Media Networking

Ninety percent of teenagers (age 13 to 17) have used social media and among 75 percent of them have an active profile online.[46] Facebook is the most popular social networking site among teenage users followed by Twitter, Google Plus, and MySpace.[47] The results of a PRC survey on privacy online and teenagers found that, in general, the moderate teen Facebook users have around 300 friends, while teen Twitter users have 79 followers.[48] Teens appear to be more likely to divulge an array of information about themselves and daily life on social media sites to expand their social networks with respect to making friends, keeping social life, and managing relationships than they did in the past. Basic profile details that teenagers usually post on the Internet are real name (92%), photos of themselves and selfies (91%), interests and hobbies (84%), date of birth (82%), school name (71%), living location (71%), relationship status (62%), e-mail address (53%), phone number (20%), and videos of themselves (24%).[49] Sixteen percent of teenagers would like to use advanced profile functions that enable the automatic inclusion of location to tag themselves with friends in a current location when they post information.[50] The majority of teenagers, however, reported that they are not very concerned about others accessing their personal data.[51]

However, social media networking is a good recourse for sexual predators and as "jackpot" for pedophiles to gain information about targeted subjects. The effect of online socialization seems to grant availability of victimization as a high-risk behavior. Trends of receiving online harassment have also increased from 2000 to 2010.[52] Reported cases of sexual predation on the Internet indicate that social media and network life appear to become a soil of sexual crime. The accounts also reflect a diverse group of predators and methods even though, according to research, most Internet predators are older men and victims are teenagers.[53] There are reports of 17 percent of teens having received contact in a way that made them uncomfortable and feel scared on the Internet.[54] Some of these cases result in arrests. A Pennsylvania man was arraigned on one count of unlawful sexual conduct with a 15-year-old girl. He had been communicating and maintaining a relationship with the girl through social media for more than a year.[55] Stephen A. Martin, 38, a male teacher, enticed an under-age girl to lure a 12-year-old boy into a relationship by making friends on Facebook. Martin possessed 9,500 child pornography pictures and around 2,000 videos were found during the investigation.[56]

Sexual predators, pornographers, and prostitution rings are rising through using social media across all kinds of ICT.[57] In 2010, the national hotline received 223,374 cases for reporting cyber-sexual exploitation of children.[58] A special agent from the Georgia Bureau of Investigation who is in charge of Child Exploitation and Computer Crime Unit indicated that sexual predators have evolved and "worked their language down to an art on how to approach children who don't think anybody else cares about their problems or wants to spend time with them."[59] As long as children routinely share personal information on social media, the likelihood of them being a target would still cause concern. In fact, pedophiles now find a cunning way to avoid charges of pornography by using stolen family and teen pictures from social media profile pages. In the United Kingdom, sex predators surf the Internet and "steal" child images that they had taken by themselves or shared by friends or copy pictures that parents have taken of their children on some special occasions that have their children dressed on beach holidays to build their own Facebook albums.[60]

Finally, the common public image of Internet predators is exemplified by those cases noted so far. For Facebook, there are around 1.1 billion people online every month[61] and a majority of them benefit from using social media. Facebook users reported that the platform helped them connect with friends, colleagues, family members, and finds friends from the past such as high school or college classmates.[62] While a portion of 901 million diverse users have utilized social media platform to do "bad" things,[63] and 81,000,000 profiles that appear in Facebook are falsified, no one is likely to ever find these out.[64] Thus, there is much evidence that sexual predators come from all walks of life. Nonetheless, there are a few commonalities among cyber predators. Internet monitors indicate that predators prefer chat rooms, personal websites, and instant messaging. Most offenders spend weeks to years cultivating a potential victim before attempting to meet him or her in person.[65] Though the rate of offending and range of offenders may be the same as the Peeping Toms and shopping mall perverts of days past, we would argue that the ingredient most unsettling to parents is the thought of such acts occurring in their homes.

Although social media is a new technological phenomenon, it is not inconsistent with over one hundred years of delinquency research that indicates that youth seeking excitement and stimulation often engage in high-risk behavior despite warnings, cautions, and restrictions to the contrary. And, following principles of risk and benefit, if offenders find it more economical and practical to use these resources for tracking and stalking potential victims, then they will utilize them until we can develop the tools to make it ineffective for them to do so.

ANONYMOUS CYBERSPACE: CHALLENGES FOR LAW ENFORCEMENT

Detecting, investigating, and prosecuting crimes committed on the Internet has posed serious challenges for law enforcement, coordinated agency efforts and time-consuming undercover work have been beneficial. In 1995, the FBI created the Innocent Images National Initiative (IINI) program to crack down on sexual predators on the Internet and to reduce the vulnerability of children lured from their families through social media networking. More than 200 FBI agents work undercover posing as teenagers/preteens on the social networking websites to identify potential sex predators. According to the FBI,[66] there was a 2,535 percent increase in child exploitation investigations between 1996 and 2009. Currently the IINI has made more than 2,000 arrests, achieved over 2,500 convictions, and identified 246 new children featured in child pornography. The operation of IINI has escalated to a global force through the launch of the Innocent Images International Task Force (IIITF) in 2004. The IIITF collaborates with 42 countries and roughly 100 international agents joined the force, which allows for transparent information to uncover the dark and anonymous cyberspace crime problems. The IIITF, within three years, had uncovered numerous suspects who traded more than 400,000 images of pornography internationally.

According to statistics on Facebook,[67] of the globally 1,310,000,000 that are active Facebook users per month, 680,000,000 are mobile Facebook users and 75 percent of users are not in the United States. Facebook users, on average, are connected to 80 different pages, groups, and events and have 130 friends per user. Approximately 205 images are uploaded per day and those images are dispersed to 54,200,000 different Facebook pages. Although those figures may not be exactly accurate due to statistical errors, it gives an idea of the hidden risk on the Internet. The accomplishment of the IINI and the IIITF is worthy of appreciation, yet, their work may just reveal the tip of an iceberg on social networking. In an anonymous cyberspace, most cybercrimes are under the deep-down water and the Internet incidents keep challenging law enforcement and legal authorities.

Concerned over how easy access to children appeared to be exploiting technology, a volunteer in a California sheriff's department decided to do something about it. Robert Lotter invented a mobile monitoring technology, RADAR, that "tracks and logs text messages, social medial conversations and phone calls on mobile devices."[68] The system provides the trail of evidence and documentation necessary in order to obtain a conviction that had been a weak link in prosecutions in the past. Free to law enforcement agencies, the software claims a 100 percent conviction rate in the thousands of cases in which it has been employed.[69]

WHAT YOU AND PARENTS CAN DO

For parents, the goal of convictions is not as meaningful as successful prevention and intervention. Unfortunately, while parents may seem concerned about Internet safety, many are not sophisticated users themselves. They are often uncertain about the specific practices that may constitute illegal activity or high-risk communication, and they are often unwilling or unable to purchase and install software mechanisms that might filter or block inappropriate sites. This means that the Internet, like other youthful activities that parents do not understand, is subject to fears and misconceptions that might be more effectively managed if parents were aware of the context of the situation and its relative risks. Forty percent of children surveyed in one study reported that they "never" use the Internet with their parents and "never" share online activities with parents or any adults at home.[70] Despite growing parents' use of social media, adoption of social networking sites, getting familiar with conversation on those sites, demographic difference (e.g., age, education, socioeconomic status) would limit parents on the degree of adoption of social media and variation of sites used.[71]

In 2011, 80 percent of parent social media users who have friended or followed their child on the same social media websites would comment on their child's posting.[72] This seems the best intentions of parents to monitor Internet access. Some teens, however, seem to prefer not being friends with their parents because they feel parents "keep an eye on them" and "some of their family are obnoxious" when responding to postings and status updates. Some teens, on the other hand, use viewer restriction features to put parents on the list of restricted profile viewers to block their parents' access to their pictures, posts, and other profile information. Therefore, being children's Facebook friends does not appear to be effective enough regarding parental control and Internet safety.

Officials recommend the following measures for promoting safe Internet use for families with children. These strategies are two-way axis and would work better when parents and children build mutual understanding of online sex predators and other potential risk of victimization in an anonymous cyberspace.

- Instruct children on avoiding the display or disclosure of personal details related to names and addresses, how to avoid posting scheduled activities, and what may be interpreted as provocative pictures or language.

- Help children set up privacy settings within home pages and profiles. Disable the functions of the automatic inclusion of location on social media sites and reduce the likelihood of tagging friends and yourself about time stamp and location. Make children leave a less traceable mark on the Internet.

- Make children aware that their "friend" may be an adult and that some strangers are not to be trusted easily; sex predators especially always lie about their age. Try not to talk to strangers online or doing through texting.

- Do not allow your children to meet with strangers that they have made friends online without permission. Be aware of mail, e-mail, gifts, small tokens, souvenirs, or packages that your children receive from strangers.

- Even though children may access the Internet outside, making the home environment monitored more easily is important. Keep computers in open areas, such as the living room, family room, or kitchen, where the content of regular use may be monitored.

- Check websites that children log onto and make children aware that you are able to track their activity and that you are doing that to protect them. More important is to make children aware of the potential risk of why they are not supposed to visit some sites.

- Parents should be conscious about finding pornographic images and files hidden in children's room. Parents should prepare to have a gentle and rational talk to children rather than scold or blame once they found some inappropriate objects.

- Turn on the free "parental control" settings installed in the computer, which could provide a basic level of managing children's use of this computer, the applications on it, and the download. Invest in advanced software that will help you to further track, monitor, filter, and control Internet access, website activities, and block high-risk sites.

- Share your information, experiences, and anything that makes you uncomfortable online with other parents and with the school. An alliance or network is much more effective and efficient than one person alone. Children need to see the unity of parents in consensus on this issue and they need to be encouraged to bring Internet problems and issues to the attention of adults.

- Arrange to spend quality time with children in meaningful activities, travel, sports, recreation, and leisure away from the computer to offset their interest and preoccupation in this form of social activity. Try to make children unplug from cell phones, tablets, and other electronic devices through which they can access the Internet in the night when you are asleep.
- Talk to your children honestly and in a nonthreatening way about their use of the Internet. Involve them in making up rules and setting parameters so that they are interested in the issues and feel some of shared power that is an important need in their lives as they develop a sense of responsibility and control over their lives.

Today, about half of the parents who have teens at home with online activities reported they use parental controls or some other household rules to monitor and regulate their children or block certain sites if necessary.[73] Eighty-four percent of students reported that they have some sort of online rules at home related to downloading music, videos, movies, or software, posing content, talking to strangers, and others.[74] Compared to those teens without parental controls or household rules in online activities, those teens with such online restriction were found be less likely to engage in risky behavior and post their contact information, seek out the SEWs, and chat with strangers on the Internet.[75] The most important thing to note is online predators need some duration of time to form a relationship with children. Before predators could move to their next step, to ask out and meet up, to introduce sexual context, and sexual content into their conversations, they need to invest time to lower children's guard and inhibitions. While these practices cannot guarantee a safe Internet experience for children, they at least serve two important functions. First, they provide some surveillance over Internet behavior before children become victimized in a predatory online relationship. Second, they provide a model for assessing the risk of activity that may require parental interventions if harmful relationships have already been established.

CONCLUSION

The difficulty in dealing with violent and sexually explicit material is the lack of consensus on what constitutes harmful or obscene material and high-risk behaviors online. There is also great variation between jurisdictions on the extent to which First Amendment protections cover the exchange of print and film between consenting adults. There is also no clarity on the degree of government regulation for what children access and the responsibility of such access on government and parents. Over the years various regulations, codes, laws, and ordinances have been promulgated in an attempt to control the distribution of violent and sexually explicit material (and to keep up with its changing themes as well as evolving technological mediums). These problems of defining and controlling not only the music and film industry but all of its bootlegged, illegally recorded, and downloaded offshoots are magnified when the Internet is concerned.

Proposed answers to censorship are parent-controlled software, generic legislation (as with the provisions in the Telecommunications Decency Act), and hardware. Software exists to censor the Internet and continues to evolve to balance the needs of access and protection. The consensus of the legal community appears to be that absolute prohibition of "indecent" materials (for both adults and children) is clearly unconstitutional. Whatever its direction, the final legislative solution will no doubt work as well in limit juveniles' access to violence and pornography as have solutions to the equally thorny problems of alcohol, drugs, and tobacco.

One of the solutions needed is illustrated by the advertising campaigns designed for the war on drugs. Exaggerated statements and stories were disseminated for scare purposes, but billed as "information." In one sense they had the intended effect, but for the wrong audience—parents. Youth were able to draw on experiences and word of mouth to determine that the statements and stories were, indeed, scare tactics and in many cases laughably so. Information on Internet risk should be informed by this experience and bear a closer resemblance to reality. The fact is that children, youth, and adults are all going to use the Internet (actually, the Internet is now a commodity and necessity). Without exaggerating risk and creating fear, the task is to determine how to manage potential risk through reasonable behavior. Governments are not going to be in the forefront of this activity, but parents will have to be, perhaps after learning to manage their own Internet risk.

DISCUSSION QUESTIONS

1. How much freedom is appropriate for children and teens on the Internet? What are the trade offs that parents face in trying to set appropriate boundaries for Internet use with their children?
2. What types of programming approaches would best provide effective and age-appropriate skills for avoiding predatory schemes and exploitative relationships in Internet communications?
3. Is cyberbullying really different from more traditional forms of school bullying? How much responsibility do school staff and administrators bear in each of the forms of bullying?

4. How effective do you think laws and regulations on the Internet have been and what other types of legislation might help reduce cyberbullying or its effects?

ADDITIONAL RESOURCES

Barlett, Christopher P., Douglas A. Gentile, Craig A. Anderson, Kanae Suzuki, Akira Sakamoto, Ayuchi Yamaoka, and Rui Katsura. "Cross-Cultural Differences in Cyberbullying Behavior A Short-Term Longitudinal Study." *Journal of Cross-Cultural Psychology* 45, no. 2 (2014): 300–313.

Connell, Nadine M., Natalie M. Schell-Busey, Allison N. Pearce, and Pamela Negro. "Badgrlz? Exploring Sex Differences in Cyberbullying Behaviors." *Youth Violence and Juvenile Justice* 12, no. 3 (2013): 209–228.

Heiman, Tali, and Dorit Olenik-Shemesh. "Cyberbullying Experience and Gender Differences among Adolescents in Different Educational Settings." *Journal of Learning Disabilities* 48, no. 2 (2013): 146–155.

Hinduja, Sameer and Justin Patchin. *Bullying Beyond the Schoolyard: Preventing and Responding to Cyberbullying*, 2nd edition. Thousand Oaks, CA: Corwin, 2014.

Kowalski, Robin, Susan Limber and Patricia Agatston. *Cyberbullying: Bullying in the Digital Age*. 2nd edition. Hoboken, NJ: Wiley Blackwell, 2012.

Obermaier, Magdalena, Nayla Fawzi, and Thomas Koch. "Bystanding or Standing By? How the Number of Bystanders Affects the Intention to Intervene in Cyberbullying." *New Media & Society* (2014): 1461444814563519.

Orel, Alexandria, Marilyn Campbell, Kelly Wozencroft, Eliza Leong, and Melanie Kimpton. "Exploring University Students' Coping Strategy Intentions for Cyberbullying." *Journal of Interpersonal Violence* (2015): 0886260515586363.

Tanrıkulu, Taşkın, Hüseyin Kınay, and O. Tolga Arıcak. "Sensibility Development Program against Cyberbullying." *New Media & Society* 17, no. 5 (2015): 708–719.

Van Ouytsel, Joris, Michel Walrave, and Heidi Vandebosch. "Correlates of Cyberbullying and How School Nurses Can Respond." *NASN School Nurse* 30, no. 3 (2015): 162–170.

Washington, Edwina. "An Overview of Cyberbullying in Higher Education." *Adult Learning*, 26, no. 1 (2015): 21–27.

Wegge, Denis, Heidi Vandebosch, Steven Eggermont, and Sara Pabian. "Popularity through Online Harm: The Longitudinal Associations between Cyberbullying and Sociometric Status in Early Adolescence." *The Journal of Early Adolescence* (2014): 0272431614556351.

Zalaquett, Carlos, and SeriaShia Chatters. "Cyberbullying in College: Frequency, Characteristics, and Practical Implications." *SAGE Open* 4, no. 1 (2014): 2158244014526721.

RELATED WEBSITES

Cyberbullying Research Center, http://cyberbullying.us/
FBI—Cracking Down on sexual Sexual Predators on the Internet, http://www.fbi .gov/news/stories/2003/december

KidsHealth: Cyberbullying, http://kidshealth.org/parent/positive/talk/cyberbul
    lying.html
ScienceDaily: Most Internet Sex Offenders Aim at Teens, http://www.sciencedaily
    .com/releases/2008/02/080218185101.htm
Stopbullying.gov, http://www.stopbullying.gov/cyberbullying/
What We've Learned about Cyberbullying, http://cyberbullying.us/weve-learned-
    cyberbullying-2013/

SUPPORTING FILMS

Cyberbully (2011)
Cyberbully (2015)
Hard Candy (2005)
Megan Is Missing (2011)
Trust (2010)

NOTES

1. Hanley (2007).
2. The White House (2011), p. 3.
3. Deutsch (2014).
4. Ibid.
5. See the National Crime Victimization Surveys on the Bureau of Justice Statistics website.
6. "Child Predators: The Online Threat Continues to Grow" (2011).
7. See the "kids-safety tips," "a parent's guide to Internet safety," "child ID app," and "safe online surfing on Internet challenge" on the FBI website.
8. Kaiser Family Foundation (2010), 2.
9. U.S. Census Bureau (2005), 6.
10. File (2013), 5.
11. Ibid., 5.
12. Madden, Lenhart, Duggan, Cortesi, and Gasser (2013), 3–4.
13. "Child Predators: The Online Threat Continues to Grow" (2011).
14. Kelly (2012).
15. National Center for Education Statistics (2013), T-1.
16. Slonje, Smith, and Frisén (2013), 30.
17. Kwan and Skoric (2013).
18. Ibid.
19. Ibid.
20. Hoffman (2010).
21. Staksrud, Ólafsson, and Livingstone (2013).
22. Nordli (2014).
23. Ibid.

24. McCoy (2014).
25. Bauman, Toomey, and Walker (2013).
26. Cash and Bridge (2009).
27. Hinduja and Patchin (2010).
28. Bauman, Toomey, and Walker (2013), 345.
29. Staksrud, Ólafsson, and Livingstone (2013).
30. Coleman (2006).
31. MediaSmarts (2014b), 2.
32. National Center for Education Statistics (2011).
33. In doing some quick online research in preparation for this chapter, we can attest that once one defeats the "safe-search" feature on common search sites (usually requiring a click on the "yes" box next to "I am an adult," "disable family filter," or "do not filter my results") there are few taboo topics and graphics not available. Before viewing this fact as an evil, it is wise to reflect on the reason these search engines exist (and have become hugely capitalized entities, as well)—the access to information of all types has become the hallmark of the 21st century.
34. Braun-Courville and Rojas (2009), p. 158.
35. Ibid.
36. Ostrow (1993).
37. Rotella (1994).
38. Associated Press (1994).
39. Fernandez and Favro (2013).
40. Madden, Cortesi, Gasser, Lenhart, and Duggan (2012).
41. Ibid., 2.
42. National School Boards Foundation (2013).
43. MediaSmarts (2014a).
44. Ibid., 21.
45. Ibid.
46. Common Sense Media (2012), 9.
47. Ibid., 9.
48. Madden et al. (2013), 6.
49. Ibid., 30.
50. Ibid., 34.
51. Ibid., 10.
52. Jones, Mitchell, and Finkelhor (2012).
53. Kornblum 2006.
54. Madden et al. (2013), 12.
55. Mallett (2014).
56. Sourtzis and Stevens (2014).
57. Acohido (2011).
58. Ibid.
59. Ibid.
60. Herbert and Glaze (2013).

61. Ibid.
62. Duggan, Ellison, Lampe, Lenhart, and Madden (2015).
63. Palis (2012).
64. Statistic Brain Research Institute (2014).
65. Mallett (2014).
66. "Testimony" (2011).
67. Statistic Brain Research Institute (2014).
68. McCoy (2014).
69. Ibid.
70. MediaSmarts (2014c), 38.
71. Madden et al. (2012).
72. Ibid., 12.
73. Ibid., 3.
74. MediaSmarts (2014c), 31.
75. Ibid.

REFERENCES

Acohido, Byron. "Sex Predators Stalk Social Media." *USA Today*, March 1, 2011, 1A.

American Community Survey Reports. *Computer and Internet Use in the United States: 2013*. By Thom File and Camille Ryan. Washington, DC: U.S. Census Bureau, 2014.

Associated Press. "Couple Guilty of Sending Pornography by Computer." *Los Angeles Times*, July 29, 1994, A10.

Bauman, Sheri, Russell B. Toomey, and Jenny L. Walker. "Associations among Bullying, Cyberbullying, and Suicide in High School Students." *Journal of Adolescence* 36, no. 2 (2013): 341–350.

Braun-Courville, Debra K., and Mary Rojas. "Exposure to Sexually Explicit Web Sites and Adolescent Sexual Attitudes and Behaviors." *Journal of Adolescent Health* 45, no. 2 (2009): 156–162.

Cash, Scottye J., and Jeffrey A. Bridge. "Epidemiology of Youth Suicide and Suicidal Behavior." *Current Opinion in Pediatrics* 21, no. 5 (2009): 613.

"Child Predators: The Online Threat Continues to Grow." *Federal Bureau of Investigation*. May 17, 2011. http://www.fbi.gov/news/stories/2011/may/predators_051711/predators_051711.

Coleman, Sandy. "Cyberspace Invaders: Internet Harassment Can Be a Kid's Virtual Nightmare." *The Boston Globe*, March 30, 2006, P1.

Common Sense Media. *Social Media, Social Life: How Teens View Their Digital Lives*. By Victoria Rideout. San Francisco, CA: Common Sense Media, 2012.

Deutsch, Lindsey. "Unfiltered YouTube Levels Playing Field." *USA Today*, December 26, 2014, 5B.

Duggan, Maeve, Nicole B. Ellison, Cliff Lampe, Amanda Lenhart, and Mary Madden. "Social Media Update." *Pew Research Center*. January 9, 2015. http://www.pewinternet.org/2015/01/09/social-media-update-2014/.

Fernandez, Lisa, and Marianne Favro. "San Jose Teacher Arrested on Child Pornography Allegations. *NBC Bay Area*. March 14, 2013. http://www

.nbcbayarea.com/news/local/San-Jose-Teacher-Arrested-With-Child-Por nography-198146921.html.

File, F. (2013). *Computer and Internet Use in the United States.* Washington, DC: U.S. Census Bureau.

Hanley, Christine. "'The Worst Was Yet to Come'; An O. C. Teen's Parents Thought They had Disconnected a Dangerous Internet Relationship. *Los Angeles Times*, June 18, 2007, B1.

Herbert, Dominic, and Ben Glaze. "Paedophiles Stealing Parents' Facebook Pictures of Their Kids to Share on Sick Pages." *Sunday Mirror*, June 23, 2013, 10.

Hinduja, Sameer, and Justin W. Patchin. "Bullying, Cyberbullying, and Suicide." *Archives of Suicide Research* 14, no. 3 (2010): 206–221.

Hoffman, Jan. "Online Bullies Pull Schools into the Fray." *New York Times*, June 28. 2010, A1.

Jones, Lisa M., Kimberly J. Mitchell, and David Finkelhor. "Trends in Youth Internet Victimization: Findings from Three Youth Internet Safety Surveys 2000–2010." *Journal of Adolescent Health* 50, no. 2 (2012): 179–186.

Kaiser Family Foundation. *Generation M2: Media in the Lives of 8- to 18-Year-Olds.* By Victoria J. Rideout, Ulla G. Foehr, and Donald F. Roberts. Menlo Park, CA: Henry J. Kaiser Family Foundation, 2010.

Kelly, Heather. "Computer Hacking for 8-Year-Olds." *CNN.* July 31, 2012. http://www.cnn.com/2012/07/31/tech/web/def-con-kids-2012/.

Kornblum, Janet. "Social Websites Scrutinized: MySpace, Other Reviewed in Crimes against Teenagers." *USA Today*, February 13, 2006, 6D.

Kwan, Grace Chi En, and Marko M. Skoric. "Facebook Bullying: An Extension of Battles in School." *Computers in Human Behavior* 29, no. 1 (2013): 16–25.

Madden, Mary, Amanda Lenhart, Maeve Duggan, Sandra Cortesi, and Urs Gasser. "Teens and Technology." *Pew Research Center.* March 13, 2013. http://www.pewinternet.org/2013/03/13/teens-and-technology-2013/.

Madden, Mary, Amanda Lenhart, Sandra Cortesi, Urs Gasser, Maeve Duggan, Aaron Smith, and Meredith Beaton. "Teens, Social Media, and Privacy." *Pew Research Center.* May 21, 2013. http://www.pewinternet.org/2013/05/21/teens-social-media-and-privacy/.

Madden, Mary, Sandra Cortesi, Urs Gasser, Amanda Lenhart, and Maeve Duggan. "Parents, Teens, and Online Privacy." *Pew Research Center.* November 20, 2012. http://www.pewinternet.org/2012/11/20/parents-teens-and-online-privacy/.

Mallett, Tanisha. "More Sexual Predators Using Social Media to Meet Juveniles." *WBNS-10TV.* October 15, 2014. http://www.10tv.com/content/stories/2014/10/15/columbus-ohio-more-sexual-predators-using-social-media-to-meet-juveniles.html.

McCoy, Tracy "The Sexual Predator App with a 100 Percent Conviction Rate." *Newsweek*, August 29, 2014, 1.

MediaSmarts. *Young Canadians in a Wired World, Phase III: Sexuality and Romantic Relationships in the Digital Age.* By Valerie Steeves. Ottawa, Canada: MediaSmarts, 2014a.

MediaSmarts. *Young Canadians in a Wired World, Phase III: Cyberbullying: Dealing with Online Meanness, Cruelty and Threats.* By Valerie Steeves. Ottawa, Canada: MediaSmarts, 2014b.

MediaSmarts. *Young Canadians in a Wired World, Phase III: Life Online.* By Valerie Steeves. Ottawa, Canada: MediaSmarts, 2014c.

National Center for Education Statistics. *Student Reports of Bullying and Cyber-Bullying: Results from the 2011 School Crime Supplement to the National Crime Victimization Survey.* By Deborah Lessne and Sayali Harmalkar. Washington, DC: National Center for Education Statistics, 2013.

National Center for Education Statistics. *Student Victimization in U.S. Schools: Results From the 2009 School Crime Supplement to the National Crime Victimization Survey.* By Jill Fleury DeVoe, Lynn Bauer, and Monica R. Hill. Washington, DC: U.S. Department of Education, 2011.

National School Boards Foundation. *Safe and Smart: Research and Guidelines for Children's Use of the Internet.* Alexandria, VA: National School Boards Foundation, 2013. http://www.grunwald.com/pdfs/Safe-and-Smart_GRUNW ALD-NSBA-Study-2000.pdf.

Nordli, Brian. "Sister's Ordeal Motivates Vegas Anti-Bullying App." *Las Vegas Sun,* September 7, 2014, A15.

Ostrow, Ronald J. "Fight against Child Pornography Waged on New Front: Computers." *Los Angeles Times,* September 1, 1993, A26.

Palis, Courtney. "Facebook Child Porn Pages: Shocking Groups Reportedly Uncovered on Social Network." *The Huffington Post,* May 7, 2012. http://www.huffingtonpost.com/2012/05/07/facebook-child-porn_n_1496530.html.

Rotella, Sebastian. "Computerized Child Porno Ring Broken." *Los Angeles Times,* September 24, 1994, A31.

Slonje, Robert, Peter K. Smith, and Ann Frisén. "The Nature of Cyberbullying, and Strategies for Prevention." *Computers in Human Behavior* 29, no. 1 (2013): 26–32.

Sourtzis, Litsa, and Sarah Stevens. "Sex Predators Using Social Media to Ensure Their Young Victims." *The Toronto Star,* February 15, 2014, A1.

Staksrud, Elisabeth, Kjartan Ólafsson, and Sonia Livingstone. "Does the Use of Social Networking Sites Increase Children's Risk of Harm?." *Computers in Human Behavior* 29, no. 1 (2013): 40–50.

Statistic Brain Research Institute. "Facebook Statistics." April 14, 2015. http://www.statisticbrain.com/facebook-statistics/.

"Testimony." Federal Bureau of Investigation. March 2, 2011. http://www.fbi.gov/news/testimony/helping-law-enforcement-find-missing-children.

The White House. (2011). *International Strategy for Cyberspace: Prosperity, Security, and Openness in a Networked World.* Washington, DC: The White House, 2011. https://www.whitehouse.gov/sites/default/files/rss_viewer/internati onal_strategy_for_cyberspace.pdf.

U.S. Census Bureau. *Computer and Internet Use in the United States: 2003.* By Jennifer Cheeseman Day, Alex Janus, and Jessica Davis. Washington, DC: U.S. Census Bureau, 2005.

Chapter 3

Juvenile Prostitution and Safe Harbor Laws

Stephanie Fahy

Minors involved in prostitution have traditionally been perceived and treated as criminals or delinquents within the criminal justice system. However, over the past decade, sparked in large part by the passage of a federal human trafficking law, there has been a movement to redefine or reclassify minors who are involved in prostitution as victims deserving of treatment as opposed to criminals or delinquents deserving of punishment. Despite the enactment of a federal law that recognizes minors involved in prostitution as sex trafficking victims, they continue to be arrested and treated as criminals or delinquents under state criminal and juvenile delinquency laws.[1]

This contradiction between the federal definition of minors involved in prostitution and the treatment of these youth under state laws prompted some states to pass what are referred to as safe harbor laws. Presently 27 states have passed safe harbor laws or laws that have some provision of safe harbor for prostituted youth. Safe harbor laws are designed to grant minors who are arrested for prostitution immunity from prosecution or redirect prostituted minors from juvenile delinquency proceedings to the child welfare system or other victim service agencies.[2]

The following sections of this chapter will discuss the prevalence of minors involved in prostitution in the United States and the characteristics of these youth. The shift in the paradigm from prosecution of criminal offenders and juvenile delinquents to the protection of victims and survivors of a crime, including the enactment of laws that are designed to shield minors involved in prostitution from prosecution, will also be discussed. For the purposes of this chapter the term "minors involved in prostitution" or "prostitution involving minors" will be used. Legally, minors involved in prostitution are victims, and these terms are less likely to have a punitive connotation as opposed to other terms that have traditionally been used to describe this phenomenon, including "teen prostitutes" and "juvenile prostitutes." Additionally, minors involved in prostitution are also described as commercially sexually exploited children or domestic minor sex trafficking victims, so these terms will be used interchangeably throughout the chapter.

PREVALENCE AND CHARACTERISTICS OF MINORS INVOLVED IN PROSTITUTION

Although estimates on the commercial sexual exploitation of children and the sex trafficking of minors in the United States exist, these estimates vary widely and have been described as unreliable guesstimates "or extrapolations based on questionable assumptions."[3] A number of challenges exist that make it difficult to obtain a reliable number of minors involved in prostitution, including unclear definitions or inconsistencies with how commercial sexual exploitation and sex trafficking of minors are defined in the field, differences in sampling methods used by various researchers, and an overall lack of evidence-based research.[4] The most commonly cited estimate is from a study by Estes and Weiner, which revealed that more than 300,000 children are at risk of commercial sexual exploitation each year in the United States.[5] This estimate has been criticized for focusing on "at-risk" youth as opposed to actual victims of commercial sexual exploitation and the approach used by the authors is susceptible to double counting youth who fall into multiple at-risk categories.[6]

Law enforcement records of minors arrested for prostitution that make up the Federal Bureau of Investigation's (FBI) Uniform Crime Reporting (UCR) program are also inadequate for understanding prevalence since estimates that rely solely on arrest records are at risk of undercounting the number of minors involved in prostitution. For example, arrest statistics report the number of arrests that law enforcement agencies made in a given year, not the number of individuals arrested nor the number of crimes committed. Additionally, minors involved in prostitution who are not arrested by law enforcement are not counted in arrest data. According to reports, minors involved in prostitution may be picked up and detained by law enforcement and not actually arrested, or they may be arrested for other crimes, including drug possession, loitering, and curfew violation.[7] Youth involved in prostitution may also lie about their age or use false identification, resulting in the misclassification of these youth as adults.[8] Minors involved in prostitution also do not come to the attention of law enforcement because of the underground nature of the phenomenon as well as the reluctance of these youth to self-identify as victims to law enforcement.[9]

Studies that have examined the characteristics of minors involved in prostitution suffer from the same methodological limitations as those studies estimating the prevalence of prostituted youth, including problems related to small sample sizes or samples of youth that are not nationally representative.[10] Additionally, many studies are qualitative in nature and based on interviews with individuals formerly or currently involved in prostitution or with professionals working in the field, who largely indicate that the vast majority of youth involved in prostitution are female.[11] Other studies that rely on police data reveal similar findings. Using UCR data, Puzzanchera examined the characteristics of juveniles arrested for prostitution in 2011 and revealed that of the 1,000 estimated prostitution arrests for that year, 76 percent of arrests involved females, 35 percent of arrests involved white youth, and nine percent of arrests involved youth younger than age 15.[12] Although research on the commercial sexual exploitation of boys is limited, recent studies have revealed that boys make up a larger percentage of youth involved in prostitution than previous studies would suggest.[13] For example, a study based on respondent-driven sampling methods as opposed to just youth identified by law enforcement or victim service providers revealed that the percentage of prostituted boys is nearly the same as the percentage of prostituted girls.[14] Another study that included a nationally representative sample of more than 13,000 adolescents found that males accounted for two-thirds of adolescents who indicated they had ever exchanged sex for drugs or money.[15]

Findings for the racial makeup of prostituted youth have been somewhat mixed. Although 64 percent of minors arrested for prostitution in 2011 were identified as black,[16] information about prostitution incidents reported by police into the National Incident Based Reporting System (NIBRS) between 1997 and 2000 revealed that more than 70 percent of prostitution incidents involving both juvenile offenders and juvenile victims involved whites.[17] A study examining the commercial sexual exploitation of children in New York, however, revealed that black youth made up a larger proportion of prostituted youth in major metropolitan areas, and white adolescents were more likely to be identified in less urban areas.[18] According to Sherman and Goldblatt-Grace, commercially sexually exploited youth typically come from minority populations, and

African American girls are arrested at a higher rate than white girls. Additionally, the age of entry for African American girls appears to be younger than the age of entry for white girls.[19]

Although findings on the gender and race of minors involved in prostitution vary, research on the commercial sexual exploitation of children largely reveals that on average individuals become involved in prostitution between the ages of 12 and 14 with the average age reported as 14.[20] A third of females participating in a study based in the Chicago Metropolitan Area reported that they became involved in prostitution before the age of 15, and another study revealed that 62 percent of 200 juvenile and adult female prostitutes in the San Francisco Bay Area became involved in prostitution before turning 16.[21] Studies also reveal similar findings about the risk factors for prostitution. These risk factors include child neglect, physical abuse and/or sexual abuse, being a runaway or homeless, and involvement in child welfare or juvenile justice systems.[22] Research examining the association between childhood maltreatment and prostitution has revealed that women arrested for prostitution or women who reported involvement in prostitution also indicated they were abused as children.[23] Child sexual abuse is strongly associated with the commercial sexual exploitation of minors, and the most common characteristic of girls involved in prostitution is a history of childhood sexual abuse.[24] Testifying before the Senate Judiciary Committee, Subcommittee on Human Rights and the Law in 2010, Rachel Lloyd, the founder of the nation's largest provider of services to commercially sexually exploited and trafficked girls, stated that although children of all races and socioeconomic backgrounds can fall victim to commercial sexual exploitation, it "disproportionately affects low-income children, children of color, children who've been in the child welfare system, children who've been in the juvenile justice system, children who rarely have a voice in public policy, [and] children who are frequently ignored."[25]

SHIFTING PARADIGMS: FROM PROSECUTION OF "TEEN PROSTITUTES" TO PROTECTION OF "DOMESTIC MINOR SEX TRAFFICKING VICTIMS"

Despite the link between early childhood victimization and juvenile involvement in prostitution, criminal justice agents have traditionally perceived and treated minors involved in prostitution as juvenile delinquents or criminals deserving of punishment. According to Sherman and Goldblatt-Grace, minors involved in prostitution are "first seen as victims in the child and family services system as a result of familial abuse. They are later seen as delinquents in our juvenile justice system, criminalized for their exploitation."[26] Furthermore, minors involved in prostitution continue to be viewed as juvenile delinquents and arrested for prostitution-related offenses despite state and federal laws that criminalize adult sexual contact with children and that define minors that are induced into prostitution as sex trafficking victims.[27] For example, all states have enacted statutory rape laws[28] that make it a crime for adults to have sexual contact with children.[29] Although statutory rape laws assume that minors are incapable of consenting to sex, some states do not distinguish between adults and minors involved in prostitution, so minors can still be arrested and charged with prostitution-related offenses. In addition to statutory rape laws, a number of federal laws designed to protect children from sexual exploitation have been passed in the United States. Among them are federal statutes that specifically address the prostitution of minors in the United States, including laws pertaining to the transportation of minors for prostitution and other criminal sexual activity,[30] which fall under the jurisdiction of the Mann Act.[31] Although the Mann Act is cited as the first law to specifically address the prostitution of juveniles in the United States, it focuses primarily on increasing penalties for individuals who sexually exploit minors and less on the physical and psychological needs of exploited youth.[32]

The passage of the Victims of Trafficking and Violence Protection Act,[33] or the Trafficking Victims Protection Act (TVPA) in 2000[34] is considered a pivotal piece of U.S. legislation that paved the way for a host of other laws and initiatives designed to recognize minors involved in prostitution as victims of a crime.[35] The TVPA refers specifically to the recruitment, harboring, transportation, provision, or obtaining of a person for one of three following purposes: (1) labor or services, through the use of force, fraud, or coercion for the purpose of subjection to involuntary servitude, peonage, debt bondage, or slavery; or (2) a commercial sex act through the use of force, fraud, or coercion; or (3) if the person is under 18 years of age, any commercial sex act, regardless of whether any form of coercion is involved. The TVPA and its subsequent reauthorizations (2003, 2005, 2008, 2013) have been called the "most significant national action" to combat the Commercial Sexual Exploitation of Children (CSEC)[36] because it defines anyone under 18 years induced to perform a commercial sex act as a victim of sex trafficking.[37]

Unlike the Mann Act, the TVPA does not require transportation across state lines to prove human trafficking.[38] The TVPA also includes enhanced penalties, including a maximum sentence of life in prison for individuals who force into prostitution children younger than 14[39] or between 14 and 18 years of age.[40] In 2005, Congress reauthorized the TVPA and in doing so officially recognized U.S.-born minors as trafficking victims by expanding the scope of the trafficking service provision to explicitly include domestic minor trafficking victims.[41] Although the initial focus of the TVPA may have been on protecting foreign-born individuals, some legislators recognized early on the connection between the international trafficking of children into the United States and commercial sexual exploitation of U.S.-born children. Most notably it defined the term "juvenile subjected to trafficking" to mean a U.S. citizen, or alien admitted for permanent residence, who is the subject of sex trafficking or severe forms of trafficking in persons that occurs, in whole or in part, within the territorial jurisdiction of the United States and who has not attained 18 years of age at the time the person is identified as having been the subject of sex trafficking or severe forms of trafficking in persons. The TVPRA (2005) also established a pilot program to provide benefits and services to juveniles subjected to trafficking, including shelter, psychological counseling, and assistance in developing independent living skills.[42]

Despite the passage of the TVPA and its recognition of minors involved in prostitution as victims there was an understanding early on that states also needed to play a significant role in combatting human trafficking.[43] The enactment of state trafficking laws was also important since most domestic juvenile prostitution prosecutions occur in state courts under state laws.[44] Since the passage of the TVPA, all 50 states in the United States have adopted human trafficking statutes or laws that criminalize human trafficking, with some states including additional provisions for victim services and training that is designed to improve the ability of law enforcement to identify and respond to victims of human trafficking.[45] States vary in their coverage, however, with some statutes not distinguishing between the sex trafficking of adults and minors.[46] Consequently, prosecutors are forced into proving minors are induced into prostitution through force, fraud, or coercion. A report that assessed the effectiveness of state laws in responding to domestic minor sex trafficking revealed that more than half of all states were failing in their efforts to address and prevent the trafficking of minors.[47] Shared Hope International published The Protected Innocence Challenge: State Report Cards on the Legal Framework of Protection for the Nation's Children in 2011. This report assessed states on six areas of law: (1) criminalization of domestic minor sex trafficking, (2) criminal provisions for demand, (3) criminal provisions for traffickers, (4) criminal provisions for facilitators, (5) protective provisions for the child victims, and (6) law enforcement and criminal justice tools to effectuate investigation and prosecutions. Twenty-six states received failing grades for adopting laws that either (1) did not align with the federal trafficking law in clearly defining a human trafficking victim as any minor under the age of 18 used in a commercial sex act without regard to use of force, fraud, or coercion, (2) did not identify CSEC as a separate and distinct offense from general sexual offenses, or (3) enacted CSEC or prostitution statutes that did not refer to the sex trafficking statute to identify the commercially sexually exploited minors as trafficking victims. Another report released by the same authors in 2014 revealed an improvement in grades; however, 34 percent of states received a grade of D or lower.[48]

ADDRESSING RISK FACTORS ASSOCIATED WITH SEXUAL VICTIMIZATION

Minors involved in prostitution who are treated as juvenile delinquents or criminals and are not provided with victim services can suffer from serious, long-lasting, and sometimes life-threatening physical health problems and psychological problems as a result of their victimization.[49] Risk factors that are associated with prostitution include physical and sexual violence, increased exposure to sexually transmitted diseases, and forced use of drugs and/or alcohol, which can in turn lead to a number of physical health problems such as cardiovascular problems, respiratory problems, liver disorders, cervical cancer, reproductive health problems, neurological problems, including seizures, human immunodeficiency virus (HIV) infection, suicide, and drug and/or alcohol addiction.[50]

Physical and sexual violence are commonplace in the lives of minors involved in prostitution particularly as more visible forms of street-level prostitution move indoors and under the radar of law enforcement.[51] Reports of violence by purchasers of sex acts, or "johns," include being stabbed or cut, gang raped, chocked and/or strangled, beaten, kidnapped, stalked, held at gun point, tied up, tortured, beaten with a baseball bat or crowbar, and run over.[52] Pimps also use violence to control and manipulate youth into having sex with "johns" and/or to enforce daily quotas, or specific amounts of money that youth are required to make performing sex acts.[53] The relationship between a pimp and a prostituted girl is similar to a relationship characterized by domestic violence in that pimps often isolate girls from family and friends and maintain control using threats and intimidation, including fear of arrest, perpetuation of shame or guilt about the victimization, and threats to withhold love and affection.[54] In addition to physical health problems minors involved in prostitution suffer from a host of mental health problems related to their victimization, including posttraumatic stress disorder, depression, anxiety disorders and/or panic attacks, self-harm behaviors, and personality disorders.[55] Prostituted youth who are controlled by pimps often experience extreme anxiety and fear, which can result in "trauma bonds."[56] Trauma bonds are compared to Stockholm syndrome, a psychological phenomenon in which hostages express empathy, sympathy and have positive feelings toward their captors, sometimes to the point of defending them. Pimp-controlled women and girls may not self-identify as victims or cooperate in law enforcement investigations against their pimps out a misguided sense of loyalty and may even express feelings of love and admiration for their pimps.[57]

SAFE HARBOR LAWS

In an effort to bring state statutes in line with the federal human trafficking law, thereby recognizing minors involved in prostitution as victims in need of services as opposed to criminals or juvenile delinquents deserving of punishment, 27 states have enacted safe harbor laws or laws that meet partial requirements of safe harbor. This includes Arkansas, California, Connecticut, Delaware, Florida, Illinois, Iowa, Kansas, Kentucky, Louisiana, Massachusetts, Michigan, Minnesota, Mississippi, Nebraska, New Hampshire, New Jersey, New York, North Carolina, Ohio, Oklahoma, Tennessee, Texas, Utah, Vermont, Washington, and Wyoming.[58] Safe harbor laws are designed to recognize minors involved in prostitution as sexually exploited victims in need of protection and services by granting them immunity from prosecution or diverting minors from juvenile delinquency proceedings and instead directing them to child welfare services.[59]

The TVPA 2013 reauthorization introduced a mandate to include safe harbor provisions in a model state law; however, the first safe harbor law was passed in New York in 2008 and went into effect in 2010.[60] The impetus for the New York State Safe Harbor for Exploited Children Act was a 2003 case involving a 12-year-old girl, Nicolette R., with a long history of physical and sexual abuse who was charged with an act of prostitution.[61] Under New York law a child who was incapable of consenting to a sexual act was also deemed capable of consenting to sexual conduct in return for a fee; thus, a child who was considered a victim of a rape could simultaneously be prosecuted for committing an act of prostitution.[62] Under the New York Safe Harbor Act, minors arrested for prostitution are presumed victims of a "severe form of trafficking" as defined in the TVPA 2000.[63] There, the term "severe forms of trafficking in persons" means (A) sex trafficking in which a commercial sex act is induced by force, fraud, or coercion, or in which the person induced to perform such act has not attained 18 years of age; or (B) the recruitment, harboring, transportation, provision, or obtaining of a person for labor or services, through the use of force, fraud, or coercion for the purpose of subjection to involuntary servitude, peonage, debt bondage, or slavery. Based on this presumption, all cases involving minors arrested for prostitution-related offenses are converted from juvenile delinquency proceedings to Persons in Need of Supervision (PINS) proceedings, which mandate diversion into specialized services.[64]

Although the New York statute is considered groundbreaking in that it marks a pivotal shift in the paradigm from prosecution to protection of minors involved in prostitution, it has been criticized for including certain conditions, including a prior arrest(s) for prostitution and a victim's refusal of services,[65] which could preclude prostituted minors from receiving a PINS certification that is required for diversion into programs with specialized services.[66] Prostituted minors who are denied PINS certification can instead be charged and adjudicated as delinquents.

Since the passage of the New York safe harbor law states have passed safe harbor laws generally fall into one of three safe harbor models: a decriminalization model, a diversion model, and a model that combines decriminalization and diversion. The New York Safe Harbor Act is modeled using diversion as opposed to decriminalization since minors can still be arrested, charged, and prosecuted as delinquents following the enactment of safe harbor laws. Massachusetts' safe harbor law is similar to the statute enacted in New York State in that it does not decriminalize prostitution for anyone under a specified age. Under Massachusetts' safe harbor law, which is part of the state human trafficking statute that went into effect on February 19, 2012,[67] minors involved in prostitution are recognized as a sexually exploited children who are eligible for diversion into service programs rather than delinquency proceedings. However, if the court finds that the child has failed to substantially comply with the requirements of services the court may re-initiate the delinquency case.

States that have enacted safe harbor laws based on a decriminalization model include Connecticut and Tennessee. Although these states have safe harbor laws that prohibit the prosecution of minors for prostitution, they have been criticized for doing little else to protect prostituted minors.[68] Connecticut passed An Act Providing a Safe Harbor for Exploited Children in February 2010.[69] The law prohibits a child under 16 years of age from being charged with prostitution[70] and minors who are 16 or 17 receive a presumption that they are victims of human trafficking although they could still enter the juvenile justice system as delinquents.[71] The Connecticut Safe Harbor Act also increases penalties for prostitution of children less than 16 years of age,[72] but it does not mandate specialized services for child sex trafficking victims who are identified by law enforcement, nor does it require a criminal investigation into individual(s) who may be suspected of prostituting youth or soliciting sex from underage youth.[73]

Other states have adopted a model that incorporates decriminalization and diversion. For example, the Illinois Safe Children Act[74] is upheld as a model approach to the safe harbor of minors involved in prostitution since they are immune from prosecution and are provided services as victims of sexual exploitation.[75] Illinois' law closely mirrors the TVPA in that it provides immunity to anyone less than 18 years old[76] and temporary protective custody in secure facilities such as shelters, hospitals, or other medical facilities.[77] Additionally, the term "juvenile prostitute" was replaced with "soliciting for a minor engaged in prostitution" in the criminal code,[78] which reinforces the original intent of Safe Harbor Legislation that prostituted minors are victims rather than criminals.[79] The Illinois Safe Children Act also requires an investigation into possible child abuse or child neglect for all minors who are taken into custody by police for prostitution or prostitution-related offenses.[80]

CONCLUSION

The passage of safe harbor laws by some states is a critical step toward recognizing minors involved in prostitution as victims of a crime in need of services rather than criminals or juvenile delinquents. However, some safe harbor models have been criticized for not doing enough to protect minors involved in prostitution. For example, a major criticism of safe harbor laws that are straight decriminalization is that they fall short of protecting minors involved in prostitution, who often require specialized services to overcome their victimization.[81] On the other hand, safe harbor laws that divert youth into specialized services but also leave the door open to prosecution run the risk of failing some youth who fall short of meeting conditional requirements for diversion, such as having a prior arrest for prostitution or not willingly complying with victim service programs. Models that both decriminalize prostitution and divert minors into specialized services appear promising; however, future studies should examine the impact of these models on the criminal justice response to minors involved in prostitution as well on the implementation of programs or interventions designed to treat these youth as victims.

DISCUSSION QUESTIONS

1. What are some of the underlying family and individual problems underlying the engagement in juvenile prostitution?
2. Have societal views on juvenile prostitution changed over time? In what ways?
3. What impact do you believe safe harbor laws will have on the problems of juvenile prostitution and the trafficking of minors in sex industries?
4. It can be argued that safe harbor laws are just the beginning of effective interventions with teens engaged in prostitution. What other services and interventions would be needed?

ADDITIONAL RESOURCES

Dorais, Michel and Patrice Corriveau. *Gangs and Girls: Understanding Juvenile Prostitution*. Montreal, Quebec, McGill Queens University Press, 2009.

Franklin, Cortney and Tasha Menaker. "The Impact of Observer Characteristics on Blame Assessments of Prostituted Female Youth." *Feminist Criminology* 10, no. 2 (2015): 140–164.

Oneil, Carle and Waln Brown. *Juvenile Prostitution*. Tallahassee, FL: William Gladden Foundation Press, 2014.

Reid, Joan. "Entrapment and Enmeshment Schemes Used by Sex Traffickers." *Sexual Abuse: A Journal of Research and Treatment* (2014): 1079063214544334.

Reid, Joan and Alex Piquero. "Age-Graded Risks for Commercial Sexual Exploitation of Male and Female Youth." *Journal of Interpersonal Violence* 29, no. 9 (2014): 1747–1777.

Salisbury, Emily, Jonathan D. Dabney, and Kelli Russell. "Diverting Victims of Commercial Sexual Exploitation from Juvenile Detention: Development of the InterCSECt Screening Protocol." *Journal of Interpersonal Violence*, 30, no. 7 (2015): 1247–1276.

RELATED WEBSITES

American Bar Association, Commission on Homelessness and Poverty, Safe Harbor Laws, http://www.americanbar.org/content/dam/aba/events/home lessness_poverty/2013_Midyear_Meeting_Safe_Harbor_Laws/rich_ho oks_wayman_powerpoint.authcheckdam.pdf

ECPAT (Ending Child Slavery at the Source) Safe Harbor Resources by State, http://www.ecpatusa.org/safe-harbor-resources-by-state

National Conference of State Legislatures, http://www.ncsl.org/research/civil-and-criminal-justice/human-trafficking-overview.aspx#Safe%20Harbor

Polaris Project: Sex Trafficking of Minors and "Safe Harbor," http://www.polaris project.org/what-we-do/policy-advocacy/assisting-victims/safe-harbor

SUPPORTING FILMS

Holly (2006)
Not My Life (2010)
Pretty Baby (1978)
Taxi Driver (1976)
Trade (2007)
What I Have Been Through Is Not Who I Am (2011), http://www.ecpatusa.org/video

NOTES

1. Clayton, Krugman, and Simon (2013), 8; Polaris Project (2011).

2. "2014 State Ratings on Human Trafficking Laws." (2014); Geist (2012), 71.

3. Crimes against Children Research Center (2008).

4. Clayton et al. (2013), 42–43; Greenbaum (2014), 246.

5. Center for the Study of Youth Policy (2001), 142.

6. Crimes against Children Research Center (2008).

7. ECPAT-USA, Inc. (2005), 22; Crimes against Children Research Center (2008); Mitchell, Finkelhor, and Wolak (2010), 33.

8. ECPAT-USA, Inc. (2005), 2; Mitchell, Finkelhor, and Wolak (2010), 33.

9. California Child Welfare Council (2013), 18.

10. Greenbaum (2014), 246; Center for Missing and Exploited Children, (1999), 2.

11. Greenbaum (2014), 246.

12. Puzzanchera (2013), 3.

13. Office of Juvenile Justice and Delinquency Prevention (2014); California Child Welfare Council (2013), 20.

14. U.S. Department of Justice (2008), 3.

15. Edwards, Iritani, and Hallfors (2006), 356.

16. Federal Bureau of Investigation (2012d).

17. Finkelhor and Ormrod (2004), 8.

18. New York State Office of Children and Family Services (2007), 86–87.

19. Sherman and Goldblatt-Grace (2011), 336.

20. Ibid., 336; ECPAT-USA, Inc. (2005), 3; Shared Hope International (2009), 30; Office of Juvenile Justice and Delinquency Prevention (2014).

21. Center for Impact Research (2002), 4; Silbert and Pines (1982), 483.

22. Clayton, Krugman, and Simon (2013), 78; Shared Hope International (2009), 31–33; New York State Office of Children and Family Services (2007), 3–4.

23. Wilson and Widom (2010), 223; Widom (1995), 6; McClanahan, McClelland, Abram, and Teplin (1999), 1608.

24. Clayton et al. (2013), 84; Sherman and Goldblatt-Grace (2011), 336.

25. Rachel Lloyd, testimony before Senate Judiciary Committee, Subcommittee on Human Rights and the Law, *In Our Own Backyard: Child Prostitution and Sex Trafficking in the United States*, 111th Cong., 2nd session, February 24, 2010, http://judiciary.senate.gov/pdf/10-02-23 Lloyd'sTestimony.pdf.

26. Sherman and Goldblatt-Grace (2011), 331.

27. Shared Hope International (2014a), 87; Clayton et al. (2013), 8; Center on Poverty and Inequality (2013), 4; Polaris Project (2011); Halter (2010), 156; Mitchell et al. (2010), 29; Raphael, Reichert, and Powers (2010), 90.

28. Commonly referred to as statutory rape laws, these statutes are codified as Statutory Rape, Sexual Abuse, Child Molestation, Unlawful Sexual Conduct with a Child, Lewd Conduct with a Minor, Sexual Assault (National District Attorneys Association (NDAA) (2010).

29. Broughton (2013), 1.

30. 18 U.S.C. § 2421–2423

31. United States White-Slave Traffic Act of 1910, 18 U.S.C. §§ 2421–2424

32. Adams, Owens, and Small (2010), 3.

33. Victims of Trafficking and Violence Prevention Act of 2000, 22 U.S.C § 7101 *et seq.* P.L. 106-386 Stat. 114 (2000):1464.-457 Stat. (2008).

34. The Trafficking Victims Protection Act (TVPA).

35. Urban Institute, Justice Policy Center (2008), 4; Shared Hope International (2009), 4–6.

36. Barnitz (2001), 602.

37. 18 U.S.C. § 1591

38. Adams et al. (2010), 3.

39. 18 U.S.C. § 1591(b)(1).

40. 18 U.S.C. § 1591 (b)(2); In 2003 Congress passed the PROTECT Act (Public Law 108–21) which increased the maximum penalty for trafficking victims between 14 and 18 years old from 20 years in prison to 40 years, and the Adam Walsh Act of 2006 (Public Law 109-248) further increased the penalty from 40 years to life in prison (Adams et al., 2010).

41. Trafficking Victims Protection Reauthorization Act (TVPRA) of 2005, 42 USC § 14044b(f) (2006).

42. 42 USC § 14044b(b).

43. "2014 State Ratings on Human Trafficking Laws."

44. Schwartz, Steffensmeier, and Feldmeyer (2009).

45. "Wyoming Becomes 50th State to Outlaw Human Trafficking" (2013).

46. "2014 State Ratings on Human Trafficking Laws."

47. Shared Hope International (2011), 13.

48. Shared Hope International, (2014a), 14.

49. Greenbaum (2014), 253; Clayton et al. (2013), 116–120; Office of Assistant Secretary for Planning and Evaluation (2010), 1–3.

50. Muftic and Finn (2013), 1862–1864; Clayton, Krugman, and Simon (2013), 116–119.

51. California Child Welfare Council (2013), 24–25.

52. Nixon, Tutty, Downe, Gorkoff, and Ursel (2002), 1027–1028.

53. Dank et al. (2014), 175.

54. President's Interagency Taskforce to Monitor and Combat Trafficking in Persons (2014), 6; Leidholdt (2011), 171–174; Raphael, Reichert, and Powers (2010), 97; Center for Missing and Exploited Children (1999), 5.

55. Clayton et al. (2013), 118–119; Office of Assistant Secretary for Planning and Evaluation (2010), 1–3.

56. U.S. Department of Health and Human Services (2007), 2; Shared Hope International (2009), 4; California Child Welfare Council (2013) 23–24.

57. Center for Missing and Exploited Children (1999), 5; Williamson and Cluse-Tolar (2002), 1083–1084; Shared Hope International (2009), 41–43.

58. "2014 State Ratings on Human Trafficking Laws."

59. Ibid.

60. Safe Harbour for Exploited Children Act (effective April 1, 2010)— amends Family Court Act §§ 311.4, 712, 732; and amends NY Social Services Law 447-a, -b.

61. In the Matter of Nicolette R., 779 N.Y.S. 2nd 487; Geist (2012), 85–86; Mullen and Lloyd (2011), 129.

62. Mullen and Lloyd (2011), 132.

63. 22 USC 7102(8);

64. N.Y. Fam. CT. Act § 311.4(3).

65. Ibid.

66. Meisner (2009).

67. On November 21, 2011, the governor of Massachusetts signed into law H. 3808, "An Act Relative to the Commercial Exploitation of People," which strengthens protections for victims of human trafficking and prostitution and increases the punishment for offenders by carrying a potential life sentence for traffickers of children. It also defines a "sexually exploited child" to include any person under the age of 18 who is a victim of sex trafficking as defined under federal law; or who engages in conduct described as sex for a fee, is a victim of being induced into prostitution, or engages in acts of common street walking or common night walking, all as defined under Massachusetts's law.

68. Geist (2012), 95.

69. Public Act No. 10–115

70. Conn. Gen. Stat. Ann. § 53a-82(a); In Connecticut the legal age for consensual sex is 16 years.

71. Conn. Gen. Stat. Ann. § 53a-82(c); Shared Hope International, Connecticut Report Card, 2014 Protected Innocence Challenge, 2014.

72. Conn. Gen. Stat. Ann. § 53a-86(a)

73. Geist (2012), 116; Shared Hope International (2014b); The Connecticut Commissioner of Children and Families may: (1) provide child welfare services for any minor child residing in the state who is identified by the Department of Children and Families as a victim of trafficking, as defined in section 46a-170 of the general statutes; and (2) provide appropriate services to a minor child residing in the state who the Department of Children and Families reasonably believes may be a victim of trafficking in order to safeguard the welfare of such minor child ("2014 State Ratings on Human Trafficking Laws.").

74. Pub. Act 96–1464, 2010

75. Geist (2012), 102–103; Annitto (2011), 52–53.

76. HB 6462 § 15(d) (Ill. 2010)

77. Annitto (2011), 53.

78. Ill. Penal Code § 11–15.1

79. Annitto (2011), 53.

80. HB 6462 § 15(d) (Ill. 2010).

81. Geist (2012), 115.

REFERENCES

Adams, William, Colleen Owens, and Kevonne Small. "Effects of Federal Legislation on the Commercial Sexual Exploitation of Children." *Juvenile Justice Bulletin*. Washington, DC: Office of Juvenile Justice and Delinquency Prevention, 2010.

Annitto, Megan. "Consent, Coercion, and Compassion: Crafting a Commonsense Approach to Commercial Sexual Exploitation of Minors." *Yale Law and Policy Review* 30, no.1 (2011): 1–66.

Barnitz, Laura. "Effectively Responding to the Commercial Sexual Exploitation of Children: A Comprehensive Approach to Prevention, Protection and Reintegration Services." *Child Welfare* 80, no. 5 (2001): 597–610.

Broughton, Grace. "Prosecuting Innocence: An Analysis of Statutory Efforts to Stop the Justice System's Re-Victimization of Exploited Youth in America's Sex Trade." *National Center for Prosecution of Child Abuse Update* 23, no. 8 (2013): 1–4.

California Child Welfare Council. *Ending the Commercial Sexual Exploitation of Children: A Call for Multisystem Collaboration in California.* By Kate Walker. Sacramento, CA: California Health and Human Services Agency, 2013.

Center for Impact Research. *Sisters Speak Out: The Lives and Needs of Prostituted Women in Chicago. A Research Study.* By Jody Raphael and Deborah Shapiro. Chicago, IL: Center for Impact Research, 2002.

Center for Missing and Exploited Children. *Prostitution of Children and Child-Sex Tourism: An Analysis of Domestic and International Responses.* By Eva Klain. Washington, DC: National Center for Missing and Exploited Children, 1999.

Center for the Study of Youth Policy. *The Commercial Sexual Exploitation of Children in the US, Canada and Mexico.* By Richard Estes and Neil Alan Weiner. Philadelphia, PA: University of Pennsylvania, 2001.

Center on Poverty and Inequality. *Blueprint: A Multidisciplinary Approach to the Domestic Sex Trafficking of Girls.* By Rebecca Epstein and Peter Edelman. Washington, DC: Georgetown Law, 2013a.

Center on Poverty and Inequality. *Blueprint: A Multidisciplinary Approach to the Domestic Sex Trafficking of Girls.* By Rebecca Epstein and Peter Edelman. Washington, DC: Georgetown Law, 2013b.

Clayton, Ellen Wright, Richard D. Krugman, and Patti Simon, eds. *Confronting Commercial Sexual Exploitation and Sex Trafficking of Minors in the United States.* Washington, DC: The National Academies Press, 2013.

Crimes against Children Research Center. *How Many Juveniles Are Involved in Prostitution in the U.S.?* By Michelle Stransky and David Finkelhor. Durham, NH: University of New Hampshire, 2008.

Dank, Meredith, Bilal Khan, P. Mitchell Downey, Cybele Kotonias, Deborah Mayer, Colleen Owens, Laura Pacifici, Lilly Yu. "Estimating the Size and Structure of the Underground Commercial Sex Economy in Eight Major US Cities." *Urban Institute.* March 12, 2014. http://www.urban.org/research/publication/estimating-size-and-structure-underground-commercial-sex-economy-eight-major-us-cities/view/full_report.

ECPAT-USA, Inc. *Who Is There to Help Us? How the System Fails Sexually Exploited Girls in the United States: Examples from Four American Cities.* By Sara Ann Friedman. Brooklyn, NY: ECPAT-USA, Inc., 2005.

Edwards, Jessica M., Bonita J. Iritani, and Denise Dion Hallfors. "Prevalence and Correlates of Exchanging Sex for Drugs or Money among Adolescents in the United States." *Sexually Transmitted Infections* 82, no. 5 (2006): 354–358.

Federal Bureau of Investigation. "Crime in the United States, 2011: Table 43." http://www.fbi.gov/about-us/cjis/ucr/crime-in-the-u.s/2011/crime-in-the-u.s.-2011/tables/table-43.

Federal Bureau of Investigation. U.S. Department of Justice, *Crime in the United States, 2010,* "*Table 43: Arrests by Race, 2011.*" Released September 2012d, http://www.fbi.gov/about-us/cjis/ucr/crime-in-the-u.s/2011/crime-in-the-u.s.-2011/tables/table-43.

Finkelhor, David and Richard Ormrod. "Prostitution of Juveniles: Patterns from NIBRS." *Juvenile Justice Bulletin*. Washington DC: Office of Juvenile Justice and Delinquency Prevention, 2004.

Geist, Darren. "Finding Safe Harbor: Protection, Prosecution, and State Strategies to Address Prostituted Minors." *Legislation and Policy Brief* 4, no. 2 (2012): 68–127.

Greenbaum, Jordan. "Commercial Sexual Exploitation and Sex Trafficking of Children in the US." *Current Problems in Pediatric Adolescent Health Care* 44, no. 9 (2014): 245–269.

Halter, Stephanie. "Factors That Influence Police Conceptualizations of Girls Involved in Prostitution in Six U.S. Cities: Child Sexual Exploitation Victims or Delinquents?" *Child Maltreatment* 15, no. 2 (2010): 152–160.

In the Matter of Nicolette R., 779 N.Y.S. 2nd 487.

Leidholdt, Dorchen. "Interviewing and Assisting Trafficking Survivors." In *Lawyer's Manual on Human Trafficking: Pursuing Justice for Victims*, 2nd edition. Edited by Jill Goodman and Dorchen Leidholdt, 169–181. New York: Supreme Court of the State of New York, Appellate Division, First Department New York State Judicial Committee on Women in the Courts, 2011.

McClanahan, Susan, Gary McClelland, Karen Abram, and Linda Teplin. "Pathways into Prostitution among Female Jail Detainees and Their Implications for Mental Health Services." *Psychiatric Services* 50, no.12 (1999): 1606–1613.

Meisner, Toolsi. "Shifting the Paradigm from Prosecution to Protection of Child Victims of Prostitution," *Update* 21, no. 8 (2009).

Mitchell, Kimberly, David Finkelhor, and Janis Wolak. "Conceptualizing Juvenile Prostitution as Child Maltreatment: Findings from the National Juvenile Prostitution Study." *Child Maltreatment* 15, no. 1 (2010): 18–36.

Muftic, Lisa and Mary Finn. "Health Outcomes among Women Trafficked for Sex in the United States: A Closer Look." *Journal of Interpersonal Violence* 28, no. 9 (2013): 1859–1885.

Mullen, Katherine and Rachel Lloyd. "The Passage of the Safe Harbor Act and the Voices of Sexually Exploited Youth." In *Lawyer's Manual on Human Trafficking: Pursuing Justice for Victims*, 2nd edition. Edited by Jill Goodman and Dorchen Leidholdt, 129–148. New York, NY: Supreme Court of the State of New York, Appellate Division, First Department New York State Judicial Committee on Women in the Courts, 2011.

National District Attorneys Association (NDAA). "Sexual Offenses against Children: Statutory Compilation, 2010." http://www.ndaa.org/pdf/Sexual%20Offenses%20Against%20Children_6-2010.pdf.

New York State Office of Children and Family Services. *New York Prevalence Study of Commercially Sexually Exploited Children Final Report*. By Frances Gragg, Ian Petta, Haidee Bernstein, Karla Eisen, and Liz Quinn. Rennsselaer, NY: New York State Office of Children and Family Services, 2007.

Nixon, Kendra, Leslie Tutty, Pamela Downe, Kelly Gorkoff, and Jane Ursel. "The Everyday Occurrence: Violence in the Lives of Girls Exploited through Prostitution." *Violence against Women* 8, no. 9 (2002): 1016–1043.

Office of Assistant Secretary for Planning and Evaluation. *Evidence-Based Mental Health Treatment for Victims of Human Trafficking*. By Erin Williamson,

Nicole Dutch, and Heather Clawson. Washington, D.C.: U.S. Department of Health and Human Services, 2010.

Office of Juvenile Justice and Delinquency Prevention. *Commercial Sexual Exploitation of Children/Sex Trafficking.* Bethesda, MD: Development Services Group, Inc., 2014.

Polaris Project. *Child Sex Trafficking At-A-Glance,* Washington, DC: Polaris Project, 2011.

President's Interagency Taskforce to Monitor and Combat Trafficking in Persons. *Federal Strategic Action Plan on Services for Victims of Human Trafficking in the United States 2013–2017.* Washington, DC: U.S. Department of Justice, U.S. Department of Health and Human Services, and U.S. Department of Homeland Security, 2014.

Puzzanchera, Charles. "Juvenile Arrests 2011." *Juvenile Justice Bulletin.* Washington, DC: Office of Juvenile Justice and Delinquency Prevention, 2013.

Raphael, Jody, Jessica Ashley Reichert, and Mark Powers. "Pimp Control and Violence: Domestic Sex Trafficking of Chicago Women and Girls." *Women & Criminal Justice* 20, no. 1 (2010): 89–104.

Schwartz, Jennifer, Darrell Steffensmeier, and Ben Feldmeyer. "Assessing Trends in Women's Violence Via Data Triangulation: Arrests, Convictions, Incarcerations, and Victim Reports." *Social Problems* 56, (2009): 494–525.

Shared Hope International. *2014 Protected Innocence Challenge: A Legal Framework of Protection for the Nation's Children.* Vancouver, WA: Shared Hope International, 2014a.

Shared Hope International. *Connecticut Report Card, 2014 Protected Innocence Challenge.* Vancouver, WA: Shared Hope International, 2014b.

Shared Hope International. *The National Report on Domestic Minor Sex Trafficking: America's Prostituted Children.* By Linda Smith, Samantha Vardaman, and Melissa Snow. Vancouver, WA: Shared Hope International, 2009.

Shared Hope International. *The Protected Innocence Challenge: State Report Cards on the Legal Framework of Protection for the Nation's Children.* Vancouver, WA: Shared Hope International, 2011.

Sherman, Francine and Lisa Goldblatt-Grace. "The System Response to the Commercial Sexual Exploitation of Girls." In *Juvenile Justice: Advancing Research, Policy, and Practice,* 2nd edition. Edited by Francine T. Sherman and Francine H. Jacobs, 331–351. Hoboken, NJ: John Wiley & Sons, 2011.

Silbert Mimi and Ayala Pines. "Entrance into Prostitution." *Youth and Society* 13, no. 4 (1982): 471–500.

"2014 State Ratings on Human Trafficking Laws." *Polaris Project.* http://www.polarisproject.org/what-we-do/policy-advocacy/national-policy/state-ratings-on-human-trafficking-laws.

Urban Institute, Justice Policy Center. *An Analysis of Federally Prosecuted Commercial Sexual Exploitation of Children (CSEC) Cases since the Passage of the Victims of Trafficking and Violence Protection Act of 2000.* By Kevonne Small William Adams, Colleen Owens, and Kevin Roland. Washington, DC: Urban Institute, Justice Policy Center.

U.S. Department of Health and Human Services. *Finding a Path to Recovery: Residential Facilities for Minor Victims of Domestic Sex Trafficking.* By Heather Clawson and Lisa Goldblatt-Grace. Washington, DC: U.S. Department of Health and Human Services, 2007.

U.S. Department of Justice. *The Commercial Sexual Exploitation of Children in New York City.* By Ric Curtis, Karen Terry, Meredith Dank, Kirk Dombrowski, and Bilal Khan. Washington, DC: U.S. Department of Justice, 2008.

Widom, Cathy. "Victims of Childhood Sexual Abuse—Later Criminal Consequences." *National Institute of Justice Research in Brief.* Washington, DC: U.S. Department of Justice, Office of Justice Programs, 1995.

Williamson Celia and Terry Cluse-Tolar. "Pimp-Controlled Prostitution." *Violence against Women* 8, no. 9 (2002): 1074–1092.

Wilson, H.W. and Cathy Widom. "The Role of Youth Problem Behaviors in the Path from Child Abuse and Neglect to Prostitution: A Prospective Examination." *Journal of Research on Adolescence* 20 (2010): 210–236.

"Wyoming Becomes 50th State to Outlaw Human Trafficking," *Polaris Project.* February 27, 2013. https://www.polarisproject.org/media-center/news-and-press/press-releases/742-wyoming-becomes-50th-state-to-outlaw-human-trafficking.

Part II

Communities and Institutions: Problems and Responses to Delinquency

PREFACE TO PART II

From the Hairbrush to the Ritalin: Changes in Views on Children Acting Out

In the early 1900s, efforts such as the Police Athletic League (PALS) program and the "Junior Police" in major metropolitan areas assumed that the attractiveness of the police image would inspire youngsters to emulate law-abiding behaviors.[1] In traditional Chicago school style, a college-educated policeman brought to the community a commitment to prevention and programming whereby the officer could potentially serve as a role model to an expanding landscape of high-risk kids. Music, drama, nature and service activities, games, and sports were featured. In Washington, DC, popular singer Ella Fitzgerald even entertained at meetings and the Federal Bureau of Investigation's (FBI) chief, J. Edgar Hoover, sent over an agent to speak to the youth.[2] Part of the pledge a youth signed when obtaining his badge would read:

(1) I will not be a first offender.
(2) I will use my influence to prevent others from becoming first offenders.
(3) I will mind my own business: tell the truth at all times and never be a tattle-tale.

As Washington explains in her thesis evaluating one of these programs, the goal was to discourage the young from engaging in crime by "making a hero of each boy who prevents a friend from stealing" and by developing systems for breaking up fights.[3] Reporting on the success of one program, Richardson says "bonfires have been reduced in the district ninety-eight percent, complaints of disorderly street gatherings have been cut to less than half, street cleaning has been lightened, fire escapes cleared, garbage cans kept in order, juvenile cigarette smoking made unpopular and a juvenile millennium all but inaugurated."[4]

Though we often talk about the way the media influences people's perceptions of social problems, it can also be argued that our popular views and beliefs about contemporary issues also influence the media. Looking at cartoons that appeared in criminal-justice-related news magazines from the 1940s and 1950s we can see how these trends in policy and programming were criticized and satirized in humor.[5] These editorial snapshots also reflect what were then the latest fads and philosophies to circulate through the professional field. Many of these progressive efforts in the 1940s incorporated the growing interest in child development and child psychology, which encouraged a more permissive style of parenting while critics launched a direct assault on the notion of "spare the rod and spoil the child." Some cartoons of the time featured child psychologists secretly using a hairbrush, or advocating the use of one as a last resort. One cartoon even showed a policeman patrolling with a hairbrush instead of a nightstick.

While media coverage of the positive effects of outreach programs and community integration efforts can spearhead new trends in treatment and practice, emphasis on negative juvenile events can be equally as influential. For example, in 1996, political scientist John DiIulio compiled a highly publicized report that predicted asocial circumstances were ripe to spawn a wave of serious juvenile super-predators who would plague American communities. Republican presidential candidate and Senate Majority Leader Bob Dole quickly adopted the "super-predator" scare scenario to propel legislators into passing The Violent Youth Predator Act of 1996, which allowed many young offenders to be tried and incarcerated as adults. In a short time, of course, criminologists were able to demonstrate that the phenomenon was not going to occur and, in many areas, violent crime by juveniles had decreased. Although DiIulio's pronouncements were widely discredited, the image and its effects lingered—as did many of the terms that, 20 years later, are still often resurrected during political campaigns and funding competitions. Still, as we will see in the chapters that follow, there is some optimism about the pendulum shifting again toward more positive preventive measures.

According to Maloney,[6] over the last two decades, practitioners and theorists have moved away from the negative connotations of always assessing youth in terms of risk and potential for failure or delinquency to focus more on positive youth development (PYD). To its advocates, PYD emphasizes skill building and character features that are associated with productive adulthoods and a positive life trajectory much like those early police-sponsored activity programs. This is in contrast to traditional anti-drug and antigang strategies like DARE and GREAT that seem to focus only on the reduction of negative behaviors.[7]

There is little disagreement that our preoccupation with combatting drugs and drug use has altered the normal functioning of schools, athletics, military operations, and law enforcement agencies, to name just a few social institutions. Therefore, the idea of *in loco parentis* as described in Dr. Cavanaugh's article is a great topic for classroom debate. Can principals and school administrators ever really argue that they are acting in place of "a parent"? Or, by duty and responsibilities, are they instead representatives of a collective school purpose? The U.S. Supreme Court has long been an opponent of strip-searching children in schools or anywhere else. The majority in *Safford Unified School District v. Redding* agreed with the circuit court finding that "it does not require a constitutional scholar to conclude that a nude search of a 13-year-old child is an invasion of constitutional rights of some magnitude." Even so, the only dissenter on the case, Justice Clarence Thomas, argued in support of strip-searching children. He said officials should have the power to insure the health and safety of students in school, without judges second-guessing them. The other justices, however, would go even further in condemning the practice, often voting to uphold liability claims against schools engaging in strip searches. More recent claims against Transportation Security Administration (TSA) officials and the random pat downs of young girls in airports will undoubtedly come before the courts.

The court's reasoning has undoubtedly been influenced in some way by expert testimony about the potential harm young girls suffer from strip searches. As Cavanaugh points out, earlier case law specifically designates that officials must weigh the risks of intrusiveness in terms of "the age and sex of the student and the nature of the infraction."[8] Emotional damage, inability to concentrate, and even subsequent dropping out of school all have been recorded as lingering consequences. An example of this comes from Savana Redding, a Supreme Court plaintiff in a strip search case discussed in Chapter 5. Savana Redding called the strip search "the most humiliating experience" of her life and, as Lithwick[9] notes, Savana, a former honor student, dropped out of school.

In this part, drug use among juveniles and case law pertaining to searches at schools are analyzed. Both problems, as explained in the chapters, are linked together. Drug use represents one of the biggest problems among juveniles and schools are one place where kids come together with regularity. In an effort to figure out a way to reduce and combat drug use (in addition to violence), schools have resorted to search policies that could be considered to violate the rights of U.S. citizens. A juvenile delinquency problem and a solution by the system are presented. Quite often, as is the case with policy creation, unintended negative consequences arise from the solution. This part touches on that conundrum.

REFERENCES

Greenberg, Martin. "A Short History of Junior Police." *The Police Chief* 75, no. 4 (April 2008). http://www.policechiefmagazine.org/magazine/index.cfm?fuse action=display_arch&article_id=1463&issue_id=42008.

Lithwick, Dahlia. "The Supreme Court Is Neither Hot Nor Bothered by Strip Searches." *Slate*, April 21, 2009. http://www.slate.com/articles/news_and_ politics/supreme_court_dispatches/ 2009/04/search_me.html.

Maloney, Shannon. *Positive Youth Development in a School-Based Setting. A Study of the Los Angeles Police Academy Magnet School Program.* Ph.D. diss., The Pardee RAND Graduate School, 2014.

McShane, Marilyn and Frank P. Williams III. "Corrections and Cartoons: An Analysis of Thematic Content, 1939–1957." Paper presented at the annual meeting of the Western Society of Criminology, Las Vegas, NV, February, 1990.

New Jersey v. T.L.O., 469 U.S. 325 (1985).

Richardson, Guy, ed. "Boy-Policemen." *Our Dumb Animals* 47, no. 12 (1915): 185.

Washington, Elizabeth Jean. "A Study of the Program and Activities of the Junior Police and Citizens Corps in Washington, DC." Master's Thesis, Atlanta University, 1945.

Chapter 4

Drugs in Homes, Schools, and Communities

Marcos Misis

Drug use among American adolescents has been a subject matter of great concern for researchers, educators, governmental entities and other social actors in the last five decades. Past research has shown that age is one of the main correlates of illegal drug use in the United States, and adolescence seems to be the heightened point of drug use in the life course.[10] Adolescence is a crucial period in the physical, psychological, and cognitive development of humans, and experimentation with drugs, due to risk-taking behavior tendencies and peer pressure, is common during these years.[11] The physical, psychological, and social consequences of drug abuse during adolescence are mostly dreadful and life-altering. Among them, school failure, development of psychiatric problems (such as depression and anxiety), personality disorders, higher risk of suicidal tendencies, contraction of HIV and other sexually transmitted diseases, disengagement from peers and community activities, and dysfunctions in the family unit seem to be the most prominent.[12]

In order to understand adolescence use of drugs, a number of self-report surveys have been used to obtain information of the use, perceptions, and availability of illegal substances, alcohol, and other drugs. Among them, the Monitoring the Future (MTF) study has been the most widely used.

The MTF has been collecting data on drug use among adolescents since 1975.[13] Other self-report surveys such as the Youth Risk Behavior Survey (YRBS), implemented by the Centers for Disease Control, have complimented the data obtained from MTF.[14]

In addition to collecting data to understand the nature and extent of drug use and abuse among American youth, governmental and private entities have created numerous school-based prevention programs to prevent and curb drug use among children and adolescents. The success of these programs is in question to this day. Some sources indicate the lack of empirical proof to verify these programs have any effect on drug use among youth, while others believe that the existence of these programs is beneficial no matter what the outcome is.

MONITORING THE FUTURE

Purpose and Design

Funded by the National Institute on Drug Abuse and conducted by the University of Michigan researchers, the Monitoring the Future (MTF) study was first put into operation in 1975 as a survey of high-school students about their drug and alcohol use. In 1976, the MTF began to select a random sample of high-school students to follow them biannually after high school in their college and/or their professional careers through the age of 55.[15] In 1991, MTF started collecting data on 8th and 10th graders. In 2014, the MTF survey obtained data of approximately 41,600 students attending 8th (15,200 students), 10th (13,300 students), and 12th (13,000 students) grades in 377 secondary schools nationwide.[16]

The MTF is administered every spring to approximately 420 high schools and middle schools in the country, both public and private. These schools are selected using a multistage random sampling scheme, which consists of three stages: (a) Stage one: certain geographical areas are selected; (b) Stage two: one or more schools are selected in the geographical area considering probability proportionate to size; and. (c) Stage 3: Classes in each school are selected. Within each school, a maximum of 350 students may be selected. In small schools, all students are included. Conversely, in larger schools, a random sample of students is used. The MTF investigators use sampling weights when analyzing the data to adjust for unequal probabilities of selection in any of the steps in the multistage random sampling scheme.[17]

Once the sample is selected, parents and students are informed about the study 10 days before the in-school administration. Parents receive in advance informed consent letters that contain means to decline their child's participation. The questionnaire administration is conducted by representatives of the University of Michigan in normal class time.

In regards to the follow-up survey, participants are mailed the question-naires together with a self-addressed, stamped envelope and a small monetary gift.[18]

Using nearly 100 questions, MTF surveys adolescents on their use of marijuana, synthetic marijuana, inhalants, lysergic acid diethylamide (LSD), cocaine, crack, amphetamines, methamphetamine, and crystal methamphetamine, heroin, narcotic drugs (such as OxyContin and Vico-din), tranquilizers, sedatives (barbiturates), ecstasy (MDMA) and other "club drugs," alcohol, cigarettes, smokeless tobacco, e-cigarettes, small cigars and tobacco using a hookah, and steroids in the last 30 days and in their lifetime.[19] In addition, MTF includes questions of the age at first use of drugs, the frequency and quantity of use, availability of drugs, peers informal rules in regards to use of drugs, perceptions of health risks due to the use of drugs, and expected future use of drugs.[20]

Strengths and Weaknesses of Self-Report Data on Youth Drug Use

Self-report surveys were implemented for the study of deviant behav-ior beginning in the 1940s and 1950s. These surveys included questions measuring illegal substances' use. Self-report surveys were an impor-tant innovation in the study of crime, as it allowed researchers to go "directly to the source" to obtain data of all kinds of crimes, including drug use.[21]

One of the main advantages of self-report surveys is that it enables researchers to make general assumptions about the behavior of a general population using a relatively small sample, provided that researchers have used the proper sampling procedures. As such, with a properly selected sample, researchers can obtain data on use of specific drugs, patterns of usage, demographic differences in drugs' use and abuse, availability of drugs, and the consequences of use and abuse of drugs among others. In addition, the flexibility of self-report instruments allows researchers to target those populations most likely to try, experience, or use drugs. To this extent, researchers can investigate the use and availability of new drugs among youth such as ecstasy, Ketamine, or GHB, which are a con-cern for society in determined periods of time.[22]

Self-report data collection methods have a number of limitations that must be considered when interpreting the results. One of the main prob-lems with self-report methods when it comes to obtaining information is the difficulty of access to some populations involved in illegal substance use and abuse. For instance, in the case of drug use among teenagers, most self-report surveys are based on middle- and high-school student popula-tions. The data obtained from this population is definitely incomplete as it does not account for high-school dropouts and those with high levels of absenteeism, as they are more likely to consume illegal drugs and alcohol than students that stay in school.[23]

Another issue of high importance is the tendency of individuals to underreport their drug use. That is, the tendency of respondents to lie, minimize, or fail to answer questions that they feel may be threatening to themselves. This issue is highly related to social desirability, which is the tendency of respondents to answer certain questions in a way they perceive it would be more socially appropriate. As such, researchers have observed that there is a tendency to underreport the consumption of harder drugs, such as heroin, cocaine, and methamphetamine, due to the higher social stigma they carry. Likewise, researchers have noted that levels of underreporting are higher among minorities, the uneducated, and those living in poverty. This pattern has been explained by the distrust these populations held against the white "powerful" majority and what it is perceived to be criminal behavior, which is highly stigmatized within the criminal justice system.[24]

All in all, although data on drug use and abuse among youth obtained from self-report instruments should be evaluated with caution, this data provides researchers and other social agents with a reasonable valid picture of substance use and abuse among youth in America. With its limitations in mind, this data can be used as a starting point for policy creation and implementation.[25]

MONITORING THE FUTURE DATA: TRENDS AND FINDINGS

Marijuana

According to the data gathered in this study, marijuana use peaked among 12th graders in 1979 with 51 percent of the students reporting use of marijuana. After 1979, its consumption declined in the next 13 years bottoming in 1992 with 22 percent of high-school seniors reporting use of marijuana. In the years 1996, 1997, and 1998, marijuana use spiked once again among students and remained fairly high until the period of 2006, when marijuana use declined considerably among students of the three grades. Marijuana use among 8th graders increased in use from 2007 to 2010, decreased marginally from 2010 to 2012, and then leveled. Among 10th graders, MTF surveys showed a slight increase from 2008 to 2012 and then leveled. Among high-school seniors, marijuana use increased from 2006 to 2011 and leveled from 2011 to 2013.[26]

In 2014, use of marijuana among surveyed students declined slightly from 26 percent in 2013 to 24 percent in the three grades combined. In all, 6.5 percent of 8th graders, 16.6 percent of 10th graders, and 21.2 percent of 12th graders reported using marijuana in the last 30 days. Around

6 percent of 12th graders reported to use marijuana every day (one in every 17 high school seniors), and 81 percent of them believed marijuana was easy to get. Interestingly, MTF data for 2014 showed that in states with medical marijuana laws, 40 percent of high-school seniors reported consumption of marijuana edibles, while 26 percent of high-school seniors in nonmedical marijuana states reported the consumption of marijuana edibles. Finally, the majority of high-school seniors believed that occasional marijuana use is not harmful, with only 16.4 percent of them stating that occasional use puts the user at great risk.[27]

Cocaine

Use of cocaine among high-school seniors grew rapidly in the late 1970s and continued stable until 1986 when consumption experienced a great decline. Between 1992 and 1999, the use of cocaine between 8th, 10th, and 12th graders almost doubled before declining by 2000. In fact, cocaine use among 8th graders peaked in 1996 with 3 percent of students reporting its use. Among 10th and 12th graders, cocaine use peaked in 1999 with 4.9 and 6.2 percent of students reporting using cocaine. Over the last 15 years, use has declined with historical lows in all three grades.[28] In 2014, only a very small minority of students reported using cocaine in the last 30 days. Only 0.5 percent of 8th graders, 0.5 percent of 10th graders, and 1 percent of 12th graders said they consumed cocaine. Annually, the percentages showed a slight increase with approximately 2.5 percent of high school seniors, 1.5 percent of 10th graders, and 1 percent of 8th graders indicating they used cocaine in the last year.[29]

Questions on perceived risks of the use of cocaine have been asked only of 12th graders. High-school seniors' perceptions stayed fairly leveled in the beginning of the 1980s until 1986 where it raised more than 14 percent in one year and continued high until 1991. Perceived risk declined discreetly from 1991 to 2000. In recent years, perceived risks of consumption of cocaine and disapproval of use have increased showing a gradual upward drift over the past five years in all grades. At last, the proportion of high-school seniors stating that it would be easy for them to get cocaine when they wanted went from 33 percent in 1977 to 48 percent in 1980. After that, it held leveled through 1982 increasing steadily to 59 percent by 1989. In 1994, perceived availability fell to about 47 percent; since 1997, perceived availability of cocaine has fallen considerably in all three grades.[30]

Crack Cocaine

Crack cocaine is derived from powder cocaine, which has been dissolved in a mixture of water and ammonia or baking soda. This mixture is boiled until it becomes a solid substance that later is divided in little chunks or rocks, which are most commonly smoked.[31]

Crack use rose up swiftly during the 1980s with a prevalence of use of around 4 percent among high-school seniors. After 1991, MTF data showed a steadily increase in the consumption of crack among adolescents. In 1998, the consumption of crack among 8th, 10th, and 12th graders peaked at 2.1, 2.5, and 2.7 percent, respectively. Since 1999, the use of crack has dropped to historical lows for 8th and 12th graders and at its lowest point among 10th graders.[32] In 2014, crack consumption among those surveyed is almost nonexistent. As such, only 0.3 percent of 8th graders and 10th graders and 0.7 percent of 12th graders reported consuming crack in the last 30 days. Furthermore, the annual consumption of crack among those surveyed is notoriously low with 0.7 percent of 8th graders, 0.5 percent of 10th graders, and 1.1 percent of 12th graders indicating consumption of crack.[33]

By 1987, high-school seniors already believed crack to be one of the most dangerous drugs on the streets with 57 percent of them seeing a great risk in even trying it. Between 1991 and 1998 there was a considerable falloff in this belief among 8th and 10th graders as use rose steadily. After leveling in 2000, 2014 has seen a rise in perceived risk of trying crack among 8th and 10th graders. Interestingly, students' perception of risk of regular use of crack fell considerably in 2014. Since 1990, students have expressed high levels of disapproval, between 80 and 90 percent, of use of crack. In 2014, disapproval of crack had leveled among 8th and 10th graders and dropped among 12th graders. Since 2000, perceptions of availability have dropped substantially, particularly among 10th and 12th graders. In 2014, perceptions of availability declined significantly as well.[34]

Heroin

Heroin use among high-school seniors fell by half between 1975 and 1979, from 1.0 to 0.5 percent, and remained at that level until 1994. Heroin consumption peaked in 1996 among 8th graders (1.6%), in 1997 among 10th graders (1.4%), and in 2000 among 12th graders (1.5%). Since 2000, the levels of consumption of heroin among adolescents has decreased consistently and remained at very low levels.[35] In 2014, very few of the surveyed students in the three grades reported using heroin. Only 0.5 percent of 8th graders, 10th graders, and 12th graders said they consumed heroin in the last 30 days. In addition, the annual consumption of heroin was really low with 0.3 percent of 8th graders, 0.4 percent of 10th graders, and 0.4 percent of 12th graders consuming heroin in 2014.[36]

In regards to the perceived risk of use of heroin among students, they have expressed over the years that heroin is one of the most dangerous drugs, which is reflected in the recorded high levels of personal disapproval of use and the minimal prevalence of use. Availability of heroin has fluctuated over time with 20 percent of 12th graders reporting it was easy to get heroin through the mid-1980s. It then increased until stabilizing at about 35 percent from 1992 through 1998. Since the late 1990s to the actuality, perceived availability of heroin had a substantial decrease in all three grades.[37]

Amphetamines

The use of amphetamines rose over the 1970s reaching its peak in 1981 at 26 percent among high-school seniors. From 1981 to 1992, the use of amphetamines steadily decreased, but increased and reached its peak in 1996, with 9.1 percent of 8th graders and 12.4 percent of 10th graders indicating the use of amphetamines. Since then, its consumption by the two lower grades students has gradually decreased. Among 12th graders, consumption of amphetamines peaked in 2002 (11.1%), and remained stable until 2009 where data has shown an increase of consumption until 2013 and a modest decrease in 2014. In 2014, 2.1 percent of 8th graders, 3.7 percent of 10th graders, and 3.8 percent of 12th graders reported consuming amphetamines in the last 30 days. Furthermore, regarding the overall consumption in the year 2014, data shows that 4.3 percent of 8th graders, 7.6 percent of 10th graders, and 8.1 percent of 12th graders used amphetamines.[38]

Perceptions of risks of use of amphetamines were fairly low in the 1980s (between 20% and 30%), and increased considerably in 1992 to almost 40 percent of students expressing concerns about amphetamines' use. Since then, levels of perceived risk have remained stable, although in 2014 a lower perception of risk was reported in comparison with other years. With reference to disapproval of amphetamine use, 12th graders have expressed continuously high levels of disapproval of even trying amphetamines. In fact, data shows a disapproval average of more than 80 percent of students since 1985. Finally, availability of amphetamines peaked in 1975 at around 70 percent of students stating that the drug was easy to get. Since then, perceived availability has been decreasing steadily to around 40 percent.[39]

Methamphetamines and Crystal Methamphetamines (Ice)

Historic use of methamphetamines has followed the same patterns of the use of amphetamines among 12th grade's students, peaking in 1981, declining until 1992, peaking again in the mid-1990s, and declining steadily from 2006 to current levels. In fact, use of all classes of methamphetamines peaked in 1996 for 8th (9.1%) and 10th graders (12.4%), and in 2002 for 12th graders (11.1%). In 2014, 2.1 percent of 8th graders,

3.7 percent of 10th graders, and 3.8 percent of 12th graders reported using methamphetamines in the last 30 days. In regards to annual use in 2014, 4.3 percent of 8th graders, 7.6 percent of 10th graders, and 8.1 percent of 12th graders reported using methamphetamines during 2014.[40]

Perceptions of risks of use of methamphetamines reached its lowest point in 2004 at around 50 percent of students expressing great concern for the use of the drug. Since then, levels of perceived risk have increased considerably, reaching its highest point in 2013 at around 75 percent. In regards to availability of methamphetamines, data showed a decrease from 30 percent in 1998 to approximately 18 percent students reporting high availability of methamphetamines in 2014.[41]

Tranquilizers

Among 12th graders, Xanax is the tranquilizer most commonly used, without prescription, followed by Valium, Klonopin, and Soma. The consumption of tranquilizers among 8th graders has remained mostly constant from 1991 to the actuality at the 3–4 percent levels. The consumption among 10th graders peaked in 2001 at 7.3 percent and has been declining since then. Among 12th graders, between the late 1970s and all of the 1980s, tranquilizers' consumption fell steadily until 1992, slowly increased, and peaked in 2002 with 7.7 percent of students indicating usage of the drug illegally. Since then, consumption among high school seniors has seen a slow decline to the actual levels.[42] In 2014, .8 percent of 8th graders, 1.6 percent of 10th graders, and 2.1 percent of 12th graders reported consuming tranquilizers in the last 30 days. Furthermore, regarding the overall consumption in the year 2014, data shows that 1.7 percent of 8th graders, 3.9 percent of 10th graders, and 4.7 percent of 12th graders used tranquilizers.[43]

In 2014, there was no data reported in regards to perceived risk of use and disapproval among the three grades. In regards to availability of tranquilizers, 12th graders' belief that tranquilizers would be fairly or very easy to get if they wanted some has fallen from 72 percent in 1975 to 14 percent by 2014. The same trend has been observed among students in the two lower grades.[44]

Other Narcotic Drugs, Including OxyContin and Vicodin

High-school seniors' use of narcotics other than heroin experienced a considerable decline from 1977 to 1992. After 1992, like other drugs, the usage of these drugs rose considerably, nearly tripling from 3.3 percent in 1992 to 9.5 percent in 2004. Since 2009, the consumption of these substances has been in decline.[45] In regards to OxyContin (a synthetic opiate), consumption peaked in 2006 for 8th and 12th graders at 2.6 and 5.5 percent respectively; 10th graders' consumption peaked in 2009 at 5.1 percent. The data for 2014 showed that 1 percent of 8th graders, 3 percent of 10th graders, and 3.3 percent of 12th graders said they consumed the drug illegally. Likewise, in terms of illegal consumption of Vicodin (another popular synthetic opiate), 1 percent of 8th graders, 3.4 percent of 10th graders, and 4.8 percent of 12th graders reported using the drug in 2014. The illegal use of Vicodin peaked in 2006 for 8th graders at 3 percent, in 2009 for 10th graders at 8.1 percent, and in 2003 for 12th graders at 10.5 percent of them reporting they have used this substance.[46]

Perceptions of narcotics other than heroin increased steadily among 12th graders from 1978 through 1989 then rose further, from 1991 through 2001, and then declined after 2006. Among 8th and 10th graders' perceived availability has been on a downward path since the late 1990s. Since 2010, all three grades' perceptions of availability of narcotics other than heroin have decreased significantly.[47]

Alcohol

Underage drinking is considered a major problem among youth in the United States. Highly related to binge drinking, the use of alcohol by minors has been linked to problems in school, legal troubles, unwanted, unplanned, and unprotected sexual activity, physical and sexual assault, higher risk for homicide and suicide, unintended accidents, memory problems, abuse of other drugs, changes in brain development, and death from alcohol poisoning. Furthermore, teenagers who start drinking before age 15 are five times more likely to develop abuse or dependency on alcohol later in life than those who begin drinking at or after the age of 21.[48]

Patterns on underage drinking are worrisome. In 2009, about 10.4 million youth between the ages of 12 and 20 drank more than "just a few sips" of alcohol. Studies have shown that by age 15, 50 percent of teenagers have had at least one drink. At the same time, by age 18, more than 70 percent of them have had at least one drink. This indicates that as kids get older, they drink more. Binge drinking is one of the characteristics of underage drinking, which means that although teenagers drink less than adults, when they drink, they do drink a higher quantity of alcohol than adults do. On average, underage drinkers have five drinks on a single occasion, which can be considered binge drinking.[49]

Historically, MTF has concentrated its efforts in obtained data of binge drinking among 8th, 10th, and 12th graders. In all three grades, annual consumption peaked in 1991 with 54 percent of 8th graders, 72.3 percent of 10th graders, and 77.7 percent of 12th graders reporting drinking alcohol.[50] Since the peak in 1991, alcohol consumption has declined to the actual levels. In 2014, 9 percent of 8th graders, 23.5 percent of 10th graders, and 37.4 percent of 12th graders reported drinking alcohol in the last 30 days.[51] Regarding the overall consumption in the year 2014, data shows that 20.8 percent of 8th graders, 44 percent of 10th graders, and 60.2 percent of 12th graders drank alcohol.[52]

Through the years MTF has been administered, the majority of high-school seniors have expressed that binge drinking on weekends has great risk. Interestingly, levels of disapproval have maintained fairly high among 8th and 10th graders at around 80 percent, and at 65–70 percent among 12th graders. In regards to availability of alcohol for minors, data suggested that parents, communities, and other social agents have been successful in reducing access to alcohol among the younger teens. However, in 2014, 12th graders' perceived availability remains high at around 88 percent of them saying that alcohol would be fairly or very easy to get.[53]

THEORIES OF DRUG USE

Theories about drug use and juveniles range from sociological explanations involving family and friends to those emphasizing biological and chemical processes in the brain and throughout the endocrine and neurological systems. Genetic links and hereditary processes are also common explanations as are psychological theories involving personality and dependence.

Sociological Theories

While parents in the past may have worried about a "bad kid" down the street influencing their children, today's youth will be impacted by the values and views of peers all over the world as social media expands messages about the acceptability of drug use. Sutherland's differential association theory explains how an excess of definitions favorable to experimenting with drugs may outweigh negative associations with drug use. The positive pressures of friends will provide not only the motives and techniques for doing so but also the social reinforcement for such experimentation.[54] Strain theories address the institutional and economic conditions that produce pressure in the form of aspirations and expectations that may confront individuals dealing with relative deprivation. It can be argued that the temporary distractions and relief that drug use may offer are difficult to overcome without broad measures of social support and resources. Life course and developmental theories deal with factors and events that might intervene to accelerate or diminish the need for illegal substances.[55]

Biological and Psychological Theories

Many of the biological or biochemical explanations of drug abuse refer to neuropathways that conduct impulses to and from the brain. Enzymes and hormones, such as testosterone, may be imbalanced, thus impeding triggers and receptors that regulate the normal functioning of the nervous system. The unique make up of each individual means that chemicals may be underproduced or overproduced, resulting in differential responses that are difficult to predict or treat. Researchers are studying both genetic predispositions for some of these markers as well as the ways these conditions can be a product of disease or injury.

Psychological theories of drug abuse often focus on the concept of an "addictive personality" as well as the reinforcement that is associated with self-medication. Posttraumatic stress is another diagnosis that commonly co-occurs in persons abusing illegal substances. Cognitive behavioral therapies are designed to facilitate rational, real-world thinking about consequences of decisions and are often used in group settings in many correctional contexts.

In popular discussions and debates, people also attempt to theorize as to whether there is evidence to support the idea that there are "gateway," or introductory and less harmful drugs that serve to pave the way for the escalation of drug use into more serious drugs. Such an idea is based on an evolutionary theory of drug abuse that suggests there is a normal progression that is commonly followed in the process of becoming addicted to drugs. The popularity of the ideas of escalation and gateway drugs are inevitably tied to their political implications and strict law enforcement policies despite the fact that they are not currently supported by consistent empirical evidence. Often these ideas are fueled by anecdotal stories and campaign rhetoric associated with getting tough on crime.[56] Much the same can be said of theorizing about the relationship between gangs, guns, drugs and violent crime.

Gang, Guns, Drugs, and Violence

There appears to be considerable agreement among law enforcement agents that drug trafficking is one of the major determinants of gang violence. Further, it is alleged that the intersection of gangs, the presence and ownership of weapons, and competitive drug dealing enhances the likelihood of violent crime.[57] Youthful, unorganized criminal activity may be less able to avoid detection and when various proactive tactics or suppression measures are used by law enforcement, such as crackdowns on street dealing, or gun possession the probability of arrest increases. Those identified by law enforcement as "known" gang members or associates are also more prone to arrest.[58] Adding to the perception that drugs are associated with gangs, guns, and violence, the media's preoccupation with extensive coverage of these high-profile incidents reinforces the image of the dangerous relationship between gangs, drugs, guns, and violence.

SCHOOL-BASED DRUG PREVENTION PROGRAMS

Most drug prevention efforts today are school programs that rely on government funding to operate. The goals of these programs are to prevent, delay or diminish the onset of drug use among children through skill building that emphasizes personal accountability and resistance to peer pressure. Some scholars and practitioners have pointed out that these programs may have a reduction effect on drug consumption in the short run, but there is no clear empirical evidence of effectiveness in the long run.[59]

Several researchers have conducted reviews of school-based drug prevention programs in the United States to identify effective practices and procedures to curb drug use among youth. Among them, Winters, Fawkes, Botzet, Fahnhorst, and August identified six characteristics of effective programs: (1) effective programs base their curriculum on reducing risk factors (e.g., reducing aggression, reducing peer delinquent's influence, and curbing impulsive-like behaviors and increasing protective factors such as strengthening children's relationship with parents and other adult role models, encouraging extracurriculum activities, and using techniques to improve children's self-esteem); (2) effective programs concentrate their efforts on the use of getaways drugs (e.g., alcohol and tobacco); (3) effective programs work with children, their parents, and their peers in order to address the risk and protective factors in school, at home and in the local neighborhood; (4) effective programs tailor their curriculums to the target population; (5) effective programs place a high priority on developing strategies to promote youth and family engagement as effectiveness of prevention programs requires a high level of engagement by its participants; and (6) effective programs balance the intensity of the program with different follow-up sessions at later periods in time to bolster the programs' impact.[60]

RESEARCH-BASED DRUG ABUSE PREVENTION PROGRAMS

Skills, Opportunity, and Recognition (SOAR)

Designed for high-risk children who attend grade and middle school, SOAR is based on interventions involving parents, teachers, and children.

These interventions try to promote early prosocial bonds, attachment and commitment to schools, and decrease delinquency.[61]

Evaluations of the program have shown a long-term positive effect for participants, including considerable reductions in antisocial behavior, alienation and teen pregnancy, and improved academic skills, commitment to school, and positive relationships with people.[62]

Project Towards No Drug Abuse (Project TND)

Developed by the University of Southern California, Project TND is an interactive classroom-based program based on more than two decades of successful research on youth drug use and abuse. Using 12 in-class sessions in high schools, Project TND focuses on three factors that predict drug use and delinquency among youth: (1) motivation factors (i.e., students' attitudes, beliefs, expectations, and desires regarding drug use); (2) skills (effective communication, social self-control, and coping skills); and, (3) decision-making (i.e., how to make decisions that lead to health-promoting behaviors).[63] Evaluations of these programs have shown positive outcomes in participants in one-year and two-year follow-ups.[64]

Project ALERT

Designed to prevent substance abuse for 7th and 8th graders, Project ALERT is a two-year program for middle-school students that reduces the onset and regular use of drugs among participants. The program is composed of 14 lessons that focus on preventing the use of alcohol, tobacco, marijuana, and inhalants. Evaluations have shown that the program has been successful in preventing the use of marijuana, decreased smoking and alcohol use, and reduced prodrug attitudes and beliefs with high- and low-risk youth from different communities.[65]

Too Good for Drugs

This is a middle-school program that also emphasizes prosocial values and attempts to address intention to experiment with alcohol, tobacco, and other illicit drugs in the future. Although there are only limited tests of this model, it involves highly interactive weekly sessions that utilize role playing, small group activities, games, discussions, and skill-building opportunities. The skills focus on decision making, communication effectiveness, and identifying and managing emotions. In an evaluation of 40 schools (20 treatment and 20 control), and over 10,000 participating students, it was found that there were more positive results for high-risk students (those with more previous experience with illicit substances) and that the effects although moderated over time, were still in evidence at one year. Also significant was that those in lower achievement groups fared better on comprehensive assessment tests after the program than their counterparts in control groups.[66]

CONCLUSIONS

As the survey data in this chapter demonstrate, drug use is a phenomenon that has plagued society for hundreds of years. Drugs of choice change, fads, and trends are evident, but experimentation appears to be stable over time.

The connection between drug use and delinquency is undisputed, as use or possession of illegal substances is automatically an offense. The reality, however, is that the relationship between drugs, delinquency, truancy, violence, and participation in gangs is murky at best. While parents and community leaders seek direct and causal links, research has been unable to uncover any particular evolution or pattern of interaction with these elements. What we do know is that zero tolerance and "Just Say No" campaigns have not worked, nor have scare tactics and negative conditioning approaches such as DARE.

Today, experts recommend more public awareness campaigns on the dangers of drug use, more funding directed at educating and assisting parents at the community level and more attempts to replicate the prevention programs that are culturally and linguistically competent as well as providing more general school-based extracurricular activities.[67] Specifically, Stagman et al.[68] are advocates for more access to confidential drug-related treatment and mental health services, particularly interventions for homeless youth, one of the highest risk groups.

Although the treatment approaches described in this article highlight contemporary best practices, questions still remain about the most economical and ethical avenues to intervention and treatment. Should all children be exposed to programming, even those who may be low risk or in need of other types of services? Are critical elements of education and academic achievement being overlooked while these activities are substituted into the curriculum? And, in order to best serve diverse segments of the population, what ethnic and cultural aspects of treatment are being incorporated into interventions to make them more relevant.

DISCUSSION QUESTIONS

1. Do you perceive that illegal drug use in our society is increasing or decreasing? What about in your community? What factors contribute to your perceptions?
2. What are the benefits of a survey such as Monitoring the Future? What are its strengths and weaknesses?

3. What theories or theory elements do you think best explain juvenile drug use? Do these factors differ from those that might explain adult drug abuse?
4. If you had to design a drug prevention program, what would you use in the curriculum and what would you specifically avoid using?

ADDITIONAL RESOURCES

Helfrich, Christine, and Lenore McWey. "Substance Use and Delinquency: High-Risk Behaviors as Predictors of Teen Pregnancy among Adolescents Involved with the Child Welfare System." *Journal of Family Issues* 35, no. 10 (2014): 1322–1338.

Pedersen, Eric, Jeremy Miles, Karen Osilla, Brett Ewing, Sarah Hunter, and Elizabeth D'Amico. "The Effects of Mental Health Symptoms and Marijuana Expectancies on Marijuana Use and Consequences among At-Risk Adolescents." *Journal of Drug Issues* 45, no. 2 (2015): 151–165.

"Principles of Adolescent Substance Use Disorder Treatment: A Research-Based Guide." *National Institute on Drug Abuse.* http://www.drugabuse.gov/publications/principles-adolescent-substance-use-disorder-treatment-research-based-guide/acknowledgements.

Taylor, Liana. *General Responsivity and Evidence-Based Treatment: Individual and Program Predictors of Treatment Outcomes during Adolescent Outpatient Substance Abuse Treatment.* PhD diss., Temple University, 2015. https://www.ncjrs.gov/pdffiles1/nij/grants/248590.pdf.

Valentine, Gill, Mark Jayne, and Myles Gould. "The Proximity Effect: The Role of the Affective Space of Family Life in Shaping Children's Knowledge about Alcohol and Its Social and Health Implications." *Childhood* 21, no. 1 (2014): 103–118.

Veliz, Philip, John Schulenberg, Megan Patrick, Deborah Kloska, Sean Esteban McCabe, and Nicole Zarrett. "Competitive Sports Participation in High School and Subsequent Substance Use in Young Adulthood: Assessing Differences Based on Level of Contact." *International Review for the Sociology of Sport* (2015): 1012690215586998.

Willging, Cathleen E., Gilbert A. Quintero, and Elizabeth A. Lilliott. "Hitting the Wall Youth Perspectives on Boredom, Trouble, and Drug Use Dynamics in Rural New Mexico." *Youth & Society* 46, no. 1 (2014): 3–29.

RELATED WEBSITES

Addiction Science Research and Education Center, http://www.utexas.edu/research/asrec/

Alcohol Policy Information System (APIS), http://alcoholpolicy.niaaa.nih.gov/

Alliance of States with Prescription Monitoring Programs, http://pmpalliance.org/

Center for Substance Abuse Treatment (CSAT), http://beta.samhsa.gov/about-us/who-we-are/offices-centers/csat

Juvenile Drug Courts: Program Profile, https://www.crimesolutions.gov/Program
    Details.aspx?ID=388
National Institute on Drug Abuse (NIDA), http://www.drugabuse.gov/
Office of National Drug Control Policy (ONDCP), http://www.whitehouse.gov/
    ondcp
Substance Abuse and Mental Health Services Administration (SAMHSA), http://
    www.samhsa.gov/

SUPPORTING FILMS

The Basketball Diaries (1995)
Boyz in the Hood (1991)
Juice (1992)
Thirteen (2003)
Traffic (2000)

NOTES

1. Greenberg (2008).
2. Washington (1945).
3. Ibid., 28.
4. Richardson (1915), 185.
5. McShane and Williams (1990).
6. Maloney (2014).
7. Ibid.
8. *New Jersey v. T.L.O.* (1985)
9. Lithwick (2009).
10. Mosher and Atkins (2014), 177.
11. National Center for Children in Poverty (2011).
12. Crowe and Sydney (2000).
13. Mosher and Atkins (2014), 181.
14. Ibid., 183.
15. "Purpose and Design."
16. Institute for Social Research (2014).
17. "Purpose and Design."
18. Ibid.
19. Mosher and Atkins (2014), 181.
20. Ibid.
21. Ibid., 178.
22. Ibid., 179.
23. Ibid.
24. Ibid., 180.
25. Ibid.
26. Institute for Social Research (2014).

27. Ibid.; "Teen Prescription Opioid Abuse, Cigarette, and Alcohol Use Trends Down"; "DrugFacts: High School and Youth Trends."

28. Institute for Social Research (2014), 20, 64.

29. Ibid., 64, 69.

30. Ibid., 20.

31. "Crack Cocaine Fast Facts."

32. Institute for Social Research (2014), 22, 64.

33. Ibid., 64, 69.

34. Ibid., 22.

35. Ibid., 28, 64.

36. Ibid., 64, 69.

37. Ibid., 28.

38. Ibid., 24, 65.

39. Ibid., 24, 25.

40. Ibid., 26, 65.

41. Ibid., 27.

42. Ibid., 32, 66.

43. Ibid., 66, 70.

44. Ibid., 32.

45. Ibid., 30.

46. Ibid., 65.

47. Ibid., 30.

48. "Fact Sheets—Underage Drinking."

49. "Underage Drinking."

50. Institute for Social Research (2014), 38.

51. Ibid., 70.

52. Ibid., 66.

53. Ibid., 38.

54. Williams and McShane (2014), 69–70.

55. Williams and McShane (2014).

56. Ibid.

57. Gordon et al. (2014); Howell and Howell (2015), 172.

58. Curry (2000).

59. RAND Corporation (2002); xv.

60. Winters, Fawkes, Botzet, Fahnhorst, and August.

61. "Skills, Opportunities, and Recognition (SOAR)."

62. "Preventing Drug Use among Children and Adolescents." (2003).

63. "About TND."

64. "Preventing Drug Use among Children and Adolescents." (2003), 33.

65. Ibid., 29.

66. C. E. Mendez Foundation (2013).

67. National Center for Children in Poverty (2011), 4.

68. Ibid.

REFERENCES

"About TND." *Project toward No Drug Abuse.* http://tnd.usc.edu/about.php.

C. E. Mendez Foundation. *Technical Report: One Year Study of the Effects of the Too Good for Drugs Prevention Program on Middle School Students.* By Tina P. Bacon, Bruce Hall, and John Ferron. Tampa, FL: C. E. Mendez Foundation, 2013. http://www.toogoodprograms.org/catalog/view/theme/mendez/files/Evaluation%20Studies/TGFD_Middle_Study_2013_March.pdf.

"Crack Cocaine Fast Facts." *National Drug Intelligence Center.* http://www.justice.gov/archive/ndic/pubs3/3978/.

Crowe, Ann H., and Linda Sydney. "Developing a Policy for Controlled Substance Testing of Juveniles." *Juvenile Accountability Incentive Block Grants Program Bulletin.* Washington, DC: Office of Juvenile Justice and Delinquency Prevention, 2000.

Curry, G. David. "Self-Reported Gang Involvement and Officially Recorded Delinquency." *Criminology* 34, no. 4 (2000): 1253–1274.

"DrugFacts: High School and Youth Trends." *National Institute on Drug Abuse.* December 2014. http://www.drugabuse.gov/publications/drugfacts/high-school-youth-trends.

"Fact Sheets—Underage Drinking." *Centers for Disease Control and Prevention.* http://www.cdc.gov/alcohol/fact-sheets/underage-drinking.htm.

Gordon, Rachel A., Hillary L. Rowe, Dustin Pardini, Rolf Loeber, Helene Raskin White, and David P. Farrington. "Serious Delinquency and Gang Participation: Combining and Specializing in Drug Selling, Theft, and Violence." *Journal of Research on Adolescence* 24, no. 2, (2014): 235–251.

Howell, James, and Megan Howell. "Gangs, Serious Gang Problems, and Criminal Justice: What to Do?" In *Critical Issues in Crime and Justice: Thought, Policy, and Practice,* 2nd edition. Edited by Mary Maquire and Dan Okada, 167–189. Thousand Oaks, CA: Sage, 2015.

Institute for Social Research. *Monitoring the Future National Results on Adolescent Drug Use: Overview of Key Findings 2014.* By Lloyd D. Johnston, Patrick M. O'Malley, Richard M. Miech, Jerald G. Bachman, and John E. Schulenberg. Ann Arbor, MI: University of Michigan, 2014. http://www.monitoringthefuture.org//pubs/monographs/mtf-overview2014.pdf.

Mosher, Clayton J., and Scott M. Atkins. *Drugs and Drug Policy.* Thousand Oaks, CA: Sage Publications, 2014.

National Center for Children in Poverty. *Adolescent Substance Use in the U.S.: Facts for Policymakers.* By Shannon Stagman, Susan Wile Schwarz, and Danielle Powers. New York: Columbia University, 2011.

"Preventing Drug Use among Children and Adolescents." *National Institute of Drug Abuse.* October, 2003. http://www.drugabuse.gov/sites/default/files/preventingdruguse.pdf.

"Purpose and Design." *Monitoring the Future.* http://monitoringthefuture.org/purpose.html.

RAND Corporation. *School-Based Drug Prevention: What Kind of Drug Use Does It Prevent?* By Jonathan P. Caulkins, Rosalie Liccardo Pacula, Susan Paddock, and James Chiesa. Santa Monica, CA: RAND, 2002.

"Skills, Opportunities, and Recognition (SOAR)." Office of Juvenile Justice and Delinquency Prevention. https://www.nationalgangcenter.gov/SPT/Prog rams/118.

Teen Prescription Opioid Abuse, Cigarette, and Alcohol Use Trends Down." *National Institute of Health.* http://www.nih.gov/news/health/dec2014/nida-16.htm.

"Underage Drinking." National Institute on Alcohol Abuse and Alcoholism. http://www.niaaa.nih.gov/alcohol-health/special-populations-co-occurr ing-disorders/underage-drinking.

Williams, Frank P., and Marilyn McShane. "Youth, Drugs, and Delinquency." In *Controversies in Juvenile Justice and Delinquency.* Edited by Peter Benekos and Alida Merlo, 69–88. Cincinnati, OH: LexisNexis, 2004.

Williams, Frank P., and Marilyn McShane. *Criminological Theory,* 6th edition. Upper Saddle River, NJ: Pearson, 2014.

Winters, Ken C., Tanya Fawkes, Andria Botzet, Tamara Fahnhorst, and Gerald August. "Project Synthesis: A Synthesis Review of Effective Drug Use Prevention Programs in the United States." *Mentor Foundation.* http://www .mentorfoundation.org/uploads/ProjectSynthesis_Brochure.pdf.

Chapter 5

School Searches: Balancing Delinquency and Privacy

Michael Cavanaugh

> The right of the people to be secure in their persons, houses, papers, and effects, against unreasonable searches and seizures, shall not be violated, and no warrants shall issue, but upon probable cause, supported by oath or affirmation, and particularly describing the place to be searched, and the persons or things to be seized.[1]

Juvenile delinquency has been a focus of criminologists throughout the years.[2] While great strides have been made in this area, there is still not one unifying theory to explain juvenile delinquency. While location-specific theories have emerged (see Routine Activities, Broken Windows, and Environmental Criminology), some researchers have offered ways to reduce crimes in certain locations through target hardening and increasing guardianship.[3] One location specifically important in juvenile delinquency is schools.

School-aged juveniles are required to attend school. Therefore, juvenile students are required to attend school (public or private) from first grade up until graduating from high school. During the school year, usually from August until May, juveniles attend about 180 days of classes. Considering that school lasts about eight hours a day, not including afterschool programs, juveniles spend about half of their waking hours at school when it is in session. Because so much time is spent at schools, research has delved into the delinquency at schools.[4]

School violence has been widely reported by media, although research suggests that violence in schools is grossly exaggerated. A large group of research has been conducted on school-related deaths, weapon-carrying among students and assaultive behavior, and teacher victimization by students.[5] Another, and more pervasive, problem in school is drug possession, use, and abuse. This has shown to be more of a problem at schools and statistics show why. For example, The Monitoring the Future survey, which asks high-school students about their drug use, finds that 49 percent of seniors have used illicit drugs (not including alcohol or tobacco) in their lifetime.[6]

Drugs and violence, especially involving weapons, have become a major focus for school administrators. While other delinquent problems such as gangs, vandalism, and theft exist, these administrators have focused much of their attention in trying to reduce or eliminate drugs and weapons on their campuses. The administrative reactions to drugs and weapons are the focus of this chapter. Search policies at schools, zero tolerance policies related to delinquent behavior, the introduction and proliferation of school police, and problem behavior being handled by the formal criminal justice system are discussed.

SEARCHES

One way schools have responded to the delinquency problems, specifically weapons and drugs, is by instituting search policies for students. Beyond the schoolhouse gates, a police officer routinely needs probable cause or a warrant to search a person, their belongings, and vehicles. This is not the case of searches of juveniles in schools. The Supreme Court of the United States has touched on school searches four times in its history and through these rulings, schools are allowed to conduct warrantless searches on students, absent probable cause. The Court indicated that the special needs of school administrators allow them to dispense with the warrant and probable cause requirements of the Fourth Amendment. A brief explanation of the four cases is presented.

New Jersey v. T.L.O. (1985)[7]

This case was the first case where the Supreme Court used the "special needs" exception to justify school searches. T.L.O. was a 14 year-old freshman at Piscataway High school when she was caught with another student smoking in the girls' bathroom. The teacher that caught the girls brought them to the assistant principal, Theodore Choplick. Choplick asked the two girls about the situation, and the other girl admitted to the allegation of smoking in the bathroom. T.L.O. denied the allegation and Choplick brought her into the office, where he took possession of her purse. He looked inside the purse and pulled out a pack of cigarettes and confronted T.L.O. with what he had found. He also saw rolling papers, which he equated with marijuana. He then performed a more invasive search of the purse and found marijuana, a pipe, and evidence that linked T.L.O. to selling drugs, including two letters, a business ledger on an index card, and a roll of one-dollar bills. After T.L.O.'s mother and the police were notified, T.L.O. was brought to the police station, where she confessed to dealing drugs at the high school.

Delinquency charges were levied against T.L.O. in juvenile court for the marijuana possession, and she filed a motion to suppress the evidence and the confession on the basis of an illegal search. The juvenile court denied the motion and ultimately found her to be delinquent. In the ruling, the juvenile court conceded that the Fourth Amendment applies to school searches but that reasonable suspicion, not probable cause, guides the searches of students by school officials. The juvenile court found it reasonable for Choplick to search T.L.O.'s purse. T.L.O. appealed, and the Appellate Division affirmed the lower court's decision on the search but remanded the case back to juvenile court to see whether T.L.O.'s Fifth Amendment rights were violated during the confession. T.L.O. appealed the case to the New Jersey Supreme Court. The New Jersey high court determined that the search of the purse had no relation to the accusation of smoking in the bathroom, as the possession of cigarettes was not against school rules but smoking in the bathroom did violate school rules. Additionally, the court found that Choplick lacked reasonable suspicion to search the purse, as he did not have information that the cigarettes would be in the purse. Furthermore, the court ruled that the rolling papers did not justify a more invasive search in the purse. The state appealed, and the United States Supreme Court granted certiorari.

The Supreme Court ruled against T.L.O. The Court rejected the *in loco parentis* doctrine (a long-held legal principle in which the state acts in the best interest of the child in the absence of the parent), finding that the school officials are acting in the interest of the state, thus triggering Fourth Amendment protections. The Court determined, however, that the Fourth Amendment's warrant and probable cause requirements were overly burdensome for school officials because of their lack of knowledge and training in the law. Because the Fourth Amendment prohibits searches that are unreasonable, the Court created a two-prong test for determining the reasonableness of a school search.

First, the search must be justified at its inception and second, the scope of the search must be reasonably related to the object of the search. Applying the test to the search of T.L.O's purse, the Court determined that Choplick had reasonable grounds for suspecting that T.L.O. had cigarettes in her purse. Furthermore, the discovery of rolling papers in the search for cigarettes, gave reasonable suspicion to Choplick to suspect that T.L.O. had marijuana in the purse. This allowed Choplick to perform a more invasive search on the purse, rendering the scope valid and the evidence admissible. The U.S. Supreme Court reversed the New Jersey Supreme Court's ruling. Of special note was the concurring opinion by Justice Blackmun, which has been cited to justify other school searches. Blackmun argued for the application of the "special needs" exception when he wrote, "The special need for an immediate response to behavior that threatens either the safety of school children and teachers or the educational process itself justifies the Court in exempting school searches from the warrant and probable-cause requirement, and in applying a standard determined by balancing the relevant interests."[8]

Vernonia School District 47J v. Acton (1995)[9]

In this case, the Court used the balancing test, developed in T.L.O. to further restrict Fourth Amendment protections for students. James Acton was a seventh-grade student who decided to play football in the fall of 1991. Two years earlier, the Vernonia school board approved a drug testing policy for all students participating in interscholastic athletics. The policy was implemented because the school district had seen a rise in drug use among the student population, finding athletes among the leaders in the student drug culture. Furthermore, the risk of injury for athletes was increased with drug use.

The policy called for all students engaging in athletics to sign a consent form and be drug tested, prior to participation in the sport. Random drug testing also occurred once a week throughout the season. Acton was denied participation in football because he and his parents failed to sign the consent form agreeing to the urinalysis. Acton and his parents filed suit in federal court, claiming the drug tests violated the Fourth and Fourteenth Amendments to the U.S. Constitution. The district court dismissed the suit, but the U.S. Court of Appeals for the Ninth Circuit reversed, finding the drug test was a violation of the Fourth and Fourteenth Amendments. The U.S. Supreme Court granted certiorari.

The Court reversed the Ninth Circuit's decision. In allowing the school to conduct suspicionless, random drug testing on the athletes, the Court explained that reasonableness of the search depended on balancing the legitimate interests of the school and the privacy interests of the student athletes. As for the privacy interests of the athletes, they have a lower expectation of privacy than the rest of the student body because of the implicit contract between athletes and the school for having good grades

and conduct and communal aspects of athletics, showering and undress-
ing together. The Court also found that the district had articulated a
pervasive drug problem at the school and showed that the athletes were
participating and, in some cases, leading the drug culture. The method of
the urinalysis was also considered, and the Court determined the method
to be minimally intrusive. According to the Court, the test was conducted
in accordance with normal bathroom behavior and did not reveal any
sensitive information, only the presence or absence of drugs. As a result,
the drug testing of athletes was considered constitutional because the
school had a legitimate educational interest in drug testing athletes, the
testing was relatively unobtrusive, athletes had a lowered expectation of
privacy, and the search was not for law enforcement purposes (special
needs).

Board of Education of Independent School District No. 92 of Pottawatomie County v. Earls (2002)[10]

In the city of Tecumseh, Oklahoma, the school district decided to implement drug testing for all students participating in extracurricular activities at all middle and high schools. Extracurricular activities in the district
included all sports teams, clubs, and groups with school affiliation. The
policy in question required students to submit to drug testing prior to
participation in the extracurricular activity, permitted random drug testing of students during the duration of the activity, and allowed for drug
tests based on reasonable suspicion of drug use.

Two students, Earls and James, through their parents, filed a 42 U.S.C.
§ 1983 lawsuit, alleging a violation of their Fourth Amendment rights by
the school district. The U.S. District Court for the Western District of Oklahoma decided in favor of the school district, allowing the drug testing to
continue; however, the U.S. Court of Appeals for the Tenth Circuit reversed
the lower court's decision. The Tenth Circuit found that the school district did not show a pervasive drug problem in the school district, as the
Vernonia[11] case demonstrated. The district appealed the decision, and the
U.S. Supreme Court granted certiorari.

In a majority opinion written by Justice Thomas, the Court relied heavily on the Vernonia and T.L.O. decisions.[12] The reasonableness standard
was utilized because precedent allowed the Court to dispense with the
probable cause and warrant requirements for searches of students. The
Court balanced the privacy interests of the students against the school
district's interests in protecting the students from drugs. Justice Thomas
explained that students participating in extracurricular activities have a
lower expectation of privacy than other students, similar to the dimin-
ished expectation of privacy for athletes. Likewise, the urinalysis was
minimally intrusive, only tested for the presence of drugs, not revealing

sensitive medical issues, and possessed a non–law enforcement purpose (special needs). Finally, the need for drug testing was important because the district showed an increased problem with drug use. As a result, the drug testing of students participating in extracurricular activities was considered constitutional.

Safford Unified School District No. 1 v. Redding (2009)[13]

This case looked at the constitutionality of a strip search of a 13-year-old girl for prescription-strength ibuprofen. The assistant principal, Kerry Wilson, at Safford Middle School learned from a student that a female student, named Marissa, was handing out white pills at school. The school nurse was able to identify the pill as a prescription strength, 400 mg, ibuprofen. Marissa was brought to the principal's office and Wilson noticed the student had a binder that contained knives, cigarettes, and a lighter. Marissa was asked to empty her pockets and her wallet and Wilson located a number of pills. Marissa told Wilson that Savana Redding had given her the pills and the binder. Savana was brought to see Wilson, who then confronted her with the evidence. Savana indicated that she had loaned the binder to Marissa and that she had no knowledge of the pills. A female assistant, Helen Romero, came into the office and she and Wilson searched Savana's book sack for more pills but did not find any. At Wilson's direction, Romero took Savana to the school nurse to search her clothes for pills. Nurse Peggy Schwallier and Romero had Savana strip down to her bra and underpants. Savana was asked to shake her bra and pull the elastic out on her underpants, exposing her breasts and pelvic region. The search proved fruitless. Savana and her mother filed suit against the district, Wilson, Schwallier, and Romero for a violation of Savana's Fourth Amendment rights in the U.S. District Court for the District of Arizona. The district court found the search to be constitutional, and the decision was appealed to the Ninth Circuit Court of Appeals. The appeals court affirmed, and then decided to hear the case en banc. The en banc ruling found the search to be unconstitutional, but granted qualified immunity to all but Wilson. The case was appealed to the U.S. Supreme Court, and the Court decided to hear the case.

In a majority opinion, the U.S. Supreme Court affirmed part of the appeals court decision and reversed part of the decision. The Court found the search performed on Redding to be unconstitutional. Using the reasonableness standard set forth in the previous schools search cases, the Court found that the search was unreasonable because there was no reason to fear a danger from the drugs and there was no reason to suspect that Redding had the drugs hidden in her underwear. Even though there was a violation of Savana's constitutional rights, however, the individual defendants were granted qualified immunity because the right was not clearly established at the time of the search.

WHY DO THESE CASES MATTER?

These cases reflect a trend of diminishing the constitutional rights of students.[14] Children are in compulsory primary and secondary education often from the age of five until age 18. School is where most socialization occurs for children, and these kids learn how to follow rules the society sets down. School represents their first interaction with the "state" or "government," and these lessons follow them throughout their lives.

Additionally, the problems of violence and drugs have been deemed serious by the public. In response to tragedies like Columbine and others before and after it, schools have been taking a hard-line stance to weapons and drugs on campus. More and more school districts have created zero tolerance policies dealing with violence and drugs on campus. Not too long ago, fights that happened in school would have been handled informally by the principal and the two fighting students may have been sent back to class after a stern "talking to" by the principal. Today, the likelihood of that happening is almost slim to none. The more likely scenario is that both students would be arrested for assault, both would be suspended from school for a set period of time, and both may be recommended for expulsion. While "kids may be kids" and do stupid things, they are being increasingly punished like adults without all of the procedural safeguards guaranteed to adults.

The growing police presence at schools also factors into these cases. The rationale behind *T.L.O.* was that the warrant and probable cause could be dispensed with because school officials were not trained law enforcement officers. Schools now have security guards, resource or liaison officers, and some school districts even have their own police forces. Lower courts have applied the reasonable suspicion standard to police officers searching students at schools, even though the *T.L.O.* rationale does not seem to apply. While school often represents juvenile's first interaction with the "state" or "government," juveniles first contact with law enforcement often are these police officers at school. First impressions last a lifetime, and negative interactions with police can lead a juvenile down a bad path.

These three factors are all intertwined. Fewer rights at schools, more police presence, and increased punishment combine together for a combustible cocktail. Scholars have been fairly critical of these factors. The Latin term *in loco parentis* loosely translates to the state as the parent. This is the basis of the juvenile justice system, with the state supposedly acting in the best interest of juveniles when acting as the parent. Likewise, *in loco parentis* is often used in schools, with school officials taking charge of students while enrolled in school. The question remains as to whether the loss of Fourth Amendment rights, increased police presence, and increased formal punishments are in the best interests of students?

LITERATURE

Much of the literature has been critical of the loss of rights for juveniles in the schools. The earlier research focused on the *T.L.O.* decision and lamented the reasonable suspicion standard. Scholars claimed that students' privacy rights were limited,[15] students no longer have constitutional protections at school,[16] and the Fourth Amendment does not apply to students in schools.[17] Other articles tried to argue for limited use of the reasonable suspicion standard,[18] the requirement of individualized suspicion in school searches,[19] and for schools to use multiple standards based on whether it was a major or minor violation.[20]

Some of the later work on this topic has shifted to become more critical of the rationale behind the use of reasonable suspicion and the later use of the "special needs" exception in *Vernonia* and *Earls*.[21] Vaughn and del Carmen explain that the "special needs" exception to the warrant and probable cause requirement is a tool for society to control disruptive groups' behavior rather than individual behavior.[22] This exception is not an individualized form of justice and suspicionless searches ultimately undermine the relationships with students and school officials, doing much more harm than good.[23]

This notion of harm is echoed in a good portion of the research on this topic. After expanding juvenile rights (even in schools) in the 1960s and 1970s, society has seen a minimization of juvenile rights and an increase in punishment for these juveniles.[24] Because of school officials' dual purpose of educating and protecting students, it has been argued that either students should have all rights guaranteed by the constitution and the increased punishments, or schools should dispense with the lessened rights notion and focus entirely on *in loco parentis*.[25] When school officials truly act in the best interest of the child, then the harsh punishments and zero tolerance penalties would not come into play. As Levin said, "where in loco parentis no longer is relevant, then constitutional protections become more important."[26]

This dual responsibility of education and protection, while noble, make each task infinitely more difficult. These two responsibilities often have competing goals and sometimes are incompatible with each other. The debate among scholars as to what is more important tends to mimic the debates being held in the public on other criminal justice issues such as terrorism, gun control, stop and frisk. It is the old argument of social order versus individual rights. The minimization of students' rights is problematic because of the lack of remedies available to them.[27] In fact, Bethel argues for liability to attach when school officials fail to protect students while on campus.[28] Others go further claiming that the emphasis on school order maintenance over students' constitutional rights has led to the decline of the American educational system.[29]

Regardless of the scholarly debate over individual rights and social order in schools, the reality is that schools have focused on the social order narrative. This can be evidenced by the influx of law enforcement personnel in schools across the country. Brown examined the influx of police at schools and determined that they were fairly rare prior to the 1990s.[30] Accordingly, the proliferation of police, especially school resource officers, happened as a result of the downfall of the Drug Abuse Resistance Education (D.A.R.E.) program.[31] School officials came to rely on officers in schools and lobbied for keeping police in the schools.[32] Other scholars argue that the increase of law enforcement was based on other factors. Some posit that the increase was due to more violations of criminal laws.[33] Others have claimed that the increase can be attributed to the fact that school officials were handling incidents, like fighting, with more formal criminal justice responses rather than handling them informally like they have done in the past.[34]

Regardless of why police have been increased on elementary, middle, and high school campuses, the fact is that they are in schools. Two questions then remain to be answered. What role do security guards, resource officers, and school police play on campus? And, what level of suspicion should be required when police search a student? To answer the first question, Bough claims three roles for police officers at schools: law enforcement, counselor, and teacher.[35] Brown also claims three duties: educational, correctional, and law enforcement. Specifically asking school principals, school resource officers, and law enforcement administrators how they view the resource officer's role on campus, all mentioned multiple roles.[36]

As to what level of suspicion should apply to student searches performed by law enforcement at schools, the court cases are mixed.[37] There are three general recommendations provided by scholars. One recommendation is that a bright line ruling be created in which all searches performed by law enforcement require probable cause.[38] An alternative recommendation finds that the level of suspicion required (probable cause or reasonable suspicion) should be based on who employs and pays for the officer's salary.[39] This means that if the police department pays the salary, probable cause should apply, but if the school district pays the salary then reasonable suspicion would apply.[40] The final recommendation is based on the officer's role at the school. If the officer is primarily a law enforcement agent then probable cause would apply, but if that officer's role is a teacher or counselor then reasonable suspicion would be applicable.[41]

The remaining question is simply, "Why should this matter?" An argument can be made that society needs to protect all students and law enforcement can help in that respect. One may be hard pressed to find disagreement with that statement. In fact, scholars have mentioned the positive impact of law enforcement at schools, including helping deescalate situations with their training.[42] However, there is a negative side as well. Increased criminalization of school misbehavior has led to more students becoming involved in the juvenile justice system.[43] Furthermore, this increased criminalization and law enforcement on campus has led to high-security educational settings that some have compared to prisons.[44]

A number of security measures have been undertaken at schools to reduce violence and drugs. Metal detectors are prevalent at a number of schools and students may have to walk through them in the mornings before schools starts. In many facilities, CCTV cameras have been installed in the hallways at some schools and security and school officials can watch for problem behaviors from a central location. Other less-known measures have been implemented including mandating that students wear or present IDs, requiring clear or mesh backpacks, and installing lockless lockers.[45] These security features combined with suspicionless searches (drug tests, locker sweeps, drug dog sweeps, metal detectors) and lowered Fourth Amendment protections are comparable to prisons.[46]

CONCLUSION

Because of these search policies and law enforcement, students can become alienated from the educational environment causing more behavioral problems.[47] Ultimately, Hutchinson and Pullman find that these restrictions can cause a student to rebel to such a degree that it causes a violent event.[48] The power gap between students and school officials has been expanded through increased law enforcement, fewer Fourth Amendment rights, and formal criminal justice handling of situations.[49] Beger explains that juveniles in schools have the worst of both worlds—fewer rights and increased punishment.[50] Arguments have been made that the loss of Fourth Amendment rights is more likely to make students unsafe, not the violence or drugs in the schools.[51]

The general public sees these policies as a good tool for protecting our students, although this may actually be a false sense of security.[52] Students do not seem to find that these measures actually make the schools safer.[53] School shootings are extremely rare events. Preventing them is a laudable goal, but some of these incidents will occur even with these policies in place.[54] The end result, according to some research, is that these policies negatively affect the learning environment.[55] Additionally, these stringent security measures are more prevalent at inner city schools.[56] Those policies that reflect more punitive, zero tolerance, or uniform reactions to misbehavior may create or increase disproportionate minority contact (DMC) with the juvenile justice system.[57]

What can be done? Restoration of full Fourth Amendment protections may be a solution, although one that will undoubtedly face opposition from social order advocates. Less police presence in schools may allow schools to informally handle misbehavior, but, again, public opposition seems likely. More discretion (fewer zero tolerance policies) for school officials in handling school problems may seem like a solution, but when the public sees a principal handing down a suspension to a six-year-old for chewing a pop tart into a gun,[58] discretion is unlikely something the public will support. Less contact with juvenile justice system is probably the best option. It will take a combination of changes, but in the best case scenario, the schools can begin to focus on education again. A divided focus on education and security renders the school an expert on neither. A sole focus on education will allow the school to achieve what it is supposed to: educating children.

DISCUSSION QUESTIONS

1. What do you think are the proper circumstances to warrant school locker searches? What limits should be imposed on such searches?
2. Is the doctrine of in loco parentis still valid today? How do recent opinions of the U.S. Supreme Court seem to view this concept?
3. Do privacy rights seem to offset concerns about school safety and the potential for school crime and violence?
4. Give some examples of how school safety measures might vary from elementary school to middle school to high school and explain your justification for the differences.

ADDITIONAL RESOURCES

Annitto, Megan. "Consent Searches of Minors." *New York University Review of Law & Social Change* 38 (2014): 1–50.

Black, Derek. "The Constitutional Limit of Zero Tolerance in Schools." *Minnesota Law Review* 99, no. 3 (2015): 823–904.

Ferrara, Christopher. Customizable "'Sexual Orientation Privacy' for Minor School-children: A Law School Invention in Search of a Constitutional Mandate." *Journal of Law and Education* 43, no. 1 (2014): 65–78.

Fuentes, Annette. *Lockdown High: When the Schoolhouse Becomes a Jailhouse.* Brooklyn, NY: Verso, 2013.

McCarthy, Martha. *Public School Law: Teachers' and Students' Rights,* 7th edition. Upper Saddle River, NJ: Pearson, 2013.

Nance, Jason. "School Surveillance and the Fourth Amendment." *Wisconsin Law Review* 2014, no. 1 (2014): 79–137.

Nolan, Kathleen, and Paul Willis. *Police in the Hallways: Discipline in an Urban High School*. Minneapolis, MN: University of Minnesota Press, 2011.

Tiller, Benjamin. "The Problems of Probable Cause: Meneese and the Myth of Eroding Fourth Amendment Rights for Students." *Saint Louis University Law Journal* 58 (2014): 589–615.

Ward, Stephanie. "Schools Start to Rethink Zero Tolerance Policies." *ABA Journal*. http://www.abajournal.com/magazine/article/schools_start_to_ rethink_zero_tolerance_policies/

RELATED WEBSITES

Department of Education—Report on School Climate and Discipline, http://www 2.ed.gov/policy/gen/guid/school-discipline/index.html

National Association of School Psychologists, Zero Tolerance, http://www.nasp online.org/resources/factsheets/zt_fs.aspx

National Youth Rights Association, http://www.youthrights.org/

Southern Poverty Law Center—Students: Know Your Rights, http://www.splcen ter.org/what-we-do/lgbt-rights/students-know-your-rights

Student Rights Handbook—ACLU, https://acluvt.org/pubs/students_rights/intro duction.php

SUPPORTING FILMS

April Showers (2009)
Bowling for Columbine (2002)
Heart of America (2002)
Zero Day (2003)

NOTES

1. U.S. Constitution Amend IV.

2. Burgess and Akers (1966); Cohen (1955); Gottfredson and Hirschi (1990); Hirschi (1969); Moffitt (1993).

3. Brantingham and Brantingham (1981); Cohen and Felson (1979); Wilson and Kelling (1982).

4. Justice Policy Institute (2000).

5. Chang, Chen, and Brownson (2003); U.S. Department of Education (2003); Nansel, Overpeck, Haynie, Ruan, and Scheidt (2003).

6. Institute for Social Research (2015).

7. *New Jersey v. TLO* (1985).

8. Ibid., 353.

9. *Vernonia v. Acton* (1995).

10. *Board of Education of Independent School District No. 92 of Pottawatomie County v. Earls* (2002).

11. *Vernonia v. Acton* (1995).

12. *New Jersey v. T.L.O.* (1985); *Vernonia v. Acton* (1995).

13. *Safford Unified School District No. 1 v. Redding* (2009).

14. *Bethel School District No. 403 v. Fraser* (2006); *Hazelwood School District v. Kuhlmeier* (1988); *Morse et al. v. Frederick* (2007); *Tinker v. Des Moines Independent Community School District* (1969).

15. Lincoln (1988).

16. Crace (1986).

17. Harris (1985); Purkey (1987).

18. Bankhead (1985).

19. Gardner (1988).

20. Mooney (1985).

21. *Vernonia v. Acton* (1995); *Board of Education of Independent School District No. 92 of Pottawatomie County v. Earls* (2002).

22. Vaughn and del Carmen (1997).

23. Levitas (2009).

24. Dale (1992).

25. Hickman (1986).

26. Levin (1986), 1680.

27. Feld (2011).

28. Bethel (2004).

29. Dupre (1996).

30. Brown (2006).

31. Ibid.

32. Ibid.

33. Stefkovich and Miller (1999); Bough (1999).

34. Kagan (2004).

35. Bough (1999).

36. Lambert and McGinty (2001).

37. *People v. Pruitt* (1996); *State v. Dilworth* (1996).

38. Price (2009).

39. Campbell (2003).

40. Ibid.

41. Bough (1999).

42. Logan and Davis (2011).

43. Torres and Stefkovich (2009).

44. Bracy (2010).

45. Addington (2009).

46. "Texas Department of Criminal Justice: Offender Orientation Handbook" (2015).

47. Hyman and Perone (1998).

48. Hutchinson and Pullman (2007).

49. Ehrensal (2003).

50. Beger (2003).

51. Beger (2002).

52. Jacobs (2000).
53. Bracy (2011).
54. Jacobs (2000).
55. Finley (2006).
56. Hirschfield (2008).
57. Piquero (2008).
58. McGregory (2014).

REFERENCES

Addington, Lynn A. "Cops and Cameras: Public School Security as a Policy Response to Columbine." *American Behavioral Scientist* 52, no. 10 (2009): 1426–1446.

Bankhead, Missy Kelly. "New Jersey v. T.L.O.: The Supreme Court Limits School Children's Fourth Amendment Rights When Being Searched by Public School Officials." *Pepperdine Law Review* 13, no. 1 (1985): 87–108.

Beger, Randal R. "Expansion of Police Power in Public Schools and the Vanishing Rights of Students." *Social Justice* 29, no. 1 (2002): 119–130.

Beger, Randal R. "The 'Worst of Both Worlds': School Security and the Disappearing Fourth Amendment Rights of Students." *Criminal Justice Review* 28, no. 2 (2003): 336–354.

Bethel, Alison "Keeping Schools Safe: Why Schools Should Have an Affirmative Duty to Protect Students from Harm by Other Students." *Pierce Law Review* 2, no. 2 (2004): 183–204.

Bethel School District No. 403 v. Fraser, 478 U.S. 675 (1986).

Board of Education of Independent School District No. 92 of Pottawatomie County v. Earls, 536 U.S. 822 (2002).

Bough, Andrea G. "Searches and Seizures in Schools: Should Reasonable Suspicion or Probable Cause Apply to School Resource/Liaison Officers?" *University of Missouri Kansas City Law Review* 67 (1999): 543–563.

Bracy, Nicole L. "Circumventing the Law: Students' Rights in Schools with Police." *Journal of Contemporary Criminal Justice* 26, no. 3 (2010): 294–315.

Bracy, Nicole L. "Student Perceptions of High-Security School Environments." *Youth and Society* 43, no. 1 (2011): 365–395.

Brantingham, Paul J., and Patricia L. Brantingham. *Environmental Criminology.* Thousand Oaks, CA: Sage Publications 1981.

Brown, Ben. "Understanding and Assessing School Police Officers: A Conceptual and Methodological Comment." *Journal of Criminal Justice* 34, no. 6 (2006): 591–604.

Burgess, Robert L., and Ronald L. Akers. "A Differential Association-Reinforcement Theory of Criminal Behavior." *Social Problems* 14, no. 2 (1966): 128–147.

Campbell, Christoper Z. "The Effective Use of School Resource Officers: The Constitutionality of School Searches and Interrogations." *School Law Bulletin* 34, no. 1 (2003): 13–17.

Chang, Jen Jen, John J. Chen, and Ross C. Brownson. "The Role of Repeat Victimization in Adolescent Delinquent Behaviors and Recidivism." *Journal of Adolescent Health* 32, no. 4 (2003): 272–280.

Cohen, Albert K. *Delinquent Boys*. Glencoe, IL: Free Press 1955.

Cohen, Lawrence E., and Marcus Felson. "Social Change and Crime Rate Trends: A Routine Activity Approach." *American Sociological Review* 44, no. 4 (1979): 588–608.

Crace, Joe. "Student Searches: Leaving Probable Cause at the Schoolhouse Gate." *Stetson Law Review* 15, (1986): 467–487.

Dale, Michael J. "The Supreme Court and the Minimization of Children's Constitutional Rights: Implications for the Juvenile Justice System." *Hamline Journal of Public Law and Policy* 13, no. 2 (1992): 199–228.

Dupre, Anne Proffitt. "Should Students Have Constitutional Rights? Keeping Order in the Public Schools." *George Washington Law Review* 65, no. 1 (1996): 49–105.

Ehrensal, Patricia A. L. "The Three Faces of Power: The U.S. Supreme Court's Legitimization of School Authority's Parental, Police, and Pedagogic Roles." *Educational Administration Quarterly* 39, no. 2 (2003): 145–163.

Feld, Barry C. "T.L.O and Redding's Unanswered (Misanswered) Fourth Amendment Questions: Few Rights and Fewer Remedies." *Mississippi Law Journal* 80, no. 3 (2011): 847–954.

Finley, Laura L. "Examining School Searches as Systematic Violence." *Critical Criminology* 14, no. 2 (2006): 117–135.

Gardner, Martin R. "Student Privacy in the Wake of T.L.O.: An Appeal for an Individualized Suspicion Requirement for Valid Searches and Seizures in the Schools." *Georgia Law Review* 22, (1988): 897–947.

Gottfredson, Michael, and Travis Hirschi. *A General Theory of Crime*. Palo Alto, CA: Stanford University Press 1990.

Harris, M. Teresa. "*New Jersey v. T.L.O.*: New Standard of Review or New Label?" *American Journal of Trial Advocacy* 9 (1985): 157–170.

Hazelwood School District v. Kuhlmeier, 484 U.S. 260 (1988).

Hickman, Michael J. "The Supreme Court and the Decline of Students' Constitutional Rights: A Selective Analysis." *Nebraska Law Review* 65 (1986): 161–187.

Hirschfield, Paul J. "Preparing for Prison? The Criminalization of School Discipline in the USA." *Theoretical Criminology* 12, no. 1 (2008): 79–101.

Hirschi, Travis. *Causes of Delinquency*. Berkeley, CA: University of California Press 1969.

Hutchinson, Lisa, and Wesley E. Pullman. "Socialization or Prisonization? Utilizing Sykes' 'Pains of Imprisonment' to Examine Deprivations in America's Public Schools." *Critical Criminology* 15, no. 2 (2007): 171–184.

Hyman, Irwin A., and Donna C. Perone. "The Other Side of School Violence: Educator Policies and Practices That May Contribute to Student Misbehavior." *Journal of School Psychology* 36, no. 1 (1998): 7–27.

Institute for Social Research. *Monitoring the Future National Survey Results on Drug Use: 1975–2014: Overview, Key Findings on Adolescent Drug Use*. By Lloyd D. Johnston, Patrick M. O'Malley, Jerald G. Bachman, and John E. Schulenberg. Ann Arbor: MI: University of Michigan, 2015.

Jacobs, Timothy L. "School Violence: An Incurable Social Ill That Should Not Lead to the Unconstitutional Compromise of Students' Rights." *Duquesne Law Review* 38 (2000): 617–662.

James, Richard K., Joan Logan, and Scott A. Davis. "Including School Resource Officers in School-Based Crisis Intervention: Strengthening Student Support." *School Psychology International* 32, no. 2 (2011): 210–224.

Justice Policy Institute and Children's Law Center. *School House Hype: Two Years Later.* By Kim Brooks, Vincent Schiraldi, and Jason Zeidenberg. Washington, DC: Justice Policy Institute, 2000.

Kagan, Josh. "Reappraising T.L.O's 'Special Needs' Doctrine in an Era of School-Law Enforcement Entanglement." *Journal of Law and Education* 33, no. 3 (2004): 291–325.

Lambert, Regina D., and Dixie McGinty. "Law Enforcement Officers in Schools: Setting Priorities." *Journal of Educational Administration* 40, no. 3 (2001): 257–273.

Levin, Betsy. "Educating Youth for Citizenship: The Conflict between Authority and Individual Rights in the Public School." *Yale Law Journal* 95, no. 8 (1986): 1647–1680.

Levitas, Kerem Murat. "York v. Wahkiakum School District and the Future of School Searches under the Washington State Constitution." *Washington Law Review* 84 (2009): 93–125.

Lincoln, Eugene A. "Searches and Seizures in Public Schools: Going beyond the Supreme Court's Ruling in New Jersey v. T.L.O." *Journal of Negro Education* 57, no. 1 (1988): 3–10.

McGregory, Kathleen. "Bill Targets Kids' Right to Bear Pop-Tart Guns." *Tampa Tribune*, February 13, 2014, 7B.

Moffitt, Terrie E. "Adolescent Limited and Life Course Persistent Antisocial Behavior: A Developmental Taxonomy." *Psychological Review* 100, no. 4 (1993): 674–701.

Mooney, Susan M. "New Jersey v. T.L.O.: The School Search Exception to Probable Cause." *New England Law Review* 21, (1985): 509–543.

Morse et al. v. Frederick, 551 U.S. 393 (2007).

Nansel, Tonja R., Mary D. Overpeck, Denise L. Haynie, W. June Ruan, and Peter C. Scheidt. "Relationships between Bullying and Violence among U.S. Youth." *Archives of Pediatric and Adolescent Medicine* 157, no. 4 (2003): 348–353.

National Center for Education Statistics. *Indicators of School Crime and Safety: 2003.* By Jill F. Devoe, Katharin Peter, Phillip Kaufman, Sally A. Ruddy, Amanda K. Miller, Mike Planty, Thomas D. Snyder, and Michael R. Rand. Washington, D.C.: U.S. Department of Education, 2003.

New Jersey v. T.L.O., 469 U.S. 325 (1985).

People v. Pruitt, 662 N.E.2d 540 (Ill. App. 1996).

Piquero, Alex R. "Disproportionate Minority Contact." *The Future of Children* 18, no. 2 (2008): 59–79.

Price, Peter. "When Is a Police Officer an Officer of the Law? The Status of Police Officers in Schools." *Journal of Criminal Law and Criminology* 99, no. 2 (2009): 541–570.

Purkey, Charlotte H. "Fourth Amendment Protections in the Elementary and Secondary School Settings." *Mercer Law Review* 38, (1987): 1417–1437.

Safford Unified School District No. 1 v. Redding, 557 U.S. 364 (2009).

State v. Dilworth, 661 N.E.2d 310 (Ill. 1996).

Stefkovich, Jacqueline A., and Judith A. Miller. "Law Enforcement Officers in Public Schools: Student Citizens in Safe Havens?" *Brigham Young University Education and Law Journal* 1, (1999): 25–69.

"Texas Department of Criminal Justice: Offender Orientation Handbook." *Texas Department of Criminal Justice.* January, 2015. http://www.tdcj.state.tx.us/documents/Offender_Orientation_Handbook_English.pdf.

Tinker v. Des Moines Independent Community School District, 393 U.S. 503 (1969).

Torres, Mario S. and Jacqueline A. Stefkovich. "Demographics and Police Involvement: Implications for Student Civil Liberties and Just Leadership." *Educational Administration Quarterly* 45, no. 3 (2009): 450–473.

Vaughn, Michael Scott, and Rolando V. del Carmen. "The Fourth Amendment as a Tool of Actuarial Justice: The 'Special Needs' Exception to the Warrant and Probable Cause Requirements." *Crime and Delinquency* 43, no. 1 (1997): 78–103.

Vernonia School District 47J v. Acton, 515 U.S. 646 (1995).

Wilson, James Q., and George L. Kelling. "Broken Windows." *Atlantic Monthly* 249 (1982): 29–38.

Part III

Keeping Youth with Special Needs Out of the Juvenile Justice System

PREFACE TO PART III

"There Ain't Enough Jesus": Special Needs Youth as Victims and Offenders

In Fannin County, Texas, two special education staff members were found guilty of unlawful restraint, causing exposure to serious bodily injury of a disabled student, and were sentenced to probation. A surveillance tape "videoed" 40 minutes of physical and emotional abuse by the two employees including threats, choke holds, slaps, and sitting on the 10-year-old on the floor. Federal lawsuits against the district and several employees are pending. The released video publically shocked viewers with the teacher vilifying the child, "There ain't enough Jesus to fix you."[1]

In 2010, Steven Eugene Washington was killed by Los Angeles gang enforcement officers because he looked suspicious. The fact that he was fearful of strangers, nervously touching himself, and looking around anxiously are all fairly normal for someone with his disabilities, but on the street after midnight, the patrolmen were alerted to the potential of a confrontation. The conduct of the autistic young man can be scrutinized and interpreted over and over but the problem is that the lack of understanding of special populations within the community will mean that these tragedies occur again and again.

Whether in the seclusion of a classroom or out on the streets of the city, youth with special needs face many challenges in being recognized as victims, which speaks volumes about the health and well-being of our justice system. Across the country, cases of abuse and maltreatment go unreported, or unsubstantiated. And, according to the most recent government data, while children with disabilities are less likely to be reported as maltreated, the injuries they do suffer as a consequence are more serious.[2] These data also do not take into account the frequency with which the abuse of children including those with disabilities go unreported, either because the youth is not able to self-report or because the person responsible for reporting their victimization, such as a parent or teacher, is involved in the abuse.

Unfortunately, somewhere along the path of abuse and victimization, hundreds of youth fall into the justice system as special needs offenders. Scholars estimate that more than half of those in the system have behavioral health problems,[3] and up to 30 percent of those impairments are designated as serious. The most common diagnoses within the behavioral health issues are disruptive behavior disorders such as conduct disorders, mood disorders such as depression and anxiety as well as posttraumatic stress disorders (PTSD). As discussed by Merlo and Benekos in Chapter 1, exposure to trauma and abuse is now acknowledged as a condition warranting intervention and treatment. The chapters in this part look more closely at some of these special circumstances, of homelessness, runaways, child abuse and maltreatment, the problem of associating disabilities such as autism spectrum disorders with delinquency, and even the challenges faced by children who have lost parents to incarceration. Although we have made some strides in recognizing the link between victimization and subsequent delinquency as we saw in the case of reconceptualizing juvenile prostitution in Part I, there are still much to be done in order to mitigate the damage done to children by raising public awareness about special needs youth and by programming for resiliency. And, as we will see, family intervention options provide perhaps the best opportunities for prevention and therapeutic services.

In developing intervention strategies for children of incarcerated parents, it is difficult to prioritize among the many legal, economic, emotional and relationship problems that these families face. As Pech and Bloom explain, this "shadow population" is at risk for problems at home, among friends and at school. The stress created from being separated from parents in prison and jail may be further heightened by formal legal proceedings initiated over child custody or even termination of parental rights. In a majority of states, incarceration is grounds for divorce and, in many states, the court may terminate a parent's custodial rights over a child upon conviction of a felony or imprisonment. A conviction may also serve as grounds for a finding of unfitness in a custody or adoption proceeding. While most children are taken into care by a remaining spouse, grandparent, or other family member, it is also possible that parental ties may be formally and permanently severed. Allowing families opportunities to maintain ties is a logical and economical intervention effort that could provide substantial cost savings in the years ahead.[4]

It can be argued that for far too long corrections officials have been paralyzed by public stinginess and vindictive tirades about why criminals with disabilities should not get rehabilitative services and programming if the law-abiding poor are denied. The problem is in the false dichotomy—the poor should not be denied either. Early screening and access to program models that have been identified as evidence-based are cost saving measures. The problem is that no one, least of all offenders, seems able to obtain assistance and treatment from the state. We have become a soulless machine that blames and punishes without humanitarian concern for the reformation and reintegration of the wayward. These are the people we once took great pride in turning around and starting on the path of good citizenship. At one time, we showcased our ability to transform the errant back into a contributing and productive member of society. Today there seems to be only an unforgiving litany of just desserts and cold hard consequences. Perhaps it is time to break the pattern of institutional defeatism, to abandon the system of complex processing that only serves to discard and abandon those in need. Perhaps it is time to recommit to rehabilitation.

This part presents a focus on juveniles who are victims, or more likely to become victims, of circumstance. Traqina Emeka (Chapter 6) discusses the problems with abused juveniles and juveniles who are homeless, either runaways or those in difficult familial situations. Juveniles suffering through these traumas can act out sometimes resulting in their formal entrance into the juvenile justice system. Alexandria Pech and Barbara E. Bloom, in Chapter 7, discuss the severe disadvantage of children growing up with incarcerated parents, and find the lack of resources available to these children can result in negative consequences later in life, including involvement in the juvenile justice system, although that link may be mediated by other intervening variables. The final chapter in this part (Chapter 8), by Rebecca Pfeffer, chronicles those youth unlucky enough to be born with an intellectual disability, specifically autism spectrum disorders. While the research shows these youth to be more susceptible to victimization, the research does not show the link to delinquency, contrary to media perception. All of these chapters indicate that children are resilient and while they may grow up in difficult circumstances, with help (through various programs), these kids can overcome those circumstances.

REFERENCES

Christian, Carol. "There Ain't Enough Jesus to Fix You." *Houston Chronicle*, March 24, 2015, http://www.chron.com/news/houston-texas/texas/article/Teacher-There-ain-t-enough-Jesus-to-fix-you-6155334.php.

Kretschmar, Jeff, Fredrick Butcher, Daniel Flannery and Mark Singer, "Diverting Juvenile Justice-Involved Youth with Behavioral Health Issues from Detention: Preliminary Findings from Ohio's Behavioral Health Juvenile Justice (BHJJ) Initiative." *Criminal Justice Policy Review* (2014), 1–24. doi:10.1177/0887403414560885.

McShane, Marilyn. *Prisons in America*. New York: LFB Scholarly Pub., 2008.

National Center for Juvenile Justice. *Juvenile Offenders and Victims: 2014 National Report*. By Melissa Sickmund and Charles Puzzanchera. Pittsburgh, PA: National Center for Juvenile Justice, 2014.

Chapter 6

Childhood Trauma: The Effects of Abuse and Homelessness

Traqina Emeka

The United States has more homeless women and children than any other modern industrialized country. The National Center on Family Homelessness estimates that about one-third of the homeless population in this country is made up of families, meaning that almost 1.6 million children each year face the trauma of having no safe place in which to sleep.[5] Poverty, unemployment, the lack of affordable housing, foreclosure, and perhaps most of all, domestic violence disrupt living arrangements and expose children to the inherent risks of homelessness.

The link between homelessness and childhood victimization is the frequency with which abused and neglected children end up on the streets either by being displaced from dysfunctional family arrangements or by running away and fleeing abusive situations. Further, the relationship between homelessness, victimization, and delinquency is often rooted in the traumatic incidents that youth experience both prior to and following life on the streets.

Cathy Spatz Widom's longitudinal study in the late 1980s[6] found that victims of child physical abuse are at greater risk for engaging in future abuse than those who have not suffered such treatment. Her research led to what is now called the "cycle of violence." At the time, Widom's work was considered groundbreaking because she examined both the short- and long-term effects of abuse. Since then, the phrase "cycle of violence" has created the myth that child victims of maltreatment will become perpetrators. Widom suggested that the available research did, in many cases, suggest a relationship; however, she questioned the relationship and the research methodologies of the empirical works that attempted to measure that relationship.[7] According to Widom, "being abused as a child may increase one's risk for becoming an abusive parent, a delinquent, or an adult violent criminal. However, on the basis of the findings from the existing literature, it cannot be said that the pathway is straight or certain. It is likely that our conceptualization of the relationship between child abuse and violence has been overly simplistic."[8]

As Martinson's *Nothing Works* conclusions about correctional rehabilitation were misunderstood and misquoted, the same can be said for Widom's work. However, there is no single explanation for the many variables that may increase the risk of crime. Criminologists caution that understanding why people commit crime is a complex formula without consistent and direct causal links. For example, Widom suggested that the relationship between child abuse and violence involves a myriad of explanations, factors, and risks, which must be taken into consideration.[9] Still, in the three decades since Widom's research, the myth of the cycle of violence continues to perpetuate a stereotype that further alienates and marginalizes victims, in this case, child victims of maltreatment. Fortunately, there is a body of research being developed that focuses on trauma and resiliency of victims; this research comes from a strengths-based perspective and it looks at ways to help victims of trauma cope rather than resort to violence.

The purpose of this chapter is (1) to trace the history of the social recognition of child abuse and neglect, (2) to define the types of child maltreatment and behaviors associated with them, (3) to provide a theoretical framework to suggest that violence is only one response to child maltreatment, and (4) to explore trauma resulting from exposure to domestic violence or child maltreatment and child homelessness as well as to recognize the significance of promoting resiliency to reduce delinquency.

HISTORICAL BACKGROUND ON CHILD ABUSE

The Dark Ages were a period of extreme hardship including starvation, disease, and a feudal economic system, for children mortality rates were high and the quality of life was low.[10] There were typically no strong emotional ties between families and very young children. Children were most often viewed as property for economic gain and for carrying on the family name or heritage. For mothers, the lack of emotional ties was most likely to provide an increased ability to cope with death if the child did not survive. Practices such as infanticide and abandonment were used if there were defects or abnormalities or the family believed the child would not survive.

During the Enlightenment or Renaissance period the portrayal of children changed from part of one's property to those who needed protection and guidance. Improvements in medicine resulted in lower mortality rates and children were acknowledged as members of the family.[11] The family was formally responsible for ensuring that children were raised properly while the school and church provided informal support. Advances in society, including the Industrial Revolution and the Renaissance, were instrumental in incorporating a strict work ethic, purity, and obedience to ensure that children were disciplined and directed in the proper manner.

As society became more socially organized, it also developed values around a system of age stratification. There were deliberate intentions to create childhood as an important phase in the formation of personality as well as the building of character through discipline. Children were viewed as developmentally different from adults and this belief prompted a structured education system and increased parental responsibility. Behaviors defined as "acceptable" were extremely narrow as more acts were defined as deviant. "Delinquency" was a term coined in response to the greater discipline and control deemed necessary to insure compliance with the norms of behavior for children.

The Massachusetts' Stubborn Child Law of 1646 opened the door to legislation that was only applicable to children, much like contemporary status offenses.[12] The stubborn child law made disobeying a parent an act punishable by death. This law was the first of many that used social control to govern the behavior of children and to outline the expectations of parents. The law was born from Puritan principles that emphasized the family, church, and community. Social concerns about child abuse were all but nonexistent as such issues were handled within the confines of the home and the community. In other words, child abuse was not a social concern but rather a family and community concern.

The end of the Civil War saw the United States experiencing social changes brought on by urbanization, industrialization, and migration. Disruption in traditional family structures and economic resources meant child abuse would soon be noticed as an element of the larger fabric of social disorganization. The impetus to a movement to recognize the plight of child abuse is often traced to a young girl named Mary Ellen Wilson. In 1874, Mary Ellen was found to be a victim of child abuse and neglect in the state of New York and was removed with some controversy from the servitude of her foster care arrangement. At that time, attempts were made to justify the intervention by the fact that there were no social services available to children, as were afforded to animals through the Society for the Prevention of Cruelty to Animals.[13] At this point in American history,

Mary Ellen's case caused a public outcry as it highlighted the issue of child abuse in American society. Subsequently, the Society for the Prevention of Cruelty to Children was created in New York City to specifically address child abuse and neglect. The view of the court and society during this time held there was no specific state duty to protect a child from abuse as this was considered the responsibility of the family, specifically the father. Although, eventually, there were laws against cruelty towards children, the enforcement and interpretations of the laws varied from jurisdiction to jurisdiction. And, as history relates, it all came too late for Mary Ellen, who was placed in an institutions for wards of the state.[14]

CHILD ABUSE IN THE 20TH CENTURY

Prior to the 1960s there were laws against cruelty to children but child abuse was not officially addressed by authorities; child discipline was generally handled by the family. However, Dr. Henry Kempe's published radiology research brought national attention to the issue of physical child abuse. His study included hundreds of cases developed from the x-rays of children with broken bones in different stages of healing. The findings of his analysis suggested what has become known as battered child syndrome or chronic child abuse. In 1974, a federal law, The Child Abuse and Neglect Prevention and Treatment Act (CAPTA), was enacted to generate awareness about child abuse and to implement methods, in each state, to track and detect suspected child abuse. In the late 1970s, the definition of child maltreatment was extended to include sexual abuse and thus, child protection statutes were expanded. Prior to that time, sexual abuse was either denied or ignored by professionals. To date, all 50 states have mandatory reporting for employees of certain occupations such as teachers, child care workers, and nurses. Child maltreatment cases are reported to child protective services (CPS) where investigations of suspected cases of maltreatment are conducted. The findings of CPS workers determine whether or not a case requires court intervention.

Today the government collects and publishes information relative to runaway, throwaway, missing, abducted, and exploited youth in a system housed under the National Center for Missing and Exploited Children. The center operates a tipline as well as a child sex trafficking response team. Their call center works with families that hope to reunify with missing children and in 2013 conducted intake on 10,094 children reported missing. According to researchers, the seriousness of runaway or throwaway cases is a complex determination based on a number of factors such as the age of the child, whether the youth has somewhere safe to go, whether he or she has been in the company of dangerous or predatory companions, and whether there has been a history of drug abuse, suicide attempts, or mental health problems. Other risks factored in are whether crimes are committed by the child or against the child in the runaway period. Overall, almost 1.7 million young people are estimated to have experienced a runaway or a throwaway event and a significant percentage of those cases were evaluated as endangered or at risk for harm. Researchers also estimate that about 21 percent of the runaway or throwaway children had been physically or sexually abused in the home before leaving or were afraid of abuse if they returned.[15]

CHILD MALTREATMENT

Victims of child maltreatment are at risk for negative outcomes including chronic health problems, mental health issues, developmental delays, poor educational well-being, and future involvement with the criminal justice, as well as other problems across the life span. Also, high crime environments, substance abuse, and living in dysfunctional families may contribute to child maltreatment. The concept of child maltreatment is an umbrella term that includes physical abuse, neglect, emotional/psychological abuse, and sexual abuse. The age of a child is an important risk factor because younger children are at a greater risk of victimization as they are less likely to be able to resist or report maltreatment. Although there are many forms of child abuse, the major categories include (1) physical abuse, (2) psychological maltreatment, (3) neglect, and (4) sexual abuse.

According to the Child Welfare Information Gateway, physical abuse is defined as nonaccidental injury and physical impairment to a child. Some examples of physical abuse include any or all of the following: breaking bones, pulling, shaking, choking, beating, burning, scalding, pushing, shoving, and kicking.[16] Some signs of a child who is possibly a victim of physical abuse may include wearing inappropriate clothing to cover injuries (wearing a sweater in the summer), unexplained or frequent injuries, fear of going home, and a child who may appear very nervous and may flinch with sudden movements.

Injury to the psychological or emotional well-being of the child as evidenced by a noticeable or subtle change in behavior is a general definition of psychological maltreatment. Psychological abuse is especially damaging because it may be difficult to detect and may coexist with other forms of abuse. The principal types of psychological abuse are mental cruelty and exploitation. Victims may suffer from low self-esteem, depression, a negative sense of identity, and the inability to form and maintain positive relationships. Other behaviors may include extremes such as being very obedient or extremely aggressive or being adult-like or infantile.[17] Also, these children may appear very withdrawn, fearful, and they may not be attached to the adults who are responsible for their direct care.

Neglect refers to the failure of a person who is directly responsible for a child to provide the food, clothing, shelter, supervision, medical care, and education needed at the basic level of care. Some examples of neglect include the failure to provide adequate housing, appropriate clothing, hygiene, and supervision, as well as the failure to provide medical care or to treat illness. Others who neglect a child may allow chronic truancy or absence from school. Child neglect is the most prevalent from of child maltreatment in the United States.

Child sexual abuse is any interaction between a child and an adult (or another child) in which the child is used for the sexual stimulation of the perpetrator or an observer.[18] Sexual abuse includes both touching and nontouching behaviors. It must be noted that a child cannot give consent to any type of sexual behavior or activity simply because of the status as a minor. Some examples of child sexual abuse include masturbation, fellacio, cunninglus, digital penetration, sexual penetration, kissing, flashing, or exposure to pornography and inappropriate touching or fondling of a child's genitals, breast, or buttocks. Child victims of sexual abuse may exhibit inappropriate sexual behavior, masturbation, problems sitting or standing, and genital problems. Posttraumatic stress disorder, behavioral changes, as well as promiscuity may result from sexual abuse. Some behavioral signs of child sexual abuse may include: depression, anxiety, anger, loss of appetite, withdrawal from normal activities, substance abuse, self-mutilation, fear of certain places or people, bed-wetting, thoughts of suicide, and acting out sexually and using language that is not age-appropriate.[19]

Child maltreatment prevention strategies to reduce abuse may include programming for dysfunctional parents, eliciting support from schools and law enforcement, and following youth from birth to childhood. Such strategies would likely increase awareness about child maltreatment and possibly address those issues that could prevent abuse. Today, policies and programs are tied to theoretical beliefs about the root causes and most dangerous effects of child abuse. Some theories are directly tied to the traits or pathologies of the individual perpetrator while others address broader social and environmental conditions that allow abuse to occur and perhaps go undetected. Still others, like general strain theory look at how abuse victims may become involved in delinquency.

GENERAL STRAIN THEORY AND DELINQUENCY IN ABUSED CHILDREN

Robert Agnew's general strain theory (GST) can be used to explain why a juvenile may become frustrated and angry when they feel they have been intentionally mistreated. Although there are different versions of strain theory, each logically assumes that strain does not always lead to delinquency. General strain theory is a social, psychological theory that examines emotions and how juveniles conceptualize treatment by others or their individual situation as compared to others.[20] When a juvenile experiences strain or stress, such as trauma or maltreatment, they may become upset and engage in acts of delinquency to reduce or escape strain. This could likely explain the myth of the cycle of violence. However, it must be noted that delinquency is not necessarily the result of strain; it is one possible outcome out of many.

General strain theory is considered a theory of delinquency because it can be used to explain why some juveniles become involved in acts of delinquency as a result of experiencing child maltreatment. Even more importantly, general strain theory can explain why a juvenile may choose not to commit an act of delinquency subsequent to child maltreatment. According to general strain theory, delinquency is not dependent on the amount of strain a person experiences, rather the risk of delinquency is determined by the amount of coping mechanisms available to individuals and their threshold or tolerance levels when dealing with depression or stress.[21]

The presence of negative events and child maltreatment experiences may appear inescapable for juveniles because they have little control. Because of their lack of control, some juveniles may commit delinquent acts to reduce strain or even seek revenge over those who have abused them. GST asserts that anger and frustration are the driving forces behind strain, and that delinquency may occur when there are few opportunities or skills for coping with strain.

According to GST, there are three types of strain: (1) the failure to achieve goals, (2) the loss of positive stimuli, and (3) the presentation of negative stimuli.[22] In an attempt to explain the response to, and the trauma of child maltreatment, it appears that the loss of positive stimuli and the presentation of negative stimuli would most likely describe strain as a result of child abuse, parental neglect, and negative relations with others. The focus on negative events and situations allows for measuring delinquency with increased amounts of anger and strain.

It can be argued that the more coping mechanisms available to victims of child maltreatment, the lower their risks of delinquency will be. GST holds there are two different categories for coping mechanisms, criminal and noncriminal behaviors. Delinquency results when a juvenile has poor coping skills, limited resources, and a lack of social support. Individual coping resources such as interpersonal skills, self-regulation, and problem-solving skills may enable juveniles to use their individual traits to reduce strain and minimize delinquent responses to strain. Conventional social support includes having support from intimate others and institutions to reduce strain.

General strain theory implies then that the traumas children face when they are victims of homelessness and maltreatment may explain why delinquency results. Of particular importance for program planners and agents of the juvenile justice system is the issue of how to increase the resiliency of children who experience traumatic stress.

THE EFFECTS OF TRAUMATIC STRESS ON CHILDREN

The consequences of child maltreatment tend to vary based upon multiple factors that include the type of trauma, whether the trauma is acute or chronic, maltreatment type, co-occurrences of maltreatment, and the individual characteristics of the child (e.g., age and development). GST incorporates the psychological aspect of behavior in the use of terms such a coping mechanisms and emotional support. According to the mental health literature, traumatic stress can be caused by experiencing serious injury to self, witnessing the serious injury or death of another, or threats of serious injury or death to self or others. Most traumatic events can be placed into one of two categories: (1) acute traumatic events and (2) chronic traumatic events.[23] An acute traumatic event is one in which there is generally a single occurrence. In some cases, homelessness may be an example of an acute traumatic event. In this way, the single event of losing a stable living environment can be a source of child stress.

A chronic traumatic event is one in which there are several occurrences or episodes. Generally, victims of child maltreatment are likely to suffer from multiple occurrences of traumatic events. Along with trauma from maltreatment, other co-occurring sources of child stress may include poverty, school failure, divorce, loss, separation from family, and other events that may result in the loss of positive stimuli and the presentation of negative stimuli. Child traumatic stress may differ greatly from adult stress because a child has fewer faculties in place to deal with trauma. For example, an infant cannot communicate needs, there are very few abilities in place for the infant to cope with stress; the available coping strategy is to cry. As an individual grows and develops, so does the ability to cope with stress. In other words, the child has not developed the skills to understand and deal with the resulting trauma.

Coping with Trauma

Many experts, including Widom, point out that not all victims of child maltreatment will commit criminal or delinquent acts. In fact, many victims of child maltreatment do not engage in violence at all. In more recent research, Widom and her colleagues explored the role of individual variables, family variables, and neighborhood variables to explain resiliency to child maltreatment.[24] Their study was based on 676 documented cases of child maltreatment, specifically physical abuse, sexual abuse, and neglect. These cases filed in juvenile court between 1967 and 1971 and participants were interviewed approximately 22 years after their abuse cases were considered (between 1989 and 1995).[25] Findings indicated that nearly half (48%) of child maltreatment victims demonstrated resilience in adolescence and 30.2 percent did so in young adulthood. Resiliency was highest for youth in adolescence who had stable living conditions and for those with a stable partner or spouse in adulthood. These findings are in line with GST, which suggests that having social support and meaningful relationships with others helps individuals to cope with child traumatic stress.

According to Cutuli and Herbers, two of the most positive influences on resiliency are cognitive functioning and healthy functional family relationships.[26] Their research defines resilience as bouncing back from trauma, and the authors suggest that having strong bonds to functional parents creates a protective factor that can minimize the dysfunctional risk factors of poverty, criminality, and exposure to violence. These authors suggest that risk factors based upon a circumstance or multiple circumstances increase the likelihood of negative outcomes. Child trauma that occurs as an acute trauma in the midst of other types of chronic trauma may also result in poor outcomes. Further, negative results are more likely to occur when appropriate coping and resiliency skills are not present.

HOMELESSNESS AS TRAUMA

According to the National Center on Family Homelessness, children who are displaced from a residence are much less healthy than non-homeless children, more often hungry as well as nutritionally deprived, more likely to display emotional and behavioral problems, and more likely to suffer delayed development symptoms as well as learning disabilities. About one quarter of children who are homeless have lived through episodes of violence within the home and, by the age of 12, 83 percent have been exposed to a serious violent event.[27]

As explained by Mohan and Shields, children who are victims of homelessness are generally at a higher risk for poor outcomes and to experience strain most likely from the inability to control or access stable living conditions.[28] Homelessness, as well as childhood victimization, creates an uncertainty, as well as stigma, trauma, shame, and undue stress on children. In some cases, this type of victimization may result in delinquency and behavior problems if there are no interventions in place. Grineski notes that how a child responds to trauma is dependent upon the age, current living status, resiliency, family support, and the time and frequency of homeless events (acute vs. chronic).[29] He further writes that resiliency and success are based upon drawing on the child's strengths and cultivating attitudes that encourage an asset-based perspective instead of a deficit-based perspective.

Cutuli and Herbers conducted research on the resiliency of children who have faced homelessness.[30] The authors argue that the negative impact of a homeless experience can be prevented with proper parenting and a healthy adaptive system. Executive functioning is important to note in the child trauma literature as this functioning type is an umbrella term for a set of processes that include memory and the ability to control emotions and behavior. This functioning type suggests that a child has the cognitive ability to self-regulate his or her behavior and thus possesses the adaptive mechanisms to cope with trauma. The timing of the homelessness can also determine the coping adaptations in place. In line with the child trauma literature, the writers note that the earlier the homeless event, the poorer the outcome. However, it is important to provide early interventions for those children who are very young and have not yet developed the high levels of executive functioning due to cognitive development.

Family Dynamics and Programs with Potential

Family dynamics are important to victims of child maltreatment as supportive networks are seen as therapeutic for victims.[31] Healthy, intact families are those that help individual family members with their needs, have clear well-defined boundaries, provide leadership, provide opportunities for open communication, problem solving, negotiation skills, and accept changes well.[32] Dysfunctional families are those in which neither the father, mother, or direct caregiver is whole; a whole person possesses emotional, social, physical, and mental abilities and is able to balance these abilities. Ongoing stressors may increase a child's vulnerability and inhibit their ability to cope. In this way, it is very important for families to provide protective factors to protect, nurture, and promote healthy parent–child relationships.

In many cases, it is very difficult to get parents to engage in parenting skills programs to support their children after episodes of child maltreatment. Parents may not embrace programs that take a deficit perspective, suggesting that they lack the skills to be effective parents. In an effort to get buy in from parents, it is best to use the protective factors approach and focus on the skills that a parent possesses, as a starting point.[33] Programs offered to parents should be specific to the needs of the parent, child, and the family. Programs that are responsive to cultural differences, incorporate home visits, and provide parent education and prevention strategies are considered common approaches for the family.[34]

Because military veterans are at high risk for homelessness special programs (e.g., Community Circles of Support for Veterans' Families) have been developed to address posttraumatic stress disorders, enhance communications within the family, and increasing public awareness of the needs of veterans and their families. Other programs target the mother and child bond and emphasize child development and substance abuse counseling as part of the family preservation strategy (Strengthening At Risk and Homeless Young Mothers and Children). Also fulfilling an important role, the Institute for Children, Poverty & Homelessness provides independent research on effective public policy and programs that impact the homeless.

CONCLUSION: FOCUS ON RESILIENCY

Attachment to healthy, functional relationships and activities are critical in developing coping and resiliency skills for victims of child trauma, including children who are victims of homelessness. Evans and Burton suggest that treatment for victims of child maltreatment and trauma should be tailored to the specific type of victimization.[35] Realistically, a one-size-fits-all approach to early intervention and treatment does not address specific trauma and thus resiliency may be more difficult or hampered. Trauma-informed services should incorporate screening tools and address the behaviors that need to be treated. Accordingly, individualized treatment and an intensive holistic treatment approach should be used for traumatized children.[36] Although the executive functioning is lower for very young victims of child trauma, poor outcomes can be reduced with intensive psychological treatment. Commenting on the options available for working with victims of child trauma, Ziegler explained, "the best evidence-based practice will likely be ineffective in the hands of an incompetent adult, while a skilled adult can make a difference with any number of approaches, with or without research support."[37] In other words, one of the realities of working with children who have experienced trauma, including child maltreatment and homelessness, is to understand the importance of having a toolkit and use the appropriate tool to meet the needs of the child. The holistic approach includes all facets of a child; the whole child must be supported to increase the resiliency to cope with a child traumatic stressor to reduce the risk of delinquency.

DISCUSSION QUESTIONS

1. What are some of the strengths and weaknesses of the concept of a "cycle of violence" for explaining delinquency?
2. How effective do you think attempts to address child maltreatment and abuse have been in this country over the years and what factors seem to make the problem harder or easier to address?

3. If one were to adopt a general strain theory approach to delinquency interventions, what kinds of efforts and specific programs should be implemented? What would their goals be?
4. What is resiliency? Are some children more prone to being resilient, why or why not?

ADDITIONAL RESOURCES

Geiger, Jennifer Mullins, and Lisa Ann Schelbe. "Stopping the Cycle of Child Abuse and Neglect: A Call to Action to Focus on Pregnant and Parenting Youth in and Aging Out of the Foster Care System." *Journal of Public Child Welfare* 8, no. 1, (2014): 25–50.

Kelley, Michelle, Hannah Lawrence, Robert Milletich, Brittany Hollis, and James Henson. "Modeling Risk for Child Abuse and Harsh Parenting in Families with Depressed and Substance-Abusing Parents." *Child Abuse and Neglect* 43 (2015): 42–52.

McGuire-Schwartz, Mandy, Latoya A. Small, Gary Parker, Patricia Kim, and Mary McKay. "Relationships between Caregiver Violence Exposure, Caregiver Depression, and Youth Behavioral Health among Homeless Families." *Research on Social Work Practice* (2014): 1049731514553921.

Nowakowski, Eva, and Karen Mattern. "An Exploratory Study of the Characteristics That Prevent Youth from Completing a Family Violence Diversion Program." *Journal of Family Violence* 29, no. 2 (2014): 143–149.

Routt, Gregory, and Lily Anderson. *Adolescent Violence in the Home: Restorative Approaches to Building Healthy, Respectful Family Relationships.* New York: Routledge, 2015.

Sandy, Marie. "Pushed by Angels and Hellbent on Better: Mothers Describe Getting to the Other Side of Family Homelessness." *Humanity & Society* 38, no. 4 (2014): 388–413.

Snyder, Susan M., and Darcey H. Merritt. "Do Childhood Experiences of Neglect Affect Delinquency among Child Welfare Involved Youth?" *Children and Youth Services Review* 46 (2014): 64–71.

Wessells, Michael. "Bottom-Up Approaches to Strengthening Child Protection Systems: Placing Children, Families, and Communities at the Center." *Child Abuse and Neglect* 43 (2015): 8–21.

RELATED WEBSITES

America's Youngest Outcasts, http://www.homelesschildrenamerica.org/
Annual Report of the National Center for Missing & Exploited Children, http://www.missingkids.com/AnnualReport
Association of Family and Conciliation Courts, http://www.afccnet.org
Community Shelter Board—Homelessness . . . Through the Eyes of a Child, http://csb.org/files/media/homelessness/?gclid=CNr42uX11cUCFVKDfgodVycAMA
National Alliance for Family Court Justice, http://www.nafcj.net

National Center for Children Exposed to Violence (NCCEV): Child Development-Community Policing Program, http://medicine.yale.edu/childstudy/com munity/cdcp.aspx

National Center on Family Homelessness, http://www.familyhomelessness.org/

SUPPORTING FILMS

Frontline: Poor Kids, PBS, November 20, 2012
Homeless: The Motel Kids of Orange County (2010)
Life at 5: Resilience (Films Media Group) (2010)
The Pursuit of Happiness (2006)
This Boy's Life (1993)

NOTES

1. Christian (2015).
2. National Center for Juvenile Justice (2014), 21.
3. Kretschmar, Butcher, Flannery, and Singer (2014).
4. McShane (2008).
5. National Center on Family Homelessness (2011a, 2011b).
6. Widom (1989a, 1989b).
7. Ibid.
8. Widom (1989a), 24.
9. Widom (1989a).
10. Empey (1978).
11. Ibid.
12. Sutton (1998).
13. Costin (1991).
14. Ibid.
15. Hammer, Finkelhor, and Sedlak (2002).
16. Child Welfare Information Gateway (2014).
17. Ibid.
18. Ibid.
19. Ibid.
20. Agnew and White (1992); Broidy (2001).
21. Brezina (1996).
22. Agnew and White (1992).
23. Cutuli and Herbers (2014).
24. DuMont, Widom, and Czaja (2007).
25. Ibid.
26. Cutuli and Herbers (2014).
27. National Center on Family Homelessness (2009).
28. Mohan and Shields (2014).
29. Grineski (2014.)
30. Cutuli and Herbers (2014).

31. Ziegler (2015).
32. Clement (2002).
33. Counts, Buffington, Chang-Rios, Rasmussen, and Preacher (2010).
34. Portwood, Lambert, Abrams, and Nelson (2011).
35. Evans and Burton (2013).
36. Ziegler (2015).
37. Ibid., 42.

REFERENCES

Agnew, Robert, and Helen R. White. "An Empirical Test of General Strain Theory." *Criminology* 30 (1992): 475–499.

Brezina, Timothy. "Adapting to Strain: An Examination of Delinquent Coping Responses." *Criminology* 34 (1996): 39–60.

Broidy, Lisa. M. "A Test of General Strain Theory." *Criminology* 39 (2001): 9–35.

Child Welfare Information Gateway. *Child Abuse and Neglect Fatalities 2012: Statistics and Interventions.* Washington, DC: U.S. Department of Health and Human Services, Children's Bureau, 2014.

Clement, Mary. *The Juvenile Justice System,* 2nd edition. Boston, MA: Butterworth/Heinemann, 2002.

Costin, Lela B. "Unraveling the Mary Ellen Legend: Origins of the Cruelty Movement." *Social Science Review* 65, no 2 (1991): 203–223.

Counts, Jacqueline M., Elenor S. Buffington, Karin Chang-Rios, Heather N. Rasmussen, and Kristopher J. Preacher. "The Development and Validation of the Protective Factors Survey: A Self-Report Measure of Protective Factors against Child Maltreatment." *Child Abuse & Neglect* 34 (2010): 762–772.

Cutuli, J. J., and Janette Herbers. "Promoting Resilience for Children Who Experience Family Homelessness: Opportunities to Encourage Developmental Competence." *Cityscape: A Journal of Policy Development and Research* 16, no.1 (2014): 114–139.

DuMont, Kimberly A., Cathy S. Widom, and Sally Czaja. "Predictors of Resilience in Abused and Neglected Children Grown-Up: The Role in Individual and Neighborhood Characteristics." *Child Abuse and Neglect* 31 (2007): 255–274.

Empey, LaMar. *American Delinquency: Its Meaning and Construction.* Homewood, IL: The Dorsey Press, 1978.

Evans, Carolyn, and David Burton. "Outcomes of Child Maltreatment and Trauma—Five Types of Child Maltreatment and Subsequent Delinquency: Physical Neglect as the Most Significant Predictor." *Journal of Child and Adolescent Trauma* 6 (2013): 231–245.

Grineski, Steve. "The Multi-Dimensional Lives of Children Who Are Homeless." *Critical Questions in Education* 5 (2014): 203–217.

Hammer, Heather, David Finkelhor, and Andrea Sedlak. "Runaway/Thrownaway Children: National Estimates and Characteristics." *NISMART.* Washington, DC: Office of Juvenile Justice and Delinquency Prevention, 2002.

Mohan, Erica, and Carolyn Shields. "The Voices behind the Numbers: Understanding the Experiences of Homeless Students." *Critical Questions in Education* 5 (2014): 182–202.

National Center on Family Homelessness. *Annual Report. Working to End Family Homelessness*. Newton, MA: National Center on Family Homelessness, 2009.

National Center on Family Homelessness. *The Characteristics and Needs of Families Experiencing Homelessness: Fact Sheet*. Needham, MA: National Center on Family Homelessness, 2011a. http://www.familyhomelessness.org/media/306.pdf.

National Center on Family Homelessness. *America's Youngest Outcasts*. Newton, MA: National Center on Family Homelessness, 2011b.

Portwood, Sharon, Richard G. Lambert, Lyndon P. Abrams, and Ellissa B. Nelson. "An Evaluation of the Adults and Children Together (ACT) against Violence: Parents Raising Safe Kids Program." *Journal of Primary Prevention* 32 (2011): 147–160.

Sutton, John. *Stubborn Children: Controlling Delinquency in the United States, 1640–1981*. Berkeley, CA: University of California Press, 1998.

Widom, Cathy S. "Does Violence Beget Violence? A Critical Examination of the Literature." *Pyschological Bulletin* 106 (1989a): 3–28.

Widom, Cathy S. "The Cycle of Violence." *Science* 244 (1989b): 160–166.

Widom, Cathy S., and Michael G. Maxfield. "An Update on the 'Cycle of Violence.'" *National Institute of Justice, Research in Brief*. Washington, DC: U.S. Department of Justice, National Institute of Justice, 2001.

Williams, Franklin P., and Marilyn D. McShane. *Criminological Theory*, 6th edition. Upper Saddle River, NJ: Pearson Publishing, 2014.

Wright, Emily, and Abigail Fagan. "The Cycle of Violence in Context: Exploring the Moderating Roles of Neighborhood Disadvantage and Cultural Norms." *Criminology* 52 (2013): 217–249.

Ziegler, Dave. "Intensive Holistic Treatment for Traumatized Children." *Reclaiming Children and Youth* 23, no. 4 (2015): 40–43.

Chapter 7

Children of Incarcerated Parents: Problems and Resilience

Alexandria Pech and Barbara E. Bloom

There are 1.6 million people incarcerated in U.S. state and federal prisons.[1] Often overlooked, families and children have become a major collateral consequence of mass incarceration. More than 2.7 million children in the United States have an incarcerated parent; 2.3 percent of the U.S. child population and approximately 10 million children have experienced parental incarceration at some point in their lives.[2] Negative impacts on children and families include the following: economic instability, lack of contact between parent and children, lack of social support services, stigma and social isolation.[3] In 2007, 809,800 prisoners were parents.[4] Sixty-five percent of women in state prison had minor children.[5] In 2008, there were close to 1.6 million children with incarcerated fathers and close to 150,000 children with incarcerated mothers.[6] Furthermore, parental incarceration affects more black and Hispanic parents compared to their white counterparts. Consequently, one in 15 black children has an incarcerated parent. One in 41 Hispanic children have an incarcerated parent compared to 1 in 115 white children who have an incarcerated parent.[7]

PARENTAL INCARCERATION AND
THE IMPACT ON CHILDREN

Children face a variety of risks when their parents are incarcerated. To explain the impact of parental incarceration, one study examined the association between children's health and parental incarceration.[8] The findings revealed that children with incarcerated parents, in comparison to children without incarcerated parents, had worse health outcomes. Children with incarcerated parents were four times more likely to experience depression, behavior or conduct problems, twice as likely to suffer from learning disabilities, attention deficit disorder (ADD)/attention-deficit hyperactivity disorder (ADHD) and anxiety. Physical health ailments, such as, obesity, asthma, speech, hearing, and vision problems were seen in higher rates for children with incarcerated parents and there was an association between persistent school absence and parental incarceration. Finally, the study concluded that parental incarceration was by and large more detrimental to children's well-being in comparison to other adverse family experiences, such as divorce, death of a parent, witnessing domestic abuse of a parent, substance abuse, or mental illness.[9] It is important to recognize that past studies revealed that divorce was by and large the worse event that could take place in a child's life, in which case, may not be the most accurate statement based on the findings described earlier.

With regard to financial security, when a parent goes to prison, children suffer from economic instability due to a loss of income. Economic instability has been examined for a possible effect on children's health and well-being.[10] Furthermore, one study examined the possible association between mass imprisonment, parental incarceration, and child homelessness.[11] Findings supported the hypotheses that paternal incarceration puts children, especially black children, at risk for homelessness because of: loss of income, lack of social supports and the reduction of maternal abilities, such as an increase in maternal stress. Whereas maternal incarceration results in multiple living transitions or foster care placements for children.[12]

Risk factors for children with incarcerated parents intersect with children's school, community, familial environments as well as the prison system itself.[13] Research has described the process that children must go through when visiting their parent in jail.[14] Families must stand in lines for long periods of time before processing and they are subject to metal detectors and strip searches, before going through various metal gates to get to the visitation room. Research has shown that child friendly visiting can serve as a protective factor for children with incarcerated parents.[15] However, additional research has shown that the visitation process is daunting, stressful, and confusing for children. Secondary prisonization refers to non-incarcerated family members, forgoing their privacy, using limited financial resources and jeopardizing their emotional well-being to visit their incarcerated relative and feeling as if they were prisoners themselves.[16] Additionally, families are often low income and cannot afford to visit the parent who is in prison; prisons are often located hundreds of miles away from the child's primary residence, making it more difficult to facilitate parent–child bonds through visitation.

INCARCERATED MOTHERS VERSUS INCARCERATED FATHERS

Research has begun to differentiate the impact of paternal and maternal incarceration. One study used data collected from 6,146 inmates to assess the risks associated with mothers and fathers in prison.[17] Findings revealed that children of incarcerated mothers were more likely to be living in nonfamilial situations such as foster care or in the care of nonrelatives in comparison to 90 percent of children with incarcerated fathers who were more likely to live with their mothers.[18]

One research study specifically examined the effects of maternal incarceration on children's behavior.[19] Data analysis showed that children with incarcerated mothers were more disadvantaged prior to incarceration such that caregivers were depressed, had a history of incarceration, suffered from substance abuse problems, and material hardship. They concluded that children with incarcerated mothers had more attention problems, social problems, rule breaking, and cognitive issues, but these behavioral issues were likely due to adverse situations prior to a mother's incarceration.[20]

Research has been done on the possible spillover effects of maternal incarceration on children's academic outcomes.[21] After analyzing data from the National Longitudinal Study of Adolescence, findings revealed that for students with an incarcerated mother, there was a significant negative effect on the students' grade point average (GPA). In addition, the college graduation rate for students with incarcerated mothers was between 1 and 2 percent. Further findings revealed that when 10 percent of mothers in a school were incarcerated, college graduation rates dropped from 40 to 25 percent for children whose mothers were not incarcerated, suggesting that maternal incarceration does have spillover effects at the school level as well as the individual level.

Furthermore, it is crucial to analyze maternal versus paternal incarceration, in that, research has shown that when a mother goes to jail or prison, there are more negative consequences for her children. The best explanation for such differences between maternal and paternal incarceration is that mothers are most likely to be the primary caregiver of their children prior to incarceration and as a result, children with incarcerated mothers are more likely to be placed in foster care.[22] Children's placement in foster care, following maternal incarceration, has been identified as a risk factor due to the possibility that children will experience more than one placement resulting in housing instability.[23] One research study conducted qualitative interviews with 102 incarcerated mothers to examine the cycle of abuse between mothers and their children.[24] Of 102 children with incarcerated mothers, 83 percent experienced either physical abuse, sexual abuse, or witnessed violence in the home, and 55 percent of children experienced someone in the home using drugs or alcohol.

In regards to paternal incarceration, research has examined caregiver gate keeping, which develops when a non-incarcerated caregiver restricts the relationship between their child and their incarcerated father.[25] The caregiver believes they are protecting the child, but in reality, children may become distressed if they are denied access to a relationship with their incarcerated parent.[26]

In addition, a small body of research identifies the impact on boys versus girls when a father or mother goes to jail and/or prison. Sons of incarcerated fathers have been examined to find a possible association between paternal incarceration and possible behavior problems.[27] Findings revealed that separation, as a result of paternal incarceration, did not directly result in antisocial behavior. In actuality, it was factors, such as, psychopathology of the non-incarcerated caregiver, relationship with non-incarcerated caregiver, coping resources and social supports in addition to paternal incarceration that contributed to behavior disorders in sons of incarcerated fathers.[28] Sons with incarcerated mothers may be particularly at risk if they had ever witnessed their mother being abused prior to the mother's incarceration.[29]

JUVENILE JUSTICE

The early studies on juvenile justice did not include inquiry about the potential association between parental incarceration and juvenile delinquency. Questions remained as to whether or not parental incarceration influenced youth's entrance into the criminal justice system. If so, should a juvenile's parental circumstances be taken into account during sentencing?

There is an assumption that children of incarcerated parents are more likely to end up in the juvenile justice system but the research is inconsistent. Although there is literature implying that children of incarcerated parents will be guaranteed to be involved in the criminal justice system, only a small number of longitudinal studies have been conducted to support these claims.[30] Again, there is not valid support to claim a causal relationship between youth's potential criminal involvement and their parent's criminal involvement. Statements, such as these, perpetuate discrimination against children with incarcerated parents, and as a result, such discrimination has the opportunity to contribute to intergenerational incarceration.[31] This contribution is made in part by labeling theory, which explains that people will conform to negative stereotypes if they place belief in the negative stereotypes.[32] Research claims, mentioned earlier, lend themselves to children experiencing copious amounts of stigma, judgment and prejudice.[33] For example, a study conducted by Dallaire, Ciccone, and Wilson investigated teacher's expectations of children with incarcerated mothers using an experimental design.[34] Teachers were given eight vignettes, one of which was about a hypothetical student new to their classroom and living with their grandparent because their mother was "away at prison." Findings revealed that teachers rated students with incarcerated mothers as less competent in comparison to students' whose mothers were absent due to rehab, school, or other reasons. Similarly, female students with incarcerated mothers were rated by teachers as less competent in comparison to all other female students in each of the research conditions. Based on these results, the authors discussed the possibility of self-fulfilling prophecies unfolding as a result of teachers' lowered expectations, which could potentially force children to live up to the low academic standards set forth by their teachers.[35]

In past research, a study by Dannerbeck involved 1,112 adolescents and found that among this sample, 31 percent had parent(s) with a history of incarceration.[36] The study finds support for multiple hypotheses, one hypothesis being that a history of parental incarceration is associated with ineffective parenting styles and attributes. Ineffective parenting attributes, such as a lack of structure, discipline, and guidance, have been shown as a factor that contributes to juvenile delinquency because it promotes antisocial behavior in children. Antisocial behavior is often seen as a contributing factor to juvenile delinquency in its own right. A small number of studies, such as one by Murray and Farrington, investigated a similar question during their longitudinal research on the impact of parental incarceration on boys' antisocial behavior and delinquency.[37] Furthermore, their analysis of qualitative interviews supported the hypothesis that boys who had experienced the incarceration of a parent had a high rate of antisocial behavior and antisocial delinquent outcomes compared to boys who had never been separated from their parent (71% versus 19%, respectively).

Aaron and Dallaire used data from an intervention program to analyze possible correlations between parental incarceration history and children's delinquency.[38] The intervention was geared toward at-risk children in five major U.S. cities, in which, 332 children participated in the program and received aid from case managers, family court, and neighborhood services. Furthermore, the study looked at whether families with a history of parental incarceration dealt with negative family processes such as older sibling delinquency. Findings from parental and child interviews revealed that parents who experienced past incarceration reported that their children participating in the intervention program were more delinquent. Furthermore, parents reported higher levels of older sibling delinquency as well.

RISK AND RESILIENCY

Luthar and colleagues provide a definition of resilience that is relevant for this population.[39] To think about resilience is to understand that a phenomenon or process is occurring, which mimics positive adaptation despite experiences of significant adversity or trauma.[40] For children and youth who have a parent in prison, researchers have tried to discover which time period is most wrought with significant adversity or trauma: before their parent's incarceration or after their parent's arrest and subsequent sentencing? This distinction is important to determine in order for intervention services to be implemented at the most critical time.

Research has shown that there are significant aspects of instability existing within families and children of incarcerated parents even *before* the parent goes to jail or prison. Familial instability is synonymous with risks. When multiple risks are co-occurring at the same time this is known as "risk indices."[41] Understanding this concept, researchers have identified a plethora of risk indices for children with incarcerated mothers, which tend to include the following: low-income single parent households, history of parental incarceration, caregiver problems with substance abuse and caregiver unemployment, to name a few.[42] The combination of risk indices are central to examine considering past research that has shown negative child outcomes are associated with the more risk factors that a child experiences.[43] That is to say that more risks equals worse child outcomes at least in regards to intellectual outcomes and incarcerated mothers.[44]

Past research has investigated protective factors also known as modifiers that may affect the risks in a positive trajectory. Family processes, community processes and individual attributes have been analyzed as potential protective factors for children.[45] Nesmith and Ruhland conducted qualitative interviews with 34 children and outlined the many ways in which positive family processes, such as a strong bond between child and non-incarcerated caregiver helped children in any way.[46] The findings suggested that these children looked up to these adults as role models. In terms of community, the presence of an adult mentor, whether a relative or nonrelative, was helpful for children and youth to feel less marginalized and isolated due to having a parent in jail or prison.[47] Although it is crucial to understand that resilience is not in the form of a personality trait, the notion of individual attributes can play a key role as a protective factor. If children and youth are in a supportive environment, positive personal strengths can be fostered to help children and youth overcome life stressors occurring in childhood.[48] In fact, in terms of interventions, to optimize children's development, improving the amount of warmth, responsivity, stimulation, safety, and access to resources in caregiver's home and familial environment is seen as more effective for children in comparison to providing services directly to children.[49]

ISSUES IN RESEARCH

Johnston argues against numerous assumptions and conclusions made by researchers.[50] One assumption is that being an incarcerated parent automatically indicates that the parent is an inadequate caregiver. Johnston uses a study by Phillips et al. to showcase that no association exists between criminally involved parents and inadequate care of their offspring with the exception of drug addicted and mentally ill parents.[51] Additionally, the low number of visits that incarcerated mothers receive may be indicative of the fact that mothers have children with multiple partners and that they may have not lived with them prior to incarceration instead of the assumption that visitation is low due to distance of the prison.[52] Ultimately longitudinal and developmentally driven research is suggested in order to obtain the most accurate report on the effects of parental incarceration on children.

As far as academia goes, conducting studies on children is problematic since children are considered special populations according the Institutional Review Board (IRB). Furthermore, prisoners are also considered special populations, making the process more difficult to get approval from the IRB for purposes of a research study. Additionally, the process to gain access to prison facilities even with IRB approval is exhaustive and time-consuming. Entry into prison facilities requires approval from the prison administration, which is not always granted.

SUCCESSFUL RESEARCH STUDIES

The 1996 Adverse Childhood Experiences (ACE) study sought to explore the relationship between childhood abuse and household dysfunction and health risks. The study collected questionnaires from 9,508 adults seeking standard medical attention from a large Kaiser Permanente hospital. The questionnaire was broken down into seven categories of adverse childhood experiences: one being living with family members who were ever incarcerated. The results showed that among persons that experience a family member's incarceration, 62 percent of the same persons lived with someone with substance abuse. With that said, more risk exposure was equated to more likelihood of health-related issues, such as smoking, severe obesity, depressed mood as well as suicide attempts.[53] Thus, a child experiencing a family member's incarceration was also experiencing substance abuse in the home, resulting in exposure to a total of two adverse childhood experiences. Another data set with information specific to children of incarcerated parents is the Fragile Families and Child Well Being (FFCWB) study in which researchers have followed families for nine years.[54] In wave 5 alone, the number of fathers who had ever spent time in jail or prison was 719 as reported by the mother. This study has been used to investigate associations between children's behavior and paternal incarceration using secondary data analysis. Longitudinal data is difficult to collect as a result of attrition within these children and their families. Often times, children with incarcerated parents are known to move around from residence to residence. Also, many times these same participants drop out of a study once a parent is released from prison.

Another study is Project S.E.E.K., which is a longitudinal study of children with incarcerated parents. Launched in 1989–2004, Project S.E.E.K was the first extensive program for kids and involved weekly two-hour support group meetings, home visits, advocacy, referrals, stress management training for caregivers, and helping families communicate with incarcerated parents by providing supervision for child visits. Findings from interviews conducted with project S.E.E.K participants included the following: children were often given false or misleading information about their parent's incarceration, children experienced financial instability, and negative effects of incarceration were reduced as a result of receiving support and skills-improvement training from the program.

COMMUNITIES

The collateral consequences of mass incarceration not only impact families, but also communities, especially communities of color. Communities of color are often targeted by the criminal justice system due to overpolicing, racial profiling, and disparate sentencing practices. In low-income communities of color, it is documented that a disproportionate number of their citizens are behind bars. As it may be, using research to understand and analyze the negative implications for the over-reliance on incarceration and the incarceration of parents is critical in order to protect families, children and youth with parents in jail and/or prison.

Theories of intergenerational cycles of incarceration are prevalent within the population of children and youth who have a parent in prison. Intergenerational cycles of incarceration can be defined as the spillover effects of a parent's incarceration onto their children making children's involvement with the criminal justice system more likely. Consequentially, research has focused on family socialization as a factor, which results in the tolerance of deviant behaviors.[55] Incarceration is prevalent in many low-income communities, which makes prison seem like a badge of honor to some children and youth.[56] Furthermore, resources are not readily available to create community programs to reduce the likelihood of incarceration for youth. Adding to the problem are the difficulties in recruiting families to engage in community programs catered to children with incarcerated parents. It has been suggested that parental incarceration yields immense feelings of shame, guilt, and fear of rejection, which could be one reason why program participation is low.[57]

PROGRAMS FOR CHILDREN

Some examples of programs that are considered the best practices available for children of incarcerated parents are the following:

Project WHAT! is based in Oakland and San Francisco, California, to raise awareness for the needs of children with incarcerates parents by employing teenagers to train youth as advocates. Youth are trained to facilitate trainings on improving services and policies that affect children with incarcerated parents. These youth-led trainings have been presented to classrooms, local jails, conferences, law enforcement officials, and policymakers.

Girl Scouts Beyond Bars is a nationwide program established in 1992 that provides girls with incarcerated mothers the opportunity to preserve the mother–daughter bond while the mother is serving her prison sentence. The girls are able to visit their mothers twice a month to partici-pate in regular Girl Scout activities. An evaluation for the program was conducted for the 2010–2012-program cycle. Findings suggested that Girl Scout Beyond Bars enhanced mother–daughter relationships, helped girls avoid getting in trouble and develop their leadership skills. As for the incarcerated mothers, findings revealed that this program helped mothers develop effective parenting skills.

Sesame Street Little Children Big Problems Initiative is a campaign for children with incarcerated parents. The goal is to create awareness for children affected by parental incarceration by creating make-believe pup-pets with parents in prison, interactive videos geared for three- to eight-year-olds, tips for caregivers and real-life stories of parental incarceration. Sesame Street is watched by majority of children in the United States and as a result a significant amount of awareness is created because of this initiative.

Children of Promise is based in Brooklyn, New York, and provides aca-demic enrichment, mentoring, mental health services as well as helping children maintain contact with their incarcerated parent through letters, phone calls, and prison visits. Outcomes from their 2014 evaluation report revealed that, as a result of their intervention model, 75 percent of their young participants had graduated from their local school. It is unknown if the percentage is specific to high school or middle school. Children of promise has a 98 percent retention rate of their participants according to their website. They serve over 200 children through their academic, mentoring and family programs.

Big Brothers and Big Sisters provides children with incarcerated parents a real-life mentor, known as a, big brother or big sister. In regards to program evaluation most programs are not evaluated. An evaluation of the program found that child participants were 45 percent less likely to use drugs or alcohol compared to the nonparticipants within the control group.[58]

POLICIES

Some examples of policies that are considered the best practices available for children of incarcerated parents are the following:

A Bill of Rights was created by the San Francisco Children of Incarcerated Parents Partnership (SFCIPP), in order to give caregivers, court officials, and police administration a protocol of considerations to adhere to when arresting and sentencing a parent as well as during incarceration.

PROGRAMS FOR FAMILIES

Family visitation policies are a vital component to strengthening family ties between children and their incarcerated parent. Although prisons are located very far away from the child's home residence, programs, such as *Get on the Bus* that help children visit their mothers in California prisons, could be expanded to help increase parental visitation. To this end, it has been long argued that visitation rooms inside prisons need to be more child-friendly. Case management has been utilized as a tool for families dealing with parental incarceration. However, programs that extend case management for the children before and during incarceration, as well as comprehensive services for the reunification process would be more beneficial for families.

Reunification between incarcerated parents and their children can result in a range of problems related to the family dynamic without proper support. Brown and Bloom found that for many recently released mothers, there were often unresolved issues between the mother and the non-incarcerated caregiver.[59] The non-incarcerated caregiver would relinquish all parental duties upon the mother's release. As a result, mothers would become overwhelmed at this transition back to motherhood especially if they did not have the financial, parenting skills, or housing means to care for their children.

Curricula implemented into schools, community spaces, and child service providers on the unique effects that parental incarceration has on children are needed. Using Sesame Street's *Little Children, Big Challenges* toolbox would be an excellent source to model as it provides suggestions to improve parenting skills for caregivers, teaching skills for education personnel and emotional regulation skills for children, all of whom are dealing with the ramifications of an incarcerated parent in one way or another.

MOVING FORWARD: INTERVENTIONS AND ALTERNATIVES TO PARENTAL INCARCERATION

Based on the research findings, there is still a large body of work to be done. First, sentencing policies and practices need to be revised. Since research has shown that children with incarcerated mothers are more likely to end up in the foster care system, which has its own set of risks, reduction in the length of sentences needs to be considered. From what we know about adult female offenders, typically they commit non-violent low-level offenses, such as, larceny/theft; minor drug infractions and they are more likely to be the primary caregiver of their children. Instead of jail time, prosecutors can refuse to prosecute for low-level drug offenses.[60] Attention needs to be paid to the reunification process to help the child adjust to their parent coming home from prison. Innovative ways to improve visitation must be explored. Some jail and prison facilities have begun to experiment with video calling as a source of communication for inmates and their families. Perhaps this innovative method could alleviate the secondary prisonization that children experience.

In regards to interventions, Poehlmann suggests that the best time to provide support services for children is at the time when their mother is arrested and sentenced.[61] At that time point, children can be screened for any developmental challenges and given proper treatment. Also, intervention services may be best implemented before a parent's incarceration and at the familial level by improving the child's home environment to provide warmth, stability and safety.[62]

Alternatives to prison include the use of citations and release and diversion programs for low-level drug offenders and prostitution offenses, instead of jail time.[63] Instead of jail time offenders could be enrolled in community based programs to receive treatment for drug abuse and the same can be implemented for first time felony offenders who commit property crime, and in lieu of jail time, offenders would serve community service.[64]

In conclusion, previous studies have analyzed the negative impacts of parental incarceration on children. Major findings conclude that maternal and paternal incarceration have different effects for children, such that, paternal incarceration puts children at risk for homelessness whereas maternal incarceration results in foster care placement.[65] Aside from the few longitudinal studies that have analyzed the relationship between parental incarceration and juvenile delinquency, no causal relationship can be determined.[66] Past studies have shown that multiple risk factors increase the likelihood of negative child outcomes.[67] Future research should analyze how protective factors, such as healthy family relationships, effective mentoring programs, and participation in community organizations can help foster resiliency in children with incarcerated parents.

DISCUSSION QUESTIONS

1. What do you think are the most serious and difficult challenges faced by children of incarcerated parents?
2. Compare the effects of the loss of a mother to incarceration with that of the loss of a father. What factors might influence the impact of the loss of the mother relative to the absence of the father?
3. Describe the program components that you think might be most useful and effective when working with the children of incarcerated parents.
4. Explain how the age of the child interacts with the separation from a parent to result in problems in adjustment and in behavior.
5. What possible exceptions might there be to the assumption that ties between parents and their children should be maintained throughout incarceration?

ADDITIONAL RESOURCES

Eitenmiller, Katherine. "Bending the Bars for Mothers: How Prison Alternatives Can Build a Stronger Oregon." *Oregon Law Review* 92 (2014): 755–781.

Hamper, Carmen. "Can Life in Prison Be in the Best Interests of the Child?" *Ohio Northern University Law Review* 41 (2014): 201–225.

Harris, Yvette, James Graham, and Gloria Carpenter. *Children of Incarcerated Parents: Theoretical Developmental and Clinical Issues.* New York: Springer Publishing, 2010.

Loper, Ann, Victoria Phillips, Emily Nichols, and Danielle Dallaire. "Characteristics and Effects of the Co-Parenting Alliance between Incarcerated Parents and Child Caregivers." *Journal of Child and Family Studies* 23, no. 2 (2014): 225–241.

Miller, Alison L., Lauren Weston, Jamie Perryman, Talia Horwitz, Susan Franzen, and Shirley Cochran. "Parenting While Incarcerated: Tailoring the Strengthening Families Program for Use with Jailed Mothers." *Children and Youth Services Review* 44 (2014): 163–170.

Poehlman, Julie. *Children of Incarcerated Parents: A Handbook for Researchers and Practitioners.* Washington, DC: Urban Institute Press, 2010.

Reckdahl, Katy. "Prison's Long Reach into America's Classrooms." *Nation* 300, no. 1 (2015): 12–17.

Shortt, Joann Wu, Mark Eddy, Lisa Sheeber, and Betsy Davis. "Project Home: A Pilot Evaluation of an Emotion-Focused Intervention for Mothers Reuniting with Children after Prison." *Psychological Services* 11, no. 1 (2014): 1–9.

Warner, Jennifer. "Infants in Orange: An International Model-Based Approach to Prison Nurseries." *Hastings Women's Law Journal* 26 (2015): 65–147.

RELATED WEBSITES

Big Brothers Big Sisters of America, http://www.bbbs.org

Evidence-based Prevention and Intervention Support Center (EPISCenter), http://www.episcenter.psu.edu/

Fight Crime: Invest in Kids, http://www.fightcrime.org/

Is Your Child Resilient? Maureen Healy, Blog, PBS, http://www.pbs.org/this emotionallife/blogs/your-child-resilient

Promises for Families—Services for Children of Incarcerated Parents, http://promisesforfamilies.org/index.php/en/

White House Conference on Children of Incarcerated Parents, http://csgjustice center.org/nrrc/federal-interagency-reentry-council/posts/white-house-conference-discusses-challenges-faced-by-children-of-incarcerated-parents/?utm_source=CSG%20Justice%20Center%20Primary%20List& utm_campaign=2982615f71-10_1_13_NRRC_newsletter10_1_2013&utm_medium=email&utm_term=0_db9d88bcfb-2982615f71-42289209

Youth.Gov, http://youth.gov/youth-topics/children-of-incarcerated-parents

Youth Risk Behavior Surveillance System (YRBSS), http://www.cdc.gov/Healthy Youth/yrbs/index.htm

SUPPORTING FILMS

Autumn's Eyes (2006)

Mothers of Bedford (2011)

Pregnancy & Prisons (Stoneleigh Foundation) (2011) http://stoneleighfoundation .org/content/mothers-prison-documentary

When the Bough Breaks: Children of Women in Prison (2001)

NOTES

1. Glaze and Parks (2011).
2. Pew Charitable Trusts (2010).
3. Arditti (2005, 2012); Phillips and Gates (2011); Hagan and Dinovitzer (1999); Wildeman (2014).
4. Glaze and Maruschak (2008).
5. Bloom and Covington (2001).
6. Glaze and Maruschak (2008).
7. National Conference of State Legislatures (2009).
8. Turney (2014).
9. Ibid.

10. Ibid.

11. Ibid.

12. Ibid.

13. Hagan and Foster (2012); Cho (2009); Arditti (2005); Poehlmann (2005).

14. Arditti (2005).

15. Ibid.

16. Turanovic, Rodriguez, and Pratt (2012).

17. Dallaire (2007).

18. Ibid.

19. Wildeman and Turney (2014).

20. Ibid.

21. Hagan and Foster (2012).

22. Myers, Smarsh, Amlund-Hagan, and Kennon (1999).

23. Cho (2009); Johnston (2006).

24. Greene, Haney, and Hurtado (2000).

25. Nesmith and Ruhland (2008).

26. Ibid.

27. Gabel (1992).

28. Ibid.

29. Greene, Haney, and Hurtado (2000).

30. Miller and Barnes (2015); Dallaire (2007).

31. Phillips and Gates (2011).

32. Burkley and Blanton (2009).

33. Huebner and Gustafson (2007).

34. Dallaire, Ciccone, and Wilson (2010).

35. Ibid.

36. Dannerbeck (2005).

37. Murray and Farrington (2005).

38. Aaron and Dallaire (2010).

39. Luthar, Lyman, and Crossman (2014).

40. Ibid.

41. Rutter (1999).

42. Poehlmann (2005).

43. Ibid.

44. Ibid.

45. Luthar, Lyman, and Crossman (2014); Unger (2012).

46. Nesmith and Ruhland (2008).

47. Ibid.

48. Luthar, Lyman, and Crossman (2014).

49. Poehlmann (2005).

50. Johnston (2006).

51. Ibid.; Phillips, Erkanli, Keeler, Costello, and Angold (2006).

52. Johnston (2006).

53. Felitti et al. (1998).
54. Reichman, Teitler, Garfinkel, and McLanahan (2001).
55. Shlafer, Poehlmann, and Donelan-McCall (2012).
56. Phillips and Gates (2011).
57. Huebner and Gustafson (2007).
58. Grossman and Tierney (1998).
59. Brown and Bloom (2009).
60. Subramanian et al. (2015).
61. Poehlmann (2005).
62. Ibid.
63. Vera Institute of Justice (2015).
64. Ibid.
65. Wildeman (2014).
66. Dannerbeck (2005).
67. Poehlmann (2005).

REFERENCES

Aaron, Lauren, and Danielle H. Dallaire. "Parental Incarceration and Multiple Risk Experiences: Effects on Family Dynamics and Children's Delinquency." *Journal of Youth and Adolescence* 39, no. 12 (2010): 1471–1484.

Anda, Robert F., Janet B. Croft, Vincent J. Felitti, Dale Nordenberg, Wayne H. Giles, David F. Williamson, and Gary A. Giovino. "Adverse Childhood Experiences and Smoking during Adolescence and Adulthood." *Journal of the American Medical Association* 282, no. 17 (1999): 1652–1658.

Arditti, Joyce A. "Families and Incarceration: An Ecological Approach." *Families in Society: The Journal of Contemporary Social Services* 86, no. 2 (2005): 251–260.

Arditti, Joyce A. *Parental Incarceration and the Family: Psychological and Social Effects of Imprisonment on Children, Parents, and Caregivers*. New York: NYU Press, 2012.

Bloom, Barbara E., and Stephanie Covington. "Effective Gender-Responsive Interventions in Juvenile Justice: Addressing the Lives of Delinquent Girls." Paper presented at the annual meeting of the American Society of Criminology, Atlanta, GA, November 7–10, 2001.

Brown, Marilyn, and Barbara Bloom. "Reentry and Renegotiating Motherhood Maternal Identity and Success on Parole." *Crime & Delinquency* 55, no. 2 (2009): 313–336.

Burkley, Melissa, and Hart Blanton. "The Positive (and Negative) Consequences of Endorsing Negative Self-Stereotypes." *Self and Identity* 8, no. 2 (2009): 286–299.

Cho, Rosa Minhyo. "Impact of Maternal Imprisonment on Children's Probability of Grade Retention." *Journal of Urban Economics* 65, no. 1 (2009): 11–23.

Dallaire, Danielle H. "Incarcerated Mothers and Fathers: A Comparison of Risks for Children and Families." *Family relations* 56, no. 5 (2007): 440–453.

Dallaire, Danielle H., Anne Ciccone, and Laura C. Wilson. "Teachers' Experiences with and Expectations of Children with Incarcerated Parents." *Journal of Applied Developmental Psychology* 31, no. 4 (2010): 281–290.

Dannerbeck, Anne M. "Differences in Parenting Attributes, Experiences, and Behaviors of Delinquent Youth with and without a Parental History of Incarceration." *Youth Violence and Juvenile Justice* 3, no. 3 (2005): 199–213.

Felitti, Vincent J., Robert F. Anda, Dale Nordenberg, David F. Williamson, Alison M. Spitz, Valerie Edwards, Mary P. Koss, and James S. Marks. "Relationship of Childhood Abuse and Household Dysfunction to Many of the Leading Causes of Death in Adults: The Adverse Childhood Experiences (ACE) Study." *American Journal of Preventive Medicine* 14, no. 4 (1998): 245–258.

Gabel, Stewart. "Behavioral Problems in Sons of Incarcerated or Otherwise Absent Fathers: The Issue of Separation." *Family Process* 31, no. 3 (1992): 303–314.

Glaze, Lauren E., and Erika Parks. "Correctional Populations in the United States, 2011." *Population* 6, no. 7 (2011): 8.

Glaze, Lauren E., and Laura M. Maruschak. "Parents in Prison and Their Minor Children." *Bureau of Justice Statistics Special Report.* Washington, DC: US Department of Justice, Office of Justice Programs, 2008.

Greene, Susan, Craig Haney, and Aida Hurtado. "Cycles of Pain: Risk Factors in the Lives of Incarcerated Mothers and Their Children." *The Prison Journal* 80, no. 1 (2000): 3–23.

Grossman, Jean Baldwin, and Joseph P. Tierney. "Does Mentoring Work? An Impact Study of the Big Brothers Big Sisters Program." *Evaluation review* 22, no. 3 (1998): 403–426.

Hagan, John, and Holly Foster. "Children of the American Prison Generation: Student and School Spillover Effects of Incarcerating Mothers." *Law & Society Review* 46, no. 1 (2012): 3769.

Hagan, John, and Ronit Dinovitzer. "Collateral Consequences of Imprisonment for Children, Communities, and Prisoners." *Crime and Justice* 26, (1999): 121–162.

Huebner, Beth M., and Regan Gustafson. "The Effect of Maternal Incarceration on Adult Offspring Involvement in the Criminal Justice System." *Journal of Criminal Justice* 35, no. 3 (2007): 283–296.

Johnson, Elizabeth I., and Beth Easterling. "Understanding Unique Effects of Parental Incarceration on Children: Challenges, Progress, and Recommendations." *Journal of Marriage and Family* 74, no. 2 (2012): 342–356.

Johnston, Denise. "The Wrong Road: Efforts to Understand the Effects of Parental Crime and Incarceration." *Criminology & Public Policy* 5, no. 4 (2006): 703–719.

Luthar, Suniya S., Emily L. Lyman, and Elizabeth J. Crossman. "Resilience and Positive Psychology." In *Handbook of Developmental Psychopathology.* Edited by Michael Lewis and Karen Rudolph, 125–140. New York, NY: Springer Publishing, 2014.

Miller, Holly Ventura, and J. C. Barnes. "The Association between Parental Incarceration and Health, Education, and Economic Outcomes in Young Adulthood." *American Journal of Criminal Justice* (2015): 1–20. doi: 10.1007/s12103-015-9288-4.

Mumola, Christopher J. "Parents under Correctional Supervision: National Statistics." Lecture, NIDA Research Meeting, North Bethesda, MD, November 6, 2006.

Murray, Joseph, and David P. Farrington. "Parental Imprisonment: Effect on Boys' Antisocial Behaviour and Delinquency through the Life-Course." *Journal of Child Psychology and Psychiatry* 46, no. 12 (2005): 1269–1278.

Myers, Barbara J., Tina M. Smarsh, Kristine Amlund-Hagen, and Suzanne Kennon. "Children of Incarcerated Mothers." *Journal of Child and Family Studies* 8, no. 1 (1999): 11–25.

National Conference of State Legislatures. *Children of Incarcerated Parents.* By Steve Christian. Washington, DC: National Conference of State Legislatures, 2009.

Nesmith, Ande, and Ebony Ruhland. "Children of Incarcerated Parents: Challenges and Resiliency, in Their Own Words." *Children and Youth Services Review* 30, no. 10 (2008): 1119–1130.

Parke, Ross D., and K. Alison Clarke-Stewart. "The Effects of Parental Incarceration on Children." In *Prisoners Once Removed: The Impact of Incarceration and Reentry on Children, Families, and Communities.* Edited by Jeremy Travis and Michelle Waul, 189–232. Washington, DC: Urban Institute Press, 2003.

Pew Charitable Trusts. *Collateral Costs: Incarceration's Effect on Economic Mobility.* By Bruce Western and Becky Pettit. Washington, DC: Pew Charitable Trusts, 2010.

Phillips, Susan D., Alaattin Erkanli, Gordon P. Keeler, E. Costello, and Adrian Angold. "Disentangling the Risks: Parent Criminal Justice Involvement and Children's Exposure to Family Risks." *Criminology & Public Policy* 5, no. 4 (2006): 677–702.

Phillips, Susan D., and Trevor Gates. "A Conceptual Framework for Understanding the Stigmatization of Children of Incarcerated parents." *Journal of Child and Family Studies* 20, no. 3 (2011): 286–294.

Poehlmann, Julie. "Children's Family Environments and Intellectual Outcomes during Maternal Incarceration." *Journal of Marriage and Family* 67, no. 5 (2005): 1275–1285.

Poehlmann, Julie, Danielle Dallaire, Ann Booker Loper, and Leslie D. Shear. "Children's Contact with Their Incarcerated Parents: Research Findings and Recommendations." *American Psychologist* 65, no. 6 (2010): 575.

Reichman, Nancy E., Julien O. Teitler, Irwin Garfinkel, and Sara S. McLanahan. "Fragile Families: Sample and Design." *Children and Youth Services Review* 23, no. 4 (2001): 303–326.

Rutter, Michael. "Resilience Concepts and Findings: Implications for Family Therapy." *Journal of Family Therapy* 21, no. 2 (1999): 119–144.

Shlafer, Rebecca J., Julie Poehlmann, and Nancy Donelan-McCall. "Maternal Jail Time, Conviction, and Arrest as Predictors of Children's 15-Year Antisocial Outcomes in the Context of a Nurse Home Visiting Program." *Journal of Clinical Child & Adolescent Psychology* 41, no. 1 (2012): 38–52.

Turanovic, Jillian J., Nancy Rodriguez, and Travis C. Pratt. "Collateral Consequences of Incarceration Revisited: A Qualitative Analysis of the Effects on Caregivers of Children of Incarcerated Parents." *Criminology* 50, no. 4 (2012): 913–959.

Turney, Kristin. "Stress Proliferation across Generations? Examining the Relationship between Parental Incarceration and Childhood Health." *Journal of Health and Social Behavior* 55, no. 3 (2014): 302–319.

Ungar, Michael. Social *Ecologies and Their Contribution to Resilience.* New York: Springer Publishing, 2012.

Vera Institute of Justice. *Incarceration's Front Door: The Misuse of Jails in America.* By Ram Subramanian, Ruth Delaney, Stephen Roberts, Nancy Fishman, and Peggy McGarry. New York: Vera Institute of Justice, 2015.

Wildeman, Christopher. "Parental Incarceration, Child Homelessness, and the Invisible Consequences of Mass Imprisonment." *The Annals of the American Academy of Political and Social Science* 651, no. 1 (2014): 74–96.

Wildeman, Christopher, and Kristin Turney. "Positive, Negative, or Null? The Effects of Maternal Incarceration on Children's Behavioral Problems." *Demography* 51, no. 3 (2014): 1041–1068.

Chapter 8

Autism Spectrum Disorders and Juvenile Justice: The Myths of Perpetrators and Victims[1]

Rebecca Pfeffer

On December 14, 2012, a young man named Adam Lanza walked into an elementary school in Newtown, Connecticut, and fatally shot 20 first-grade students and six school employees. All of the children killed were between six and seven years old. The gravity and senselessness of this act sparked a national dialogue about how something like this could happen in the United States. Yet, the dialogue quickly changed from questioning our current national gun control policies to questioning the mental stability of the shooter. In particular, media outlets focused on a statement made by the shooter's father that Adam had been diagnosed with Asperger's syndrome, a high-functioning form of autism, when he was 13 years old. An association between violence and autism spectrum disorders (ASDs) was rapidly spread by the media as people who were eager for an explanation as to how such a tragedy could unfold accepted this correlation between autism and criminality. It was not the first time such a correlation had made headlines and it would not be the last.

On May 23, 2014, 22-year-old Elliot Rodger went on a shooting spree in Santa Barbara, California, killing six people and injuring seven others before killing himself. Again, the media was flooded with reports that Rodger had been diagnosed with Asperger's during his childhood, and many of these reports pointed to an association between this diagnosis and his severely antisocial behavior. Asperger's syndrome and other ASDs, which are developmental disabilities, were being misconstrued as a form of mental illness by the media, prompting mass concern that people with ASDs might be capable of committing terrible acts. However, this association is dangerously incorrect. There is no empirical evidence of an increased risk of violence among individuals diagnosed with ASDs, and in fact, people with autism may be even less likely to engage in criminal behavior than the general population.[2] Importantly, in addition to being less likely to engage in criminal activity, research indicates that people with autism and other intellectual and developmental disabilities are more likely to be victims of crime.[3]

This chapter will begin with an overview of what autism is and how prevalent autism spectrum disorders are in the United States. Then it will review what is known about the relationship between autism and offending behaviors as well as the correlation between autism and different forms of victimization. Some of the specific reasons that children with autism are at risk for victimization will also be discussed. The chapter will then conclude with explanations as to why the media—and the public—latched on to the notion that somehow a diagnosis of autism is correlated with violent criminal behavior, and offers suggestions for future research and policies that can better protect people with autism from both stigmatizing labels and interpersonal victimization.

WHAT IS AUTISM?

Once considered a rare disorder, autism has become the fastest-growing intellectual disability in the United States.[4] The alarming rate at which diagnoses are increasing has led experts to refer to autism as an "epidemic," a "national emergency" requiring a "national strategy."[5] As of 2014, the Centers for Disease Control and Prevention (CDC) estimates that one in 68 children in the United States is diagnosed with an ASD, a rate almost 30 percent higher than an assessment made only two years prior, which found that one in 88 children had been identified with an ASD.[6] While these statistics are alarming, many people do not understand what autism actually is.

ASDs are intellectual disabilities, which are different from mental health diagnoses as they are linked to cognitive functioning. ASDs are characterized by difficulty with social interaction, communication, and restricted or repeated behaviors.[7] People with ASDs often have communication deficits and may respond inappropriately to conversational cues, may not understand nonverbal communication, and often have difficulty building meaningful friendships with their peers.[8] In particular, a signature characteristic of ASDs is a lack of theory-of-mind, or mindblindness, the inability to read or properly interpret the feelings or behavior of others.[9]

ASDs occur in all racial, ethnic, and socioeconomic groups, yet four out of five affected individuals are male.[10] The cause of autism remains unknown. There is substantial debate as to whether there are actually more people who have autism born each year or if the rise in prevalence is due in part to changes in diagnostic practices. No matter the reason, the fact remains that we now recognize more individuals with autism in the United States than ever before. National special education statistics showed a 657 percent increase in students with autism between 1993 and 2003.[11] Prevalence studies from other countries have indicated similar upward trends in diagnoses in other nations around the world, including Iceland,[12] the United Kingdom,[13] and Finland,[14] among others.

THE MYTH OF AUTISM AS A CORRELATE WITH VIOLENT BEHAVIOR

The speculation that the cause of the violent behaviors by mass shooters Adam Lanza and Elliott Rodger was their alleged ASD diagnosis was not a new phenomenon. In fact, when Asperger's syndrome was first described in a paper published by Austrian pediatrician Hans Asperger in 1944, he referred to the disorder as "autistic psychopathy," because many of the presenting clinical features were seen as similar to those in psychopathic individuals including lack of empathy, inappropriate or one-sided interaction, little or no ability to form friendships, and poor verbal communication.[15] Importantly, there were other features that did not overlap with psychopathy, including repetitive speech, intense attention to certain topics, and limited imaginative activities. But the clinical similarities between ASDs and psychopathy seemed noteworthy to researchers. Yet, as autism diagnoses were rare during this time and for years to come, the question remained unanswered as to whether ASDs, which at the time were not well understood, had the same level of correlation with antisocial behavior as psychopathy did.

Most research conducted between the 1940s and today that investigated whether ASDs are correlated with violent tendencies focused on people diagnosed with Asperger's syndrome, rather than those with other ASD diagnoses associated with lower cognitive functioning. Asperger's syndrome is a condition that was until recently considered a distinct, high-functioning form of autism, but in 2013 it was folded into the umbrella diagnosis of ASD in the most recent version of the American Psychiatric Association's Diagnostic and Statistical Manual of Mental Disorders (DSM-V).[16] Early research on the correlation between autism and criminal behavior suggested that people who had been sent to secure units for acts of violence should be screened for indicators of Asperger's.[17] Yet, the majority of the research on the correlation between Asperger's syndrome and criminality was anecdotal, based on individual or small case study samples. One such case study, published in 1985, concluded, "We submit the speculation that this association between Asperger's syndrome and violent behavior is more common than has been recognized and that more such individuals are to be found in long-term care institutions of various sorts."[18]

A seminal article on this correlation written by British child psychiatrist and researcher Simon Baron-Cohen in 1988 broadened the fear over the possibility that autistic youth may be violence prone as he extended the possibility of violent behavior in children with Asperger's syndrome (at the time considered to be a form of high-functioning autism) to children with all forms of autism. The article, which was also based on an anecdotal case study, concluded that the subject displayed violent behavior as a result of his inability to appreciate other people's points of view due to a deficit in social cognition. As it was unclear to Baron-Cohen whether this young man's diagnosis ought to have been autism or Asperger's syndrome, he warned that, ". . . because of the doubt over whether the diagnosis of this case should be Asperger's syndrome or autism, the claims made in this paper regarding violence in Asperger's syndrome may be equally relevant in regarding violence in autism."[19]

To date, several theorists have purported that people with autism spectrum disorders may be more likely to offend for a variety of reasons. Some of the reasons offered for this possible connection include that people with ASDs are often socially awkward and misunderstood, that they tend to have poor impulse control, that they lack the capacity for empathy, that they fail to understand social cues, and that they may not understand the connection between their behaviors and the implications of those behaviors. While these may represent correlates of offending behavior in the general neurotypical population, the association between these characteristics and offending among the population of people with ASDs has been mostly unsubstantiated in the literature.[20] Yet, sensationalized media reports often fuel the perceived association between autism and offending.

Some studies attempt to explore the relationship between autism and offending by conducting population studies in jails, prisons, or specialized hospitals for offenders in which they screen all inmates or clients for ASDs. Not surprisingly, many of these studies do, in fact, find an increased prevalence of ASD within these specialized settings than is found in the general population. For instance, in the United Kingdom, researchers Scragg and Shah screened 392 male patients in a psychiatric hospital and found a 1.5 percent prevalence rate of ASD among the hospitalized patients, which was a much higher prevalence rate than was found in the surrounding community using the same screening criteria (0.36%).[21] However, we must exercise caution in our interpretation of these findings since there are methodological problems inherent in such studies. Prevalence studies are typically restricted to very specialized settings, and therefore the study samples are also highly selected.[22] Adding another layer of difficulty to our ability to make inferences from these study results is the fact that there is little solid evidence about the prevalence of autism in communities. Studies focusing on diagnoses in children find very different prevalence rates than population studies among adult populations. Similarly, results of prevalence studies vary based on the diagnostic criteria utilized, which differ between nations and even between states in the United States.

More recent research questions the correlation between autism and offending. Some researchers even posit that people with ASDs are actually less likely to offend than the general population because, due to conditions inherent in their autism diagnoses, they often exercise pedantic adherence to and interpretation of rules and laws.[23] Experts in the field now note that while there has been very little credible research conducted on the link between autism and offending, a great body of research has accumulated on the vulnerability of people with ASDs to various forms of victimization.

DISABILITY AND VICTIMIZATION

Although little research has been conducted that specifically investigates the incidence of victimization among people with autism, there has been growing interest in the vulnerability of people with both physical disabilities and intellectual and developmental disabilities to victimization. In 2007, the National Crime Victimization Survey (NCVS) began collecting information on the disability status of participants. Analysts of the Bureau of Justice Statistics concluded that Americans with disabilities had a victimization rate higher than nondisabled Americans. Further, they found that people with cognitive disabilities (such as autism and other developmental disorders) experienced violent crime at a rate higher than people with other types of disabilities. Those with cognitive disabilities experienced victimization at a rate of 34.3 per 1,000 respondents, nearly double the victimization rates for other categories of disability, which ranged from 9.7 to 18.2 per 1,000 respondents.[24] In the same year, the violent crime rate overall (not just among people with disabilities) was 20.4 per 1,000 respondents.[25]

A 2012 meta-analysis funded by the World Health Organization echoed these findings. After surveying the results of 26 studies of violence against people with disabilities worldwide, which included data on 21,557 adults with disabilities, they concluded that adults with disabilities are at a higher risk of violence than are nondisabled adults.[26] Persons with mental health or intellectual disabilities, they further concluded, are more at risk than those with other types of disabilities.

Studies focusing specifically on the victimization of individuals with intellectual or developmental disabilities confirm the status of such people as among the most vulnerable in our society. In the mid-1990s, researchers Sobsey conducted an in-depth literature review and estimated that people with developmental disabilities are four to 10 times more likely to be victims of crime than are their typically developing counterparts.[27] In an earlier study, Sobsey and his colleague Doe concluded that more than 70 percent of women with developmental disabilities are sexually assaulted in their lifetime, which is a rate 50 percent higher than for women without developmental disabilities.[28] Precise estimates of victimization are hard to gauge due to the issue of underreporting and differential reporting. For instance, it has been estimated that only about 20 percent of actual incidents of sexual abuse of people with developmental disabilities are ever reported.[29] While still low, reporting rates for incidences of rape and sexual assault among the general population are moderately higher in comparison. According to NCVS data, between 2006 and 2010, 35 percent of rape or sexual assault victimizations in the United States were reported to the police.[30]

Previous research on the risk factors of youth with intellectual disabilities to victimization has identified multiple risk factors associated with the elevated rates of victimization among children with intellectual and developmental disabilities (IDD). First, it has been suggested that people with IDD are more susceptible to exploitation because they are often completely dependent on others for their well-being.[31] Caregivers include parents, bus drivers, teachers, therapists, babysitters, and any other people who are trusted with the care of persons with disabilities. Research suggests that people with intellectual disabilities are conditioned to respond passively to caregivers—to comply with and not challenge them.[32] Conversely, perpetrators, specifically of sexual abuse, often victimize those they perceive to be weaker, unable to defend themselves, and unlikely to be considered credible if accusations of abuse are made.[33]

In a 2002 study focusing on the maltreatment of children with IDD, researchers Vig and Kaminer reported that on top of certain environmental and familial risk factors that can increase the likelihood of abuse or other forms of maltreatment for all children (such as poverty, educational deprivation, social isolation, or parental substance abuse), families of children with disabilities face additional stressors.[34] Parents of children with disabilities, particularly parents who have one or more autistic child, experience a great deal more stress than other parents.[35]

A study of children with Asperger's syndrome and nonverbal learning disorders cited lack of social skills as a significant risk factor for physical abuse and emotional bullying. According to caregiver reports, 94 percent of the children in this sample had been victimized by their peers; these children were described as "perfect victims" because of their profound deficit in social skills.[36] This lack of social skills has significant consequences; deficits in self-protective skills, social skills, and supportive peer networks can increase a child's risk for peer bullying and assault.[37] While many children with intellectual disabilities are still socially capable, communication and social deficits are central to ASDs, rendering these children particularly vulnerable to peer victimization.

Wilson, Seaman, and Nettlebeck (1996) specifically investigated whether interpersonal competence impacts an individual's vulnerability to criminal exploitation. This research involved a sample of people with IDDs to see if those who had been criminally victimized were distinct from those not victimized in terms of social competence.[38] The results indicated that the group of victims indeed showed poorer social competence, regardless of IQ, again indicating that lack of social understanding among youth with autism may increase vulnerability to victimization.

VICTIMIZATION OF YOUTH WITH AUTISM

Recognizing that children with autism may be even more vulnerable to interpersonal victimization than their peers with other intellectual and developmental disabilities, a study was conducted that focused exclusively on the victimization of children with ASDs.[39] In this study, 262 parents or caretakers of children with autism responded to a survey collecting information about the frequency that youth had been victims of a number of different offenses both within the last year and in their lifetimes. The children were between five and 18 years old and had a wide range of autism diagnoses and reported ability levels. The study found extremely elevated rates of victimization among the autistic sample. Nearly three quarters (74.3%) of the study sample had been assaulted or bullied within the last year, while 84 percent had experienced such an incident at least once in their lifetime. The most frequently reported forms of assault and bullying that were reported by parents to have occurred to their children within the last year included emotional bullying (52.8%), assault without a weapon (38.4%), and bullying (32.8%).

Almost half of the study sample (49.0%) had experienced an incident of robbery, theft, or vandalism within the last year, while almost two-thirds (64.2%) had been the victim of a property crime in their lifetime. Robbery, or the act of having something taken from the child by force, was the most common form of property victimization among the children in this study. Of the sample, 34.4 percent had been the victim of a robbery within the last year, while nearly half (49.2%) had something taken from them by force at some point in their lifetime.

The results of this study indicate that more than four of five children with autism in this study sample had experienced a victimization experience within the last year. Of the children from this study sample who been victimized, a great majority had experienced more than one incident of victimization in the last year (92%).

This study also involved in-depth semistructured interviews with the parents of youth with autism who were able to provide some insight into the unique vulnerabilities of children with ASDs. In an article specifically addressing these risk and protective factors, Pfeffer[40] reports that there were four main risk factors identified by parents that they felt contribute to their vulnerability to victimization. These risk factors include (1) dependence on others for safety and well-being, (2) a lack of trustworthy friends despite strong desire for social acceptance, (3) a lack of a sense of danger, often manifesting in trust of strangers, and (4) little or no verbal proficiency. With what has been discussed in the broader literature on vulnerability of people with disabilities to victimization, all of these risk factors are inherent to ASDs and therefore warrant careful consideration in terms of preventing the victimization of this special population.

DISCUSSION

It is clear that sensationalized media depictions of the correlation between autism and offending are, at the very least, uninformed, and are in fact harmful to our social understanding of the true vulnerability of autistic youth. When we, as a society, become overtaken with fear of something unknown, there is less reliance on empirical evidence and rationale, which can be extremely harmful to affected groups. In this case, it seems that an increasing awareness of the growing prevalence of autism diagnoses in the United States, combined with a dearth in understanding of how autism is distinct from mental illness, contributes to a moral panic that youth with autism may be capable of committing violent acts.

The notion that Asperger's syndrome, or any other specific autism diagnosis, may make a person inherently violent is both dangerous and uninformed. This speculation does a massive disservice to autistic youth and their families, and it likely makes it more difficult for this population to be recognized for how vulnerable they actually are. It is important that media outlets be more responsible in their reporting and define autism as it is clinically categorized—as an intellectual disability, and not as a form of mental illness. While in some individual cases, there may be overlap between autism and mental health diagnoses, they are not synonymous and should not be understood as such.

There is a need for much more research on the victimization of youth with ASDs. As the current literature finds that autistic youth are extremely vulnerable to victimization for a number of reasons, we still know very little about the impacts that such experiences can have on these individuals. In particular, the little research that has been conducted specifically on the victimization of youth with autism finds that there is a great incidence of co-occurring victimization among autistic youth.[41] In populations of neurotypical children who endure co-occurring victimization, practitioners find high incidences of enduring stress and elevated rates of posttraumatic stress disorder (PTSD).[42] We know very little about how the experience of victimization impacts children with autism in the long term, and responding to PTSD in children with autism, who have, by definition, a challenging set of communication difficulties, will require a specialized and informed response.

DISCUSSION QUESTIONS

1. Given that several high-profile crimes have been covered in the media involving a suspect alleged to have an autism spectrum disorder, how important do you think these disabilities are in explaining and perhaps mitigating behavior?
2. What types of programs and services might be useful to assist those with disabilities to be able to avoid becoming involved with crime and delinquency?
3. Should special circumstances be written into penal codes to enhance criminal sanctions for those who commit crimes against persons with disabilities? Should all types of disabilities be included here?
4. To what extent is bullying more frequent and aggressive for children with disabilities? What steps can parents and teachers take to decrease the occurrence of harassment that differentially abled children suffer?

ADDITIONAL RESOURCES

Cavendish, Wendy. "Academic Attainment during Commitment and Postrelease Education–Related Outcomes of Juvenile Justice-Involved Youth with and without Disabilities." *Journal of Emotional and Behavioral Disorders* 22, no. 1 (2014): 41–52.

Emerson, Eric, Jan Blacher, Stewart Einfeld, Chris Hatton, Janet Robertson, and Roger Stancliffe. "Environmental Risk Factors Associated with the Persistence of Conduct Difficulties in Children with Intellectual Disabilities and Austistic Spectrum Disorders." *Research in Developmental Disabilities* 35, no. 12 (2014): 3508–3517.

Hart, Angie, Becky Heaver, Elinor Brunnberg, Anette Sandberg, Hannah MacPherson, Stephanie Coombe, and Elias Kourkoutas. "Resilience Building with Disabled Children and Young People: A Review and Critique of the Academic Evidence." *International Journal of Child, Youth & Family Studies* 15, no. 3 (2014): 394–422.

Levin, Jack. "The Invisible Hate Crime." *Pacific Standard Magazine*, March, 1, 2011, http://www.psmag.com/politics-and-law/the-invisible-hate-crime-27984.

Mueller-Johnson, Katrin, Manuel Eisner, and Ingrid Obsuth. "Sexual Victimization of Youth with a Physical Disability: An Examination of Prevalence

Rates, and Risk and Protective Factors." *Journal of Interpersonal Violence* 29, no. 17 (2014): 3180–3206.

Reddy, Linda, Adam Weissman, and James Hale. *Neuropsychological Assessment and Intervention for Youth: An Evidence-Based Approach to Emotional and Behavioral Disorders*. Washington, DC: American Psychological Association, 2013.

Unruh, Deanne K., Jeff M. Gau, and Miriam G. Waintrup. "An Exploration of Factors Reducing Recidivism Rates of Formerly Incarcerated Youth with Disabilities Participating in a Re-Entry Intervention." *Journal of Child and Family Studies* 18, no. 3 (2009): 284–293.

Visser, E. M., H. J. C. Berger, J. B. Prins, H.M.J. Van Schrojenstein Lantman-De Valk, and J. P. Teunisse. "Shifting Impairment and Aggression in Intellectual Disability and Autism Spectrum Disorder." *Research in Developmental Disabilities* 35, no. 9 (2014): 2137–2147.

RELATED WEBSITES

Americans with Disabilities (ADA), http://www.ada.gov

Civil Rights of Institutionalized persons Act in Juvenile Correctional Facilities, http://www.ojjdp.gov/pubs/walls/sect-01.html

Educational Advocacy for Youth with Disabilities, http://www.ojjdp.gov/pubs/walls/sect-03.html

National Center on Criminal Justice & Disability, http://www.thearc.org/NCCJD

SUPPORTING FILMS

Cries from the Heart (1994)
I Am Sam (2001)
Johnny Belinda (1948)
Mercury Rising (1998)
Shine (1996)

NOTES

1. Portions of this chapter have been adapted from Pfeffer (2014). Copyright © DigitalCommons@The Texas Medical Center. Available at: http://digitalcommons.library.tmc.edu/jfs/vol14/iss1/21.

2. Mouridsen, Rich, Isager, and Nedergaard (2008); Woodbury-Smith, Clare, Holland, and Kearns (2006).

3. Bureau of Justice Statistics (2014).

4. Bartley (2006).

5. Roithmayr (2012)

6. Baio (2014).

7. American Psychiatric Association (2013b).

8. American Psychiatric Association (2013a).

9. Baron-Cohen (1995); Baron-Cohen, Leslie, and Frith (1985).

10. Rice (2007).
11. Bartley (2006).
12. Magnusson and Saemundsen (2001).
13. Powell et al. (2007).
14. Kielinen, Linna, and Moilanen (2000).
15. Asperger (1944); Baron-Cohen (1988).
16. American Psychiatric Association (2013b).
17. Mawson, Grounds, and Tantam (1985).
18. Ibid., 569.
19. Baron-Cohen (1988), 358–359.
20. Allen et al. (2008).
21. Scragg and Shah (1994).
22. Allen et al. (2008).
23. Wing (1997).
24. Bureau of Justice Statistics (2009).
25. "Key Facts at a Glance" (2015).
26. Jones et al. (2012).
27. Sobsey (1995).
28. Sobsey and Doe (1991).
29. Ryerson (1984).
30. Bureau of Justice Statistics (2012).
31. Furey, Granfield, and Karan (1994).
32. Walmsley (1989).
33. Furey, Granfield, and Karan (1994); Nettlebeck and Wilson (2002).
34. Vig and Kaminer (2002).
35. Rodrigue, Morgan, and Geffken (1990); Lessenberry and Rehfeldt (2004).
36. Little (2002).
37. Ibid.; Turner, Vanderminden, Finkelhor, Hamby, and Shattuck (2011).
38. Wilson, Seaman, and Nettelbeck (1996).
39. Pfeffer (2013).
40. Pfeffer (2014).
41. Pfeffer (2013).
42. Kilpatrick et al. (2003).

REFERENCES

Allen, David, Carys Evans, Andrew Hider, Sarah Hawkins, Helen Peckett, and Hugh Morgan. "Offending Behaviour in Adults with Asperger Syndrome." *Journal of Autism and Developmental Disorders* 38, no. 4 (2008): 748–758.

American Psychiatric Association. *Autism Spectrum Disorder: Fact Sheet.* Washington, DC: American Psychiatric Association, 2013a.

American Psychiatric Association. *Diagnostic and Statistical Manual of Mental Disorders*, 5th ed. Washington, DC: American Psychiatric Association, 2013b.

Asperger, Hans. "Die 'autisichen Pschopathan' in Kindesalter." *Archiv fur Psychiatrie und Nervernkrankheiten* 177 (1944): 76–136.

Baio, John. "Prevalence of Autism Spectrum Disorders among Children Aged 8 Years: Autism and Developmental Disabilities Monitoring Network, 11 Sites, United States, 2010." *Morbidity and Mortality Weekly Report.* Atlanta, GA: Centers for Disease Control and Prevention, March 28, 2014.

Baron-Cohen, Simon. "An Assessment of Violence in a Young Man with Asperger's Syndrome." *Journal of Child Psychology and Psychiatry* 29, no. 3 (1988): 351–360.

Baron-Cohen, Simon. *Mindblindness: An Essay on Autism and Theory of Mind.* Cambridge: MA: Massachusetts Institute of Technology Press, 1995.

Baron-Cohen, Simon, Alan M. Leslie, and Uta Frith. "Does the Autistic Child Have a 'Theory of Mind'?" *Cognition* 21, no. 1 (1985): 37–46.

Bartley, Jane J. "An Update on Autism: Science, Gender, and the Law." *Gender Medicine* 3, no. 2 (2006): 73–78.

Bureau of Justice Statistics. *Special Report: Crime against People with Disabilities.* By Michael Rand and Erika Harrell. Washington, DC: Office of Justice Programs, U.S. Department of Justice, 2009.

Bureau of Justice Statistics. *Special Report: Victimizations Not Reported to the Police, 2006–2010.* By Lynn Langton, Marcus Berzofsky, Christopher Krebs, and Hope Smiley-McDonald. Washington, DC: U.S. Department of Justice, Office of Justice Programs, 2012.

Bureau of Justice Statistics. *Crime against Persons with Disabilities, 2009–2012— Statistical Tables.* By Erika Harrell. Washington, DC: U.S. Department of Justice, Bureau of Justice Statistics, 2014.

Furey, Eileen M., James M. Granfield, and Orv C. Karan. "Sexual Abuse and Neglect of Adults with Mental Retardation: A Comparison of Victim Characteristics." *Behavioral Interventions* 9, no. 2 (1994): 75–86.

Jones, Lisa, Mark A. Bellis, Sara Wood, Karen Hughes, Ellie McCoy, Lindsay Eckley, Geoff Bates, Christopher Mikton, Tom Shakespeare, and Alana Officer. "Prevalence and Risk of Violence against Children with Disabilities: A Systematic Review and Meta-Analysis of Observational Studies." *The Lancet* 380, no. 9845 (2012): 899–907.

"Key Facts at a Glance." *Bureau of Justice Statistics.* May 3, 2015. http://www.bjs.gov/glance_redirect.cfm.

Kielinen, Marko, S-L. Linna, and Irma Moilanen. "Autism in Northern Finland." *European Child & Adolescent Psychiatry* 9, no. 3 (2000): 162–167.

Kilpatrick, Dean G., Kenneth J. Ruggiero, Ron Acierno, Benjamin E. Saunders, Heidi S. Resnick, and Connie L. Best. "Violence and Risk of PTSD, Major Depression, Substance Abuse/Dependence, and Comorbidity: Results from the National Survey of Adolescents." *Journal of Consulting and Clinical Psychology* 71, no. 4 (2003): 692.

Lessenberry, Beth M., and Ruth Anne Rehfeldt. "Evaluating Stress Levels of Parents of Children with Disabilities." *Exceptional Children* 70, no. 2 (2004): 231–244.

Little, Liza. "Middle-Class Mothers' Perceptions of Peer and Sibling Victimization among Children with Asperger's Syndrome and Non-Verbal Learning Disorders." *Issues in Comprehensive Pediatric Nursing,* 25, no. 1 (2002): 43–57.

Magnusson, Páll, and Evald Saemundsen. "Prevalence of Autism in Iceland." *Journal of Autism and Developmental Disorders* 31, no. 2 (2001): 153–163.

Mawson, David C., Adrian Grounds, and Digby Tantam. "Violence and Asperger's Syndrome: A Case Study." *The British Journal of Psychiatry* 147, (1985): 566–569.

Mouridsen, Svend Erik, Bente Rich, Torben Isager, and Niels Jørgen Nedergaard. "Pervasive Developmental Disorders and Criminal Behaviour: A Case Control Study." *International Journal of Offender Therapy and Comparative Criminology* 52, no. 2 (2008): 196–205.

Nettelbeck, Ted, and Carlene Wilson. "Personal Vulnerability to Victimization of People with Mental Retardation." *Trauma, Violence, & Abuse* 3, no. 4 (2002): 289–306.

Pfeffer, Rebecca. *Autistic and At-Risk: The Public and Personal Safety of Children with Autism Spectrum Disorders.* PhD diss., Northeastern University, 2013.

Pfeffer, Rebecca. "Risk and Protective Factors for the Safety of Children with Autism: A Qualitative Study of Caregivers' Perspectives." *Journal of Family Strengths* 14, no. 1 (2014): 21.

Powell, J. E., A. Edwards, M. Edwards, B. S. Pandit, S. R. Sungum-Paliwal, and W. Whitehouse. "Changes in the Incidence of Childhood Autism and Other Autistic Spectrum Disorders in Preschool Children from Two Areas of the West Midlands, UK." *Developmental Medicine & Child Neurology* 42, no. 9 (2000): 624–628.

Rice, Catherine. 2007. "Prevalence of Autism Spectrum Disorders—Autism and Developmental Disabilities Monitoring Network, Six Sites, United States, 2000." *Morbidity and Mortality Weekly Report.* Atlanta, GA: Centers for Disease Control and Prevention, February, 9, 2007.

Rodrigue, James R., Sam B. Morgan, and Gary Geffken. "Families of Autistic Children: Psychological Functioning of Mothers." *Journal of Clinical Child Psychology* 19, no. 4 (1990): 371–379.

Roithmayr, Mark. "One in 88. We Need a Strategy." Speech, Centers for Disease Control and Prevention, Atlanta, GA, March 29, 2012.

Ryerson, Ellen. 1984. "Sexual Abuse and Self-Education for Developmentally Disabled Youth: A Priority Need." *SIECUS Report* 13, no. 1 (1984): 6–7.

Scragg, Peter, and Amitta Shah. "Prevalence of Asperger's Syndrome in a Secure Hospital." *The British Journal of Psychiatry* 165, no. 5 (1994): 679–682.

Sobsey, Dick, ed. *Violence and Disability: An Annotated Bibliography.* Baltimore, MD: Paul H. Brookes Publishing, 1995.

Sobsey, Dick, and Tanis Doe. "Patterns of Sexual Abuse and Assault." *Sexuality and Disability* 9, no. 3 (1991): 243–259.

Turner, Heather A., Jennifer Vanderminden, David Finkelhor, Sherry Hamby, and Anne Shattuck. "Disability and Victimization in a National Sample of Children and Youth." *Child Maltreatment* 16, no. 4 (2011): 275–286.

Vig, Susan, and Ruth Kaminer. "Maltreatment and Developmental Disabilities in Children." *Journal of Developmental and Physical Disabilities* 14, no. 4 (2002): 371–386.

Walmsley, S. "The Need for Safeguards." In *Thinking the Unthinkable: Papers on Sexual Abuse and People with Learning Difficulties.* Edited by Hilary Brown and Ann Craft, London, UK: FPA Educational Unit, 1989.

Wilson, C., L. Seaman, and T. Nettelbeck. "Vulnerability to Criminal Exploitation: Influence of Interpersonal Competence Differences among People with Mental Retardation." *Journal of Intellectual Disability Research* 40, no. 1 (1996): 8–16.

Wing, Lorna. "Asperger's Syndrome: Management Requires Diagnosis." *Journal of Forensic Psychiatry* 8, no. 2 (1997): 253–257.

Woodbury-Smith, M. R., I. C. H. Clare, A. J. Holland, and A. Kearns. "High Functioning Autistic Spectrum Disorders, Offending and Other Law-breaking: Findings from a Community Sample." *The Journal of Forensic Psychiatry & Psychology* 17, no. 1 (2006): 108–120.

Part IV

Race, Ethnicity, Delinquency, and Justice

PREFACE TO PART IV

In her literary classic, *Uncle Tom's Cabin*, Harriet Beecher Stowe epitomizes the human suffering of her time through the sexually abused slave Cassy, whose two young children are torn from her arms and sold off. When her next child is two weeks old, she slips him the powerful drug laudanum that passes him, she believes, safely into the gentle sleep of death. In her mind, Cassy has made the only choice she felt possible, to save him from the unbearable life of slavery in early America. As Stowe's work troubled readers of her time and stirred the passions of the abolitionist framework,[1] so today do the families of young black males agonize over the possibility of a similarly troubling death. Kimani Gray, Kendrec McDade, Victor Steen, Ramarley Graham, and Michael Brown all represent a mother's worst fears, they are all young, unarmed minority teens recently killed by police.

As tensions rise, reports criticize, and politicians press for revised policies and procedures we recognize that we are living another version of the race conflicts that dominated the civil rights era. On the anniversary of the march on Selma and the release of the movie *Selma*, we have to reflect on whether we have really come that far, and how much further we still have to go to achieve racial parity in this country. According to a recent Gallup Poll, "young black males as a group have higher unemployment, lower graduation rates, less access to healthcare and higher incarceration rates than other racial, age, and gender groups in the U.S."[2]

One could argue that cyber-technologies and streaming Internet communication seem to highlight and globalize messages of hate and intolerance that we thought were in the past or, at least, diminishing. Indeed, Gallup Poll data from 2014 indicate that an increasing number of Americans (up to 13% from 2% in 2008) now view "race relations" or "racism" as the most important problem in this country.[3] The recent shameful social media exposure of an Oklahoma University fraternity engaged in racist rantings reminds us in embarrassing ways that if we cannot educate our children against intolerance, then we have failed as a modern civilization.

At a time when we need accurate data and rigorous research on the impact of race in the justice system, we are also confronted with the realities of changing racial and ethnic population patterns that can make it difficult to have meaningful discussions of discrimination, adverse impact, profiling, and disproportionate confinement. The ways data are defined and categorized add to the ambiguity, particularly in conceptualizing multiracial identities and the tendency of many agency intake systems to classify Hispanics as whites.

What do we know about the typical juvenile youth? We know that the racial breakdown of youth varies by individual states but that, overall, the number of Hispanic juveniles in the system is growing, as is the percentage of delinquency attributed to females. Analysis of data from the Gang Resistance Education and Training (G.R.E.A.T.) program indicates that female Hispanic gang members were persuaded by their peers to join gangs, a phenomenon more common when there was less or no parental supervision.[4] In the most recent census study black children were found to be less likely than other children to be living with two parents[5] and, in addition, they had higher incident rates of maltreatment. Still, government researchers argue, the "demographic classification of juveniles is not a scientific process but a culturally related one that changes with time and place."[6]

As troubling as direct sources of bias and bigotry are, the indirect role that race plays in our perceptions of crime is equally disconcerting. As Shelden explains, race indirectly impacts the scenarios of time and place where there may be more visibility of a crime or more emphasis on a certain type of crime response.[7] The interaction of economics, high crime areas, and police dispersion come together to increase the likelihood that minority youth will be drawn into the juvenile justice system. Even more disturbing, is the finding that the child welfare system may function as a feeder into the juvenile justice system. A study examining 30 years of maltreatment cases from the Los Angeles child welfare system found that those same youth received more serious dispositions in later delinquency hearings.[8]

It is obvious that the criminal justice system must join in the conversation that includes its critical assessment and amenability to change. Only by carefully examining the motives, outcomes and, perhaps, even the unintended consequences of existing laws and procedures, can we hope to raise our children in a safe and color-blind environment. As Karina Rodriguez explains, many of those in poor neighborhoods are without legitimate social networks. They need mentors, tutors, counseling, and afterschool programs. Early childhood development programs, parenting education seminars, and drug and alcohol treatment programs for parents would improve the lives of those most often impacted by disruption and dysfunction.[9]

We must also be wary of attempts to inject programs steeped in traditional and, perhaps dated, middle-class traditions and values into contemporary inner city neighborhoods. Decades of program evaluations have determined these to have little to no effect at all as they fail to take into account the needs and cultural preferences of urban neighborhoods and minority communities. More specifically, measures to address gangs and gang activity have done little to assist low-income areas with the problems they face in providing residents safe and productive living and working environments. More arrests and harsher penalties do little to address the root causes of crime both inside and outside of the context of gangs.[10] The reality is that we can no longer afford to continue to treat just the symptoms of our inattention to the plight of our urban centers. Instead, we must meet the challenges of socially responsible economic reform and meaningful urban renewal.

The two chapters in this part deal with minority issues in the juvenile justice system. As with criminal justice in general, minorities in the juvenile justice system are overrepresented when compared to the white population. Antonio Hernandez and Judith Harris examine Hispanics, the fastest growing minority group in the United States. Examining the delinquency issue through acculturation and immigration, the authors present an analysis of a very important emerging issue in the country. Disproportionate minority contact, an issue historically impacting African Americans, is the subject of the other chapter in this part. In discussing the issues with disproportionate minority contact, John Mooradian illustrates the complexities involved in the issue. While justice is supposed to be color-blind, the juvenile justice does not always live up to that ideal.

REFERENCES

Ammons, Elizabeth. "Heroines in Uncle Tom's Cabin." *American Literature* 49, no. 2 (1977): 161–179.

McCarthy, Justin. "As a Major U.S. Problem, Race Relations Sharply Rises." Gallup Poll. December 19, 2014. http://www.gallup.com/poll/180257/major-problem-race-relations-sharply-rises.aspx?utm_source=position2&utm_medium=related&utm_campaign=tiles.

McShane, Marilyn, and Frank P. Williams "Reducing Minority Youth Gang Involvement." In *Race and Juvenile Justice*. Edited by Everett Penn, Helen Greene, and Shaun Gabbidon, 111–124. Durham, NC: Carolina Academic Press, 2006.

National Center for Juvenile Justice. *Juvenile Offenders and Victims: 2014 National Report*. By Melissa Sickmund and Charles Puzzanchera. Pittsburgh, PA: National Center for Juvenile Justice, 2014.

Rodriguez, Karina. *Latinas and Gangs*. Thesis, University of Houston-Downtown, 2010.

Ryan, Joseph P., Denise Herz, Pedro M. Hernandez, and Jane Marie Marshall. "Maltreatment and Delinquency: Investigating Child Welfare Bias in Juvenile Justice Processing." *Children and Youth Services Review* 29, no. 8 (2007): 1035–1050.

Shelden, Randall. "The Juvenile Justice System." In *Critical Issues in Crime and Justice: Thought, Policy and Practice*. Edited by Mary Maguire and Dan Okada, 345–361. Thousand Oaks, CA: Sage, 2015.

Vito, Gennaro, and Julie Kunselman. *Juvenile Justice Today*. Boston, MA: Prentice Hall, 2012.

Witters, Dan, and Diana Liu. "Young Black Males in U.S. Suffer Well-Being Deficit." Gallup Poll. March 13, 2015. http://www.gallup.com/poll/181952/young-black-males-suffer-deficit.aspx?utm_source=Well-Being&utm_medium=newsfeed&utm_campaign=tiles.

Chapter 9

Acculturation, Ethnic Bias, and Explanations of Delinquency

Antonio Hernandez and Judith Harris

With the explosion of undocumented immigrants crossing the U.S.–Mexico border, many people including citizens and government officials believe this will ultimately lead to higher delinquency rates. The fear is that expanded immigration will lead to increased gangs, drug activity and addiction, and higher illegitimate birth rates. These unsupported allegations have made immigration a hot topic at community gatherings, on social media, and in government offices around the country. To combat the problem of illegal entry, the states, with assistance from the U.S. government, have sent extra law enforcement officers, military troops, and Immigration and Customs Enforcement (ICE) agents to the border. Alongside efforts by opponents to curb illegal entry into the United States, Latinos are on pace to become the nation's largest minority group and among its fastest growing population. With the Latino population on the rise, it is important to examine immigration and dispel the myth that illegal entry by undocumented immigrants leads to higher delinquency rates in the United States.

LATINO POPULATION ON THE RISE

The United States has seen a massive influx of young immigrants, many of whom are Latino.[11] Nationally, Latinos accounts for 53 million of the total population and are projected to comprise 31 percent of the U.S. population by 2060.[12] This includes an estimated 11.6 million undocumented immigrants living in the United States.[13] Future census counts will very likely to see the number rise even further. According to U.S. population projections, the numbers will increase between 2005 through 2050 and minority groups will account for approximately 82 percent of the growth in population size, with Latinos representing a significant portion of this expansion.[14] It is important to note however, that according to Pew researchers, there has been a decline in the number of illegal Mexican-born immigrants in the United States over the last five years.[15]

ACCULTURATION AND ACCULTURATIVE STRESS

One of the keys to understanding any potential effects that immigration might have on existing culture including prevailing crime rates is the concept of acculturation. Acculturation involves the adoption of new cultural information and social skills by an immigrant group that often replaces traditional cultural beliefs, practices, and interaction patterns to varying degrees.[16] Often, these changes produce a unique type of distress known as acculturative stress.[17]

Research has found that individuals are likely to experience acculturative stress when they encounter events or circumstances (stressors) they believe are detrimental to their well-being and for which they lack the resources to cope.[18] Put another way, acculturative stress refers to the emotional reaction triggered by the individual's appraisal of specific events and circumstances in their lives. These events, typically labeled challenges or stressors, may elicit different levels of acculturative stress depending on how the individual appraises them. For example, immigration to a foreign country is believed to include many stressors because it typically involves separating from one's family and friends and learning a new language and cultural system.[19] In addition to these immigration stressors, a large portion of Latino immigrants in the United States face great difficulties related to undesirable and unstable working and living conditions.[20]

Although acculturative stress may lead to some maladaptive behaviors, the process of assimilating into American culture can also cause changes in habits and values. For example, in a study of pregnant women and drinking, researchers found that Hispanic women who had been in the country longer were more likely to drink during pregnancy than women who have not been here as long.[21] Researchers theorize that the empowerment of young immigrant women strains traditional family controls and results in more identification with the contemporary drinking values of their American peers. This scenario reflects the principles of a number of delinquency theories that specifically address culture conflict, social disorganization, and the influence of subcultures.

THEORETICAL EXPLANATIONS

The primary objective of this chapter is to explore the link between immigration and juvenile delinquency among Latinos. The Chicago school's fundamental beliefs must be strongly considered because as Shaw and McKay[22] argued, structural characteristics of particular urban neighborhoods and not the characteristics of their residents make them particularly conducive to the commission of delinquent acts. Although gangs can be found in all demographics, they are especially problematic in socially disorganized communities. Gangs arise either to take the place of weak social institutions, or because weak institutions fail to recognize the characteristics of gang behavior.

Social Disorganization Theory

Although research does indicate newly arriving immigrants contribute to a region's instability, this does not mean immigrants are responsible for any spikes in crime. The typical stereotype of the Latino immigrant is a poor, uneducated, criminal entering the United States illegally. If the individual has already broken the law by "crossing over" illegally, then he will certainly continue to commit future crimes and add to the ever growing prison population. Rather than destabilizing communities and contributing to social disorganization, immigrant concentration has been *inversely* associated with homicide and robbery. Specifically, cities that have Latinos holding political office and on the police force saw fewer homicides and robberies occur in heavily concentrated Latino communities.[23]

With property crimes (burglary, theft, and motor vehicle theft) and Latino immigrants, Stansfield, Akins, Runbault, and Hammer[24] found that there is no connection between the two. Stansfield et al. indicated there were several reasons for this: (1) they are escaping violence and economic instability in their home country and are simply trying to provide a better life for their family, (2) the neighborhoods in which they settle in are better than where they came from, and (3) although Latino immigrants accept "undesirable" or low-paying by jobs by domestic standards, the work is steady, which enables to provide for their family.[25]

Culture Conflict

Each culture dictates rules for certain expected behavior and shared values and beliefs. Enculturation is the natural and unconscious process by which we acquire our own native culture. According to Pedraza[26] upon moving to the United States, immigrants choose to settle in neighborhoods with their native people. This aids them in adjusting to the customs and practices of the host nation. Eventually, through assimilation the native culture slowly fades, merging with the new culture. After a period of time, the two cultures become indistinguishable. When immigrants experience acculturation they have three options. They can adopt a second set of cultural rules that can coexist with the rules of their native culture, replace the rules of the old culture, or modify the old rules so that they complement the new ones. There are few immigrants who are bicultural, meaning they maintain and use two cultures simultaneously with equal intensity.

Like all immigrants entering into the United States, Latinos are experiencing these same worries and stresses of adapting to a new country, while keeping their traditional practices intact. High on the list of Latino values are familism, and respect for elders, which are reinforced through a strict and controlling parenting style. Familism or family needs take precedence over the needs of the individual and is commonly regarded as the most influential factor in the lives of Latinos.[27]

As time goes by, these values that Latinos prize so highly are beginning to erode with second and third generation Latino adolescents. The emotional disconnect Latino adolescents suffer from stem from acculturation conflicts and acculturation gaps.[28] Acculturation conflicts are experienced when messages from the culture of origin and host cultures become difficult to reconcile. Acculturation gaps are the result of differences between adolescent and parent levels of culture, and origin and host culture involvement.

Subculture and Gangs

Many Latino adolescents who join gangs come from broken homes and yearn for a sense of belonging. Of the 774,000 gang members in the United States, there are approximately 36 percent below the age of 18, and 50 percent are Latino.[29] Generally, admission into a gang usually includes a type of initiation so that potential members can prove their masculinity. In the Latino culture this is known as *machismo*. The initiation may require an individual to fight gang members for a certain length of time to prove they will not cower when facing a rival gang. Other initiations may include committing a violent crime such as robbery or murder. And while Latino gangs can be found in high Latino populated areas such as Southern California and Texas, they are spreading throughout the United States. For example, the Central American gang, MS-13 has members all across the United States with their numbers steadily increasing.[30]

Gang participation is due to a number of factors including acculturative stress, which play a determining role in the social role of Latino development. One stressor for example is finding an identity in a foreign country. For the Latino teenager growing up in the United States, this is a period of heightened uncertainty. They not only have to deal with the normal pressures that are associated with teenage life, but they must search for an identity in a culture that considers them an outsider. As Malec[31] found, the Latino youth find themselves in a position of sociocultural disconnection, stranded between the traditional Latino culture and the dominant mainstream. As a result, the Latino youth searches for groups with whom they can identify with and who will give them power and respect. Gangs fill the void for those individuals who are lost between family traditions and a society that is unfamiliar to them.

Conflict Theories

Conflict theories focus on the political nature of crime and examine the creation and application of criminal law. Conflict theorists are not concerned with individual behavior, but rather with the making and enforcement of law. Additionally, they are not concerned with the behavior of the offender or the psychological effects it has on families. With regards to Latino immigration, those in power attempt to enforce immigration laws, making it difficult for Latinos to acculturate into U.S. society.

As the Latino population rises, many believe crime and disease will follow those immigrating to the United States. Stories and pictures of battles raging between law enforcement and drug cartels on the U.S.–Mexico border have many on edge. These events have prompted federal and state officials to update immigration laws in their respective areas. For example, the 287(g) program, which refers to Section 287(g) of the Immigration and Naturalization Act (1952), is one of the U.S. Immigration and Customs Enforcement (ICE) top partnership initiatives.[32] The 287(g) program allows state and a local law enforcement entity to enter into a partnership with ICE, under a joint memorandum of agreement (MOA). The state or local entity receives delegated authority for immigration enforcement within their jurisdictions. Once an undocumented immigrant is apprehended and identified, if necessary, they are removed from the United States. For the fiscal 2014 year, ICE, Customs and Border Protection (CBP), and Department of Homeland Service (DHS) removed 577, 295 undocumented immigrants.[33]

Arizona Senate Bill 1070, the Support Our Law Enforcement and Safe Neighborhoods Act, was a state legislation that empowered police to detain individuals who were not able to prove their citizenship on request.[34] Toomey et al.[35] further indicated the bill was established to increase the general feeling of safety in Arizona communities. Quite the contrary has occurred. In a survey of a community in northern Arizona, Latinos indicated they felt less safe and adolescents felt a weaker sense of identity.[36]

IMMIGRANT STATUS DETERS CRIME

According to the PEW Center,[37] the United States has one out of every 31 adults in the corrections system, either in prison, on probation, or on parole. With conventional theories of crime and incarceration predicting higher rates for young adult males from ethnic minority groups, it follows that immigrants would be expected to have higher incarceration rates than natives. In actuality, the predictions should hold true for immigrant Mexican men who compose a third of all immigrant men between 18 and 39 years of age.[38] Just the opposite occurred however, as Martinez and Valenzuela found that incarceration rates of the U.S. born (3.51%) were four times that of the foreign born (0.86%).

The lowest incarceration rates among Latin American immigrants are seen for the least educated groups. The Salvadorans and Guatemalans were at 0.52 percent, while the Mexicans came in at 0.70 percent. However, those rates increased significantly for their U.S. born co-ethnics. Most notable were the Mexican Americans whose incarceration rates increased to 5.9 percent among the U.S. born. Thus, while incarceration rates are found to be extraordinarily low among Latino immigrants, they are also seen to rise rapidly by the second generation.[39] The findings indicate incarceration rates are much lower among immigrant men than the national norm, but increase significantly among their co-ethnics by the second generation, suggesting that the process of "Americanization" leads to downward mobility and greater risks of involvement with the criminal justice system.

THE POLITICS OF IMMIGRATION

Since 2001–2013 the political climate has been in constant turmoil on both sides of the congressional aisle. Initially, S1291, 107th Congress 2001–2002, known as the Development, Relief, and Education for Alien Minors Act (DREAM) was brought to the Senate floor by Senator Orrin Hatch (R-UT).[40] The DREAM Act was an effort to amend and update the Illegal Immigration Reform and Immigrant Responsibility Act of 1996.[41] An overview of the DREAM Act recommendations are (a) undocumented youth must have come to the states before age 16, (b) the path to legalization is conditional, (c) the youth must attend college, or serve in the U.S. military for a minimum of two years, (d), and the youth must maintain good moral character. Little has changed with the DREAM requirements however; there are a couple of exceptions. An individual must now be between the ages of 12 and 35 at the time the policy was enacted. Furthermore, not only is a good moral character necessary the individual must not have a criminal record.[42] According to Camarota[43] not all immigrants are illegal. Between 2000 and 2005, 7.9 million immigrants entered the United States, only 3.7 million of them were believed to be undocumented. In a 2014 article, Michelle Rindels of the *Reno Gazette Journal* extracted statistics from a new Pew Research Study, "while unauthorized immigrants accounted for 3.5 percent of the

U.S. population of nearly 316 million in 2012, the share varied from less than 1 percent in 10 states to a high of 7.6 percent in Nevada. California and Texas, each at 6.3 percent, had the next highest shares of people there illegally."[44]

The initial mandate of the DREAM Act was to bring about some procedure of immigration reform. Illegal border crossings and alien smuggling for pay was becoming more dangerous and harder to contain. The top five districts for alien smuggling are: Southern District of Texas, smugglers arrested (N=689); Southern District of California, smugglers arrested (N=492); District of Arizona, smugglers arrested (N=423); Western District of Texas, smugglers arrested (N=298); and District of New Mexico, smugglers arrested (N=43).[45] The DREAM Act continues to cause controversy and has not been passed by Congress.

In 2012 President Obama made a bold move and created Deferred Action for Childhood Arrivals (DACA). Again, controversy has made it difficult for DACA to be implemented as both left- and right-wing politicians accuse the president of making a unilateral decision, which is to allow undocumented 15- to 31-year-olds to apply for higher education and employment. However, DACA does not necessarily lead to citizenship as suggested by the DREAM Act.[46] Opponents of DACA believe this presidential order will make illegal entry more enticing and easier to obtain. A Republican senator denounced the bill by saying, "in 2011 there were roughly 6,000 children apprehended coming in illegally"[47]; these numbers were before the DACA policy was initiated. He further stated: "The direct foreseeable consequence of that was the number of unaccompanied children skyrocket so that this year the Obama administration is estimating 90,000 kids will come, next year 145,000. That's up from just 6,000 three years ago."[48]

In 2014 the Executive Amnesty Prevention Act (EAPA, H.R.5729) was passed by Congress.[49] However, most see this as symbolic attempt rather than a bill of substance. President Obama's main objective was to remove the fear of deportation that plagued those who live and worked illegally. In addition, he also added provisos for three year work permits for the five million illegal aliens living in the United States.[50] The EAPA bill, DREAM Act, and DACA continue to have an uncertain future, leaving many illegal immigrants in a state of fear, apprehension, and little hope for acculturation.

Literature concerning undocumented youth and crime is often unclear as many institutions categorize offenders into groups of white/nonwhite. According to Alvarez-Rivera, Nobles, and Lersch,[51] this kind of categorization "blur differences that may exist among and between different racial/ethnic groups."[52] Although there is evidence of Latino crime in the literature, it is small compared to other racial and ethnic groups where the line is clearly drawn between black and white offenders.[53] The effects of acculturation are evident in a study conducted by Miller, Barnes, and Hartley.[54] Their findings show that the less assimilated a youth is into the American lifestyle the more likely they are to join a gang. Thus, Miller et al.[55] conclude that acculturation, or youth marginalization are common variables in why a Latino would join a gang and commit crime. Of interest in their findings is assimilation is more difficult when belonging to an already established subgroup and that the acculturation affects gang membership rather than the other way around.[56]

THE RISE OF UNACCOMPANIED MINORS

The risk factors for undocumented juveniles are far different in scope than for any other racial or ethnic group. Most juveniles who come into the country from over the border have problems with language and suffer what Davies and Fagan[57] recognize as culture shock. Notwithstanding, nutritional deficiencies, poor family relationships, and the history of marginalization add to problems with acculturation. Pérez, Jennings, and Gover[58] who addressed acculturation by looking at the strain theory suggest that acculturation may be a factor in the rise of crime within Latino youth culture. It is therefore not unreasonable to assume that with the exponential rise in unaccompanied minors that crime within this group will continue to rise.

Approximately 63,000 unaccompanied minors were reported and apprehended crossing the Mexico border during the first 10 months of 2014.[59] The following statistics are extracted from U.S. Border Patrol by Meyer et al.[60]

Most of these unaccompanied minors are male. However there are also increases in female border crossings. Most who have been apprehended are teenage boys, there is an increase from 9 percent in FY2013 to 16 percent in FY2014. The proportion of girls has increased from 19 percent in FY2013 to 28 percent in FY2014.[61]

Table 9.1
Apprehensions of Unaccompanied Minors by Country of Origin: FY2009–FY2014

FY2009: 19,668—Mexico*, Honduras, Guatemala, and El Salvador
FY2010: 18,634—Mexico*, Honduras, Guatemala, and El Salvador
FY2011: 16,067—Mexico*, Honduras, Guatemala, and El Salvador
FY2012: 24,481—Mexico*, Honduras, Guatemala, and El Salvador
FY2013: 38,833—Mexico*, Honduras, Guatemala, El Salvador and Other
FY2014: 62,998—Mexico*, Honduras, Guatemala, and El Salvador

* Identifies the country that had the largest number of apprehended unaccompanied minors

SANCTUARY CITIES

Across America there are hundreds of so-called sanctuary cities. These are cities where undocumented juveniles and adults are protected from having to give their country of origin when apprehended by law enforcement. Although a list of actual sanctuary cities is often subjective and fluid, political candidates have attacked the topic by using threats that immigration is somehow tied to violent crime.[62] Today, the sanctuary city debate continues across America. Katy, Texas, is on the sanctuary city list and has been fighting its removal for many years. In 1990 a group of civil rights activists sued Katy after numerous raids for illegal immigrants had taken place. One 2008 article articulates the lack of judicial oversight and highlights the problems Latino youth have with acculturation. One particular young man was well known to law enforcement having arrests for indecent exposure, and hanging around the parks. He was known by the police to be in the country illegally, and lived on the streets. However, they had no authority to initiate deportation. With the help of a U.S. representative and the Katy police chief they were able to dispel the city's sanctuary image. A collaboration between the ICE and the local police department since 2008 has cleared the way for Katy to renounce the "sanctuary city" label.[63] San Francisco is still identified as a sanctuary city although the policy is very controversial and is rarely publicly acknowledged. Statistics obtained by the *Houston Chronicle* from the San Francisco Juvenile Probation Department show how many Latino undocumented youth had criminal records. The following are a sample of undocumented juvenile statistics given to the *Houston Chronicle*:

- 185 undocumented youth held on felony charges were shielded from deportation between 2005 and the summer of 2009.
- Of the 252 who were detained 180 were suspected of drug offenses.
- 98 percent of the 252 were male and 79.4 percent were from Honduras.
- Of the 180 held on drug charges 87.8 percent were from Honduras and 178 are male.
- The total of combined drug offenses against them was 295 as many had multiple changes.[64]

POLICY IMPLICATIONS AND FUTURE RESEARCH

It is clear the political uneasiness with immigration laws and policy will continue to be at the forefront of every politician's agenda. The old "I will be tough on crime" has changed to "I will be tough on immigration" and what differentiates these two opinions is, one, the freedom to obtain legal entry into the United States, and two, what happens when immigrant families are treated as undocumented and are not able to assimilate into the American culture.

There is quite a difference between an individual being able to acculturate and one who assimilates into a new culture. The changing of one's belief system and values often occurs only with an ongoing interaction between different groups. Over time, an individual begins to learn a new language, cultural beliefs, and often the values and norms shift toward those of the dominant group.[65] Sociologists Park and Burgess[66] discuss assimilation in terms of individuals or groups beginning to make memories and their attitudes, and history together form communality.

If indeed the lack of acculturation may be an indicator of future criminality for young Latinos then perhaps it should be a priority in every school, church and community center to help them cross the divide. This would be a proactive approach by teaching the richness of acculturation. It may also help diffuse tensions, and strain within individuals and groups which may lead to criminal or deviant behavior.

President Obama in his executive immigration orders stressed that fear must be removed from the equation of all young undocumented aliens. If indeed fear of living in this country is removed, and political cohesiveness can be attained, then feasibly children will learn how to adjust to the norms of American society.

DISCUSSION QUESTIONS

1. If the United States is a country where almost everyone has immigrant ancestry, why are people so biased against immigrants? What are some of the most common biases and fears? Before you answer this question, take the Immigration Quiz offered at this PBS website: http://www.pbs.org/independentlens/blog/immigration-quiz-2
2. Explain the relationship between acculturative stress and the potential for deviance. Why do some people seem to assimilate into American society faster than others?
3. What role to gangs play in the process of acculturation and dealing with acculturative stress and how could this be addressed with interventions?
4. What factors today appear to be influencing the political focus on immigration and how do you see that changing as our society becomes more diverse?
5. Discuss the advantages and disadvantages of sanctuary cities.

ADDITIONAL RESOURCES

Alvarez-Rivera, Lorna, Matt Nobles, and Kim Lersch. "Latino Immigrant Acculturation and Crime." *American Journal of Criminal Justice* 39, no. 2 (2014): 315–330.

Bersani, Bianca, Thomas Loughran, and Alex Piquero. "Comparing Patterns and Predictors of Immigrant Offending among a Sample of Adjudicated Youth, 2014." *Journal of Youth and Adolescence* 43, no. 11 (2014): 1914–1933.

Cardoso, Jodi Berger, Alan Dettlaff, Megan Finno-Velasquez, Jennifer Scott, and Monica Faulkner. "Nativity and Immigration Status among Latino Families Involved in the Child Welfare System: Characteristics, Risk and Maltreatment" *Children and Youth Services Review* 44 (2014): 189–200.

DiPietro, Stephanie, and Jaclyn Cwick. "Gender, Family Functioning and Violence across Immigrant Generations." *Journal of Research in Crime & Delinquency* 51, no. 6 (2014): 785–815.

Hernandez, Arnold. *The Dream Act Bill of 2013 Explained.* 2013. Amazon Digital Services, Inc., 2013. http://www.amazon.com/Dream-Act-Bill-2013-Explained-ebook/dp/B00E1QS592/ref=sr_1_2?ie=UTF8&qid=1432401407&sr=8-2&keywords=Dream+Act.

Light, Michael. "The New Face of Legal Inequality: Noncitizens and the Long-Term Trends in Sentencing Disparities across U.S. District Courts, 1992–2009." *Law & Society Review* 48, no. 2 (2014): 447–478.

Moehling, Carolyn, and Anne Piehl. "Immigrant Assimilation in U.S. Prisons, 1900–1930." *Journal of Population Economics* 27, no. 1 (2014): 173–200.

Schnapp, Patrick. "Identifying the Effect of Immigration on Homicide Rates in U.S. Cities: An Instrumental Variables Approach." *Homicide Studies* 19, no. 2 (2015): 103–122.

Tapia, Mike. "U.S. Latino Arrest: An Analysis of Risk by Nativity and Origin." *Hispanic Journal of Behavioral Sciences* 37, no. 1 (2015): 37–58.

Vaughn, Michael, Christopher Salas-Wright, Brandy Maynard, Zhengmin Qian, Lauren Terzis, Abdi Kusow, and Matt DeLisi. "Criminal Epidemiology and the Immigrant Paradox: Intergenerational Discontinuity and Violence and Antisocial Behavior among Immigrants." *Journal of Criminal Justice* 42, no. 6 (2014): 483–490.

Yakhnich, Liat and Meir Teichman. "Immigrant Family in Distress: Assisting Immigrant Parents of Juvenile Delinquents." *Journal of Child, Youth & Family Studies* 6, no. 1 (2015): 1–16.

RELATED WEBSITES

Center for Immigration Studies, http://cis.org/ImmigrantCrime

Dispelling DREAM Act Myths, http://www.immigrationpolicy.org/just-facts/dispelling-dream-act-myths

The Dream Act: Myths and Facts, https://www.nafsa.org/uploadedFiles/NAFSA_Home/Resource_Library_Assets/Public_Policy/The%20DREAM%20Act%20T%20and%20M%20-%20PDF%20FOR%20WEB.pdf

List of sanctuary cities, http://www.ojjpac.org/sanctuary.asp

U.S. Demographics, http://www.census.gov/quickfacts/

SUPPORTING FILMS

Alienated: Undocumented Immigrant Youth (2005), http://www.snagfilms.com/films/title/alienated_undocumented_immigrant_youth

The Graduates (2013) (PBS), http://www.pbs.org/independentlens/graduates/

The New Americans (2004) (PBS), http://www.pbs.org/independentlens/newame
ricans/

The State of Arizona (2014) (PBS), http://www.pbs.org/independentlens/state-of-
arizona/

Welcome to Shelbyville (2011) (PBS), http://www.pbs.org/independentlens/welcome-
to-shelbyville/

NOTES

1. Ammons (1977), 161–179.
2. Witters and Liu (2015).
3. McCarthy (2014).
4. Vito and Kunselman (2012), 374.
5. National Center for Juvenile Justice (2014).
6. Ibid., 15.
7. Shelden (2015), 349–350.
8. Ryan, Herz, Hernandez, and Marshall (2007).
9. Rodriguez (2010).
10. McShane and Williams (2006), 122.
11. Edwards (2010).
12. French (2014).
13. DHS Office of Information Statistics (2009).
14. PEW Hispanic Center (2008).
15. Rindels (2014).
16. Vega, Aldrete, Kolody, and Aguilar-Gaxiola (1998).
17. Berry and Anis (1974).
18. Folkman, Lazarus, Dunkel-Schetter, DeLongis, and Gruen (1986).
19. Arbona et al. (2010).
20. Center for Economic Development (2002); Simich (2006).
21. Stoeltje (2011).
22. Shaw and McKay (1942).
23. Lyons, Velez, and Santoro (2013).
24. Stansfield, Akins, Runbault, and Hammer (2013).
25. Ibid.
26. Pedraza (2014).
27. Coohey (2001).
28. Smokowski, Rose, and Bacallo (2008).
29. Howell and Egely (2005).
30. Rankin and Torpy (2010).
31. Malec (2006).
32. "DHS Releases End of the Year Statistics" (2014).
33. Ibid.
34. Toomey et al. (2014).
35. Ibid.
36. Hardy et al. (2012).

37. PEW Hispanic Center (2009).
38. Martinez and Valenzuela (2006).
39. Rumbaut, Gonzales, Komaie, Morgan, and Tafoya-Estrada (2006).
40. "S.1291–107th Congress: Development, Relief, and Education for Alien Minors Act."
41. Ibid.
42. Mahatmya and Gring-Pemble (2014).
43. Camarota (2005).
44. Rindels (2014).
45. United States Sentencing Commission (2012).
46. Bonyanpour (2015).
47. Kenny (2014).
48. Ibid.
49. Mass (2014).
50. Ibid.
51. Alvarez-Rivera, Nobles, and Lersch (2014).
52. Ibid., 316.
53. Reid, Weiss, Alderman, and Jaret (2005).
54. Miller, Barnes, and Hartley (2011).
55. Ibid.
56. Ibid., 348
57. Davies and Fagan (2012).
58. Pérez, Jennings, and Gover (2008).
59. Congressional Research Service (2014).
60. Ibid.
61. Ibid.
62. Fikac (2014).
63. Knight (2009).
64. Hastings (2008).
65. Archuleta (2012).
66. Park and Burgess (1924).

REFERENCES

Alvarez-Rivera, Lorna L., Matt R. Nobles, and Kim M. Lersch. "Latino Immigrant Acculturation and Crime." *American Journal of Criminal Justice* 39, no. 2 (2014): 315–330.

Arbona, Consuelo, Norma Olvera, Nestor Rodriguez, Jacqueline Hagan, Adriana Linares, and Margit Wiesner. "Acculturative Stress among Documented and Undocumented Latino Immigrants in the United States." *Hispanic Journal of Behavioral Sciences* 32, no. 3 (2010): 362–384.

Archuleta, Adrian J. "Hispanic Acculturation Index: Advancing Measurement in Acculturation." *Journal of Human Behavior in the Social Environment* 22, no. 3 (2012): 297–318.

Berry, John W., and Robert C. Annis. "Acculturative Stress: The Role of Ecology, Culture and Differentiation." *Journal of Cross-cultural Psychology* 5, no. 4 (1974): 382–406.

Bonyanpour, Natassia. "Pro-Con: Should Texas Repeal the DREAM Act?" *Victoria Advocate*, January 11, 2015, https://www.victoriaadvocate.com/news/2015/jan/11/pro-con-should-texas-repeal-its-dream-act/.

Camarota, Steven A. "Immigrants at Mid-Decade: A Snapshot of America's Foreign-Born Population in 2005." *Center for Immigration Studies*. December, 2005. http://cis.org/ForeignBornPopulation2005.

Center for Economic Development. *Chicago's Undocumented Immigrants: An Analysis of Wages, Working Conditions, and Economic Contributions*. By Chirag Mehta, Nik Theodore, Iliana Mora, and Jennifer Wade. Chicago, IL: University of Illinois at Chicago, 2002.

Congressional Research Service. *Unaccompanied Children from Central America: Foreign Policy Considerations*. By Peter J. Meyer, Clare Ribando Seelke, Maureen Taft-Morales, and Rhoda Margesson. Washington, DC: Congressional Research Service, 2014.

Coohey, Carol. "The Relationship between Familism and Child Maltreatment in Latino and Anglo Families." *Child Maltreatment* 6, no. 2 (2001): 130–142.

Davies, Garth, and Jeffrey Fagan. "Crime and Enforcement in Immigrant Neighborhoods Evidence from New York City." *The Annals of the American Academy of Political and Social Science* 641, no. 1 (2012): 99–124.

DHS Office of Information Statistics. *Estimates of the Unauthorized Immigrant Population Residing in the United States: January 2008*. By Michael Hoefer, Nancy Rytina, and Bryan C. Baker. Washington, DC: Department of Homeland Security, 2009.

"DHS Releases End of the Year Statistics." *U.S. Department of Homeland Security*. December 19, 2014. http://www.dhs.gov/news/2014/12/19/dhs-releases-end-year-statistics.

Edwards, Jim. "Minority Majority." *Media Week* 20 (2010): 18–19.

Fikac, Peggy. "Sen. Patrick Linking Immigration and Violent Crime." *Houston Chronicle* January 20, 2014, B1.

Folkman, Susan, Richard S. Lazarus, Christine Dunkel-Schetter, Anita DeLongis, and Rand J. Gruen. "Dynamics of a Stressful Encounter: Cognitive Appraisal, Coping, and Encounter Outcomes." *Journal of Personality and Social Psychology* 50, no. 5 (1986): 992–1003.

French, Dana. (2014). "Hispanics Will Compromise 31% of Population by 2060." *Casual Living* 54, no. 7 (2014): 74.

Hardy, Lisa J., Christina M. Getrich, Julio C. Quezada, Amanda Guay, Raymond J. Michalowski, and Eric Henley. "A Call for Further Research on the Impact of State-Level Immigration Policies on Public Health." *American Journal of Public Health* 102, no. 7 (2012): 1250–1253.

Hastings, Karen. "Katy No Longer Sanctuary for Criminal Aliens, Says Police Chief." *Houston Chronicle*. August 20, 2008, http://www.chron.com/neighborhood/katy-news/article/Katy-no-longer-sanctuary-for-criminal-aliens-1773763.php.

Howell, James C., and Arlen Egley. "Moving Risk Factors into Developmental Theories of Gang Membership." *Youth Violence and Juvenile Justice* 3, no. 4 (2005): 334–354.

Kenny, Jack. "Obama as 'Emancipator' of Illegal Immigrants." *The New American*, September 8, 2014, 24.

Knight, Heather. "S.F. Sanctuary Policy Shielded Up to 185 Youths." *San Francisco Chronicle,* April 3. 2009, http://www.sfgate.com/crime/article/S-F-sanctuary-policy-shielded-up-to-185-youths-3246314.php.

Lyons, Christopher J., María B. Vélez, and Wayne A. Santoro. "Neighborhood Immigration, Violence, and City-Level Immigrant Political Opportunities." *American Sociological Review* 78, no. 4 (2013): 604–632.

Mahatmya, Duhita, and Lisa M. Gring-Pemble. "DREAMers and Their Families: A Family Impact Analysis of the DREAM Act and Implications for Family Well-being." *Journal of Family Studies* 20, no. 1 (2014): 79–87.

Malec, Danny. "Transforming Latino Gang Violence in the United States." *Peace Review: A Journal of Social Justice* 18, no. 1 (2006): 81–89.

Martinez, Ramiro, and Abel Valenzuela. *Immigration and Crime.* New York: NYU Press, 2006.

Mass, Warren. (2014). "House Passes Executive Amnesty Prevention Act of 2014." *The New American,* December 5, 2014, http://www.thenewamerican.com/usnews/immigration/item/19667-house-passes-executive-amnesty-prevention-act-of-2014.

Miller, Holly Ventura, J. C. Barnes, and Richard D. Hartley. "Reconsidering Hispanic Gang Membership and Acculturation in a Multivariate Context." *Crime & Delinquency* 57, no. 3 (2011): 331–355.

Park, Robert E., and Ernest W. Burgess. *Introduction to the Science of Society.* Chicago: University of Chicago Press, 1924.

Passel, Jeffrey, and D'Vera Cohn. "U.S. Population Projections, 2005–2050." *Pew Research Center.* February 11, 2008. http://www.pewhispanic.org/2008/02/11/us-population-projections-2005-2050/.

Pedraza, Francisco I. "The Two-Way Street of Acculturation, Discrimination, and Latino Immigration Restrictionism." *Political Research Quarterly* 67, no. 4 (2014): 889–904.

Pérez, Deanna M., Wesley G. Jennings, and Angela R. Gover. "Specifying General Strain Theory: An Ethnically Relevant Approach." *Deviant Behavior* 29, no. 6 (2008): 544–578.

PEW Hispanic Center (2008). *The PEW Hispanic Center report: U.S. Population Projections, 2005–2050.* http://www.pewhispanic.org/files/reports/85.pdf.

PEW Hispanic Center. *A Portrait of Unauthorized Immigrants in the United States.* Washington DC: PEW Hispanic Center, 2009.

Rankin, Bill, and Bill Torpy. "It's a Dead End in MS-13." *The Atlanta Journal Constitution.* April 4, 2010, http://www.ajc.com/news/news/local/its-a-dead-end-in-ms-13/nQdtt/.

Reid, Lesley Williams, Harald E. Weiss, Robert M. Adelman, and Charles Jaret. "The Immigration–Crime Relationship: Evidence across US Metropolitan Areas." *Social Science Research* 34, no. 4 (2005): 757–780.

Rindels, Michelle. "Nevada Has Top Share of Unauthorized Immigrants." *Reno Gazette Journal,* November 23, 2014, 15A.

Rumbaut, Ruben G., Roberto G. Gonzales, Golnaz Komaie, Charlie V. Morgan, and Rosaura Tafoya-Estrada. "Immigration and incarceration: Patterns and Predictors of Imprisonment among First and Second Generation Young Adults." In *Immigration and Crime.* Edited by Ramiro Martinez and Abel Valenzuela, 64–89. New York: NYU Press, 2006.

"S.1291–107th Congress: Development, Relief, and Education for Alien Minors Act." *Govtrack.us.* http://www.govtrack.us/congress/bills/107/s1291.

Shaw, Clifford R. and Henry D. McKay. *Juvenile Delinquency and Urban Areas.* Chicago, IL: C.C. Thomas Publishing, 1942.

Simich, Laura. "Hidden Meanings of Health Security: Migration Experiences and Systemic Barriers to Mental Well-Being among Non-Status Migrants in Canada." *International Journal of Migration, Health and Social Care* 2, no. 3 (2006): 16–27.

Smokowski, Paul R., Roderick Rose, and Martica L. Bacallao. "Acculturation and Latino Family Processes: How Cultural Involvement, Biculturalism, and Acculturation Gaps Influence Family Dynamics." *Family Relations* 57, no. 3 (2008): 295–308.

Stansfield, Richard, Scott Akins, Rubén G. Rumbaut, and Roger B. Hammer. "Assessing the Effects of Recent Immigration on Serious Property Crime in Austin, Texas." *Sociological Perspectives* 56, no. 4 (2013): 647–672.

Stoeltje, Melissa Fletcher. "Study Links Assimilation, Drinking While Pregnant." *Houston Chronicle,* November 14, 2011, B3.

Toomey, Russell B., Adriana J. Umaña-Taylor, David R. Williams, Elizabeth Harvey-Mendoza, Laudan B. Jahromi, and Kimberly A. Updegraff. "Impact of Arizona's SB 1070 Immigration Law on Utilization of Health Care and Public Assistance among Mexican-Origin Adolescent Mothers and Their Mother Figures." *American Journal of Public Health* 104, no. S1 (2014): S28–S34.

United States Sentencing Commission. *Quick Facts Alien Smuggling Offenses.* Washington, DC: United States Sentencing Commission, 2012.

Vega, William Armando, Ethel Alderete, Bohdan Kolody, and Sergio Aguilar-Gaxiola. "Illicit Drug Use among Mexicans and Mexican Americans in California: The Effects of Gender and Acculturation." *Addiction* 93, no. 12 (1998): 1839–1850.

Chapter 10

When Minority Exceeds Majority: Understanding and Addressing Disproportionate Minority Contact in the Juvenile Justice System[1]

John K. Mooradian

If you want to stimulate controversy in personal conversations or on social media, all you have to do is solicit opinions about abortion, gun control, the definition of marriage, or American involvement in the Middle East. In the field of juvenile justice, you can do the same thing by raising the topic of disproportionate minority contact (DMC).

DMC means that the percentages of minority youth who contact stages of the juvenile justice system exceed their percentage of the general population, and implies that this disparity is a problem. In fact, this disparity indicates that the proportions of minority youth exceed the proportions of majority youth across the juvenile justice continuum.

DMC is a controversial issue because it forces juvenile justice professionals and community members to confront issues of protection and punishment under the dark shadow of race. Existence and persistence of DMC contradicts the claim that America has entered a "postracial" phase.

UNDERSTANDING THE PROBLEM OF DMC

Minority overrepresentation in the juvenile justice system was initially recognized as a problem in the 1988 amendments to the United States Juvenile Justice and Delinquency Prevention Act of 1974.[2] This recognition involved a directive to individual states participating in the Title II, Part B, Formula Grants Program, to reduce disproportionate confinement of all government-defined minority groups in any jurisdiction in which it was found.[3] Initial recognition of overrepresentation focused singularly on disproportionate minority confinement in secure settings, but, driven by data, it was broadened in 2002, to include disparities at all levels of contact between minority youth and elements of the juvenile justice system.[4]

Consequently, the U.S. Justice Department's Office of Juvenile Justice and Delinquency Prevention (OJJDP) identifies nine such contact points (juvenile arrests, referrals to juvenile court, diversions from juvenile court, predisposition detentions, petitions to juvenile court, adjudications by juvenile court, adjudications that result in probation, adjudications that result in secure placement, and transfer/waiver to criminal court),[5] and concludes that disproportionate minority representation is evident at nearly all of these contact points.[6] The most crucial contact points may be arrest, adjudication, placement, and waiver, because they mark decisions that significantly escalate limitations on personal freedom.[7] In addition, police contacts during arrests also pose particular risks to minority youth, but data are difficult to obtain.

DMC as an Intractable Problem

Given the federal mandate, and the passage of two decades, it would be reasonable to expect that significant reductions in DMC have been achieved. As shown in Table 10.1, using federal data,[8] however, that's not really the case. The columns for minority youth for the selected years of 1991, 2001, and 2011, indicate that their percentage of total juvenile arrests actually increased 4 percent to 34 percent over 20 years; their percentage of total juvenile court adjudications fluctuated about 3 percent, but ended in 2011 about one point higher than 1991 at 38 percent; and their percentage of total out-of-home placements fluctuated downward about 6 percent, but rose in 2011 to the same percentage as 1991 at 43 percent. The only notable reduction is shown in waivers to adult court, with a large drop from 51 percent in 1991, to 36 percent in 2001, followed by a sharp rise to 44 percent in 2011.

Similar data for white youth show that they composed 80 percent of the general population aged 10–17 in 1991, 78 percent in 2001, and 76 percent in 2011. They made up 70 percent of the arrests in 1991, 70 percent in 2001, and 66 percent in 2011. White youth comprised 63 percent of adjudications

Table 10.1
Percentages of Minority and Black Youth Contacting Selected Stages of the Juvenile Justice System

Year	General Population Age 10–17		Juvenile Arrests		Juvenile Court Adjudications		Out-of-Home Placements		Waivers to Adult Criminal Court	
	Minority (%)	Black (%)	Minority (%)	Black (%)	Minority (%)	Black (%)	Minority (%)	Black (%)	Minority (%)	Black (%)
1991	20	15	30	28	37	34	43	39	51	49
2001	22	16	30	27	34	31	37	34	36	34
2011	24	17	34	31	38	35	43	40	44	41

in 1991, 66 percent in 2001, and 62 percent in 2011. They made up 57 percent of placements in 1991, 62 percent in 2001, and 57 percent in 2011. Their percentages for waiver to adult court were 49 percent in 1991, 58 percent in 2001, and 52 percent in 2011. Contrary to percentages of minority youth, percentages of white youth at each of these contact points fall beneath their percentage of the general population, and progressively decrease as youth go deeper into the system.

Table 10.1 also shows data for black youth, who represent the greatest number of minority youth in the juvenile justice system.[9] (It is important to note that the FBI protocol for national Uniform Crime Reports does not require jurisdictions to report arrest data on Hispanic youth.[10] Hispanic youth are identified at the adjudication and placement stages, however, and data at those levels are available.) Despite the fact that they comprised only 17 percent of the general population aged 10–17 in 2011, black youth made up 31 percent of juvenile arrests; 35 percent of juvenile court adjudications; 40 percent of out-of-home placements; and 41 percent of waivers to adult criminal court.

These percentages indicate that black youth are more likely than white youth to be arrested, and that they are more likely to encounter restrictive responses at subsequent levels of the juvenile justice system than white youth. As is the case with minority youth as a whole, the percentages for black youth have evidenced no appreciable reduction at these stages over the past 20 years, except at waiver to adult criminal court. In addition, increasing percentages for black youth across the arrest, adjudication, and placement stages indicate that they are more likely than white youth to encounter increasingly punitive responses as they move through the system.

Evolving Measures of DMC

Although percentages of minority and majority youth at each stage are easily interpretable, OJJDP has encouraged the use of two proportional indexes to facilitate comparisons of minority to majority youth. These indexes have been used to make comparisons at various contact points, but add some complications to understanding the problem because they use different strategies to present slightly different views of the issue.

The initial index is known as the disproportionate representation index (DRI).[11] It is computed by dividing the percentage of a given group of youth at each stage by their percentage of the general population. Using 2011 data, the DRI for minority youth is 1.4 at the arrest stage; 1.6 at the adjudication stage; and 1.8 at the placement stage. For black youth, the DRI is 1.8 at arrest; 2.0 at adjudication; and 2.4 at placement. Corresponding values for white youth are 0.9 at arrest; 0.8 at adjudication; and 0.8 at placement. These values indicate that the proportions of minority, especially black, youth increase across these contact points. Proportions for white youth, on the other hand, are much smaller at arrest, and decline at adjudication and placement. Comparing DRI values for minority and black youth to white youth indicates that minority and black youth are significantly overrepresented at these points, and that they are likely to encounter increasingly punitive decisions.

A newer index has been developed to directly compare the rates for all or specific minority group youth to white youth at each stage of contact. It is called the relative rate index (RRI).[12] The RRI is based on a sequenced set of calculations that begins by dividing the number of youth who are arrested by their number in the general population, to obtain a rate. Dividing the arrest count of white youth in 2011 by their count in the general population aged 10–17 yields a white arrest rate of 36.0 arrests for every 1,000 white youth. In the same year, the black arrest rate was 78.8 arrests for every 1,000 black persons aged 10–17 in the U.S population. Dividing the rate for black youth by the rate for white youth produces an RRI of 2.2. This indicates that the black arrest rate in 2011 was more than double the white rate, and is interpreted to show a racial disparity. RRI values for arrests, adjudications, and out-of-home placements comparing black to white youth for 1991, 2001, and 2011 are displayed in Table 10.2. The RRIs for black youth replicate the patterns of the percentages shown earlier.

The RRI for each stage of contact is affected by the number of youth involved at the preceding stage, so that number replaces the general population number as the denominator in subsequent calculations. Therefore, the RRI presents the degree of racial disparity at a particular stage in the juvenile justice system as a combination of the disparities introduced at earlier stages with that added at the stage under examination. Interpretation, however, requires care. It may appear that the RRI of 0.9 at the adjudication stage indicates no disparity, but it simply shows that no additional disparity occurs at adjudication. (A value of 1.0 would indicate that the disparity of the arrest stage is maintained without additional disparity being added at the adjudication stage.)

Table 10.2
Relative Rate Indexes for Black Youth Contacting Selected Stages of the Juvenile Justice System

Year	Arrest	Adjudication	Out-of-Home Placement
1991	2.1	1.0	1.3
2001	1.9	0.9	1.2
2011	2.2	0.9	1.2

The U.S. Department of Justice supports use of the RRI, but issues cautions.[13] Variations in local and state data collection procedures and reporting systems, and definitions of arrest, adjudication, and placement affect accuracy of the RRI, and interpretation of meaningful differences in minority and white rates is difficult.[14] To date, only 29 states have provided RRI data for all nine of the federally identified contact points.[15] Nonetheless, the RRI has become the standard for national reports of DMC.

More recent efforts to understand DMC highlight limitations of general measures of disparities between races (like the DRI and the RRI). Efforts are underway to compare youth who are "similarly situated" across several variables, including type of offense, family characteristics, community characteristics, and juvenile justice system characteristics, who differ only on the variable of race, in order to improve policy and practice.[16]

ADDRESSING THE PROBLEM OF DMC

Efforts to address the problem of DMC have been implemented at national, state, and local jurisdiction levels of the juvenile justice system, and published in the juvenile justice literature. One set of contributions to this body of literature consists of overarching reduction models.

The OJJDP, for example, encourages states to apply its five-stage DMC reduction model, which includes identification of the degree of DMC in a given state or jurisdiction; assessment/diagnosis of mechanisms contributing to DMC in that location; implementation of interventions to reduce DMC; evaluation of the impact of these interventions; and ongoing monitoring of systemic trends in DMC in the state or jurisdiction over time.[17]

An additional reduction model centers on evaluation, and specifies seven steps, including defining the problem, implementing evidence-based programming, developing program logic models to guide evaluation, identifying measures to track DMC, collecting and analyzing data from those measures, reporting findings to constituencies, and reassessing program logic in light of new understandings.[18] These models are designed to structure state and local decision making, without prescribing particular actions.

Other sources within the literature, however, identify causes of DMC, and describe initiatives to reduce DMC. They are summarized next, and extended with additional recommendations.

Identified Causes of DMC

Juvenile justice professionals and researchers have compiled long lists of presumed causes of DMC. These lists cluster into four categories, which include characteristics of individual offenders, features of community contexts, differential effects of juvenile justice policy, and differential decision making within the juvenile justice system.

When investigating individual youth characteristics related to DMC, most researchers have focused on offense histories. Early efforts to investigate offense patterns concluded that minority youth are more likely to be involved in drug related offenses,[19] become active in gangs,[20] and commit violent crimes[21] than white youth. White youth are more likely to commit sexual assault and arson, while black youth are more likely to commit robberies and drug trafficking.[22] Research also indicates that the families of delinquents share common characteristics, including very high or very low family cohesion, and very rigid or very chaotic approaches to discipline.[23]

Research indicates that community contexts impact DMC primarily through youth exposure to poverty and violence, which are, unfortunately, highly correlated with race.[24] The National Centers for Disease Control indicate that homicide is the leading cause of death for African Americans between the ages of 10 and 24.[25] Within a context of limited opportunities, shootings by civilians and police, drug and gang-related murders, and a persistent threat of violent attacks, youth often learn to adapt to inhospitable environments by adopting antisocial attitudes and behaviors.[26] Exposure to violence also correlates with trauma and its sequelae, which include adjustment problems, depression, anxiety, and antisocial behavior, in addition to posttraumatic stress disorder.[27] Additionally, efforts to improve community institutions, such as "zero tolerance" drug and weapon policies in schools, can serve as "push out" policies that result in unintentionally harsher treatment of minority youth, and further limit prosocial opportunities.[28]

Juvenile justice policy has also been shown to impact youth differentially by race.[29] Attention has been focused on mandatory sentencing or other judicial rules, and risk scales, which were initially instituted to combat unintentional racial bias.[30] Unfortunately, they may actually unintentionally contribute to DMC. For example, it was found that laws like one enacted in Minnesota, which set mandatory sentences for possession of derivatives of cocaine differentially impacted the races because white people tended to possess and use powdered cocaine (with a five-year sentence), while black people tended to possess and use crack (which carried a 20-year sentence for an equivalent amount).[31] Risk assessment scales were also instituted to increase the fairness of commitment, detention, and postadjudication placement decisions. These scales are usually constructed with correlates of community risk, such as the number of police contacts a youth has on his or her record, or the offender's family characteristics. Consequently, some of these scales require detention under conditions like lack of two parents or one biological parent.[32]

Differential decision making is particularly difficult to assess and to address. Illustrating this difficulty, a unique experiment presented two randomized groups of "ethnically diverse" police officers with one hypothetical case. Before reading the case, one group was "subliminally primed" with racially neutral words and the other with words relating to the category "black." Those in the racially primed group reported more negative ratings of the offender in the hypothetical case, and predicted higher recidivism and recommended harsher penalties. The police officers' self-reported racial attitudes failed to explain group differences.[33] Another study found that probation officers were more likely to attribute delinquent behavior among African American youth to internal factors such as irresponsibility, while they explained delinquent behavior by white youth with external factors such as poverty.[34] Each of these studies represents elements of the literature that implicate personal bias as a factor leading to DMC.

Looming over—or perhaps entwined within—all of these causes is racism.[35] Discussing DMC without considering the larger issue of racism is disingenuous. Racism is an ideology that operates at the meta-level of social systems, and pervades American social ecology. Racism consists of a belief that people of a different race are inherently inferior to one's own race, and it uses power to systematically disenfranchise, degrade, or divert resources from the subject group.

For purposes of this chapter, racism may be thought of as taking two primary forms. Overt racism is constructed from hate, and perverts perceptions of people whom the perpetrator assigns to a devalued category. Overt racism manifests in direct discrimination that targets persons or structures which represent the assigned group. Overt racism is openly offensive and oppressive, and is evidenced by explicit expressions of disdain through stereotypic descriptors, or perpetration of physical violence. Few observers imply that overt racism governs juvenile justice decisions or results in DMC, but its total absence as a factor is in doubt.

Covert racism, on the other hand, is pervasive and much harder to detect and deter. Although covert racism may be deliberate, it often operates beneath the awareness of its perpetrators, so it may be doubly hidden. Covert racism is constructed from fear, and distorts the reality of other people's values and experience to match one's own. Covert racism is insidiously offensive and oppressive, and is evidenced by inequitable opportunity structures, disparate resource allocation, and cultural imperialism that imposes dominant values on minority cultures or communities. Covert racism underlies what has been termed "racial bias" and "institutional racism".

Initiatives to Reduce DMC

Efforts to reduce DMC have been undertaken with federal and foundation funding.[36] Given the intractable nature of DMC, it may be useful to consider additional extensions. Such efforts can focus on improving data collection and reporting; reducing racial bias in police, probation, and judicial decision making; employing effective treatment intervention for juvenile offenders and their families; enhancing community capacity building; and maximizing multilevel multisystem coordination.

Improving Data Collection and Reporting at State and Local Levels

Federal data are dependent on state and local jurisdiction reports. Because all efforts to reduce DMC are also dependent on accurate information, improving the quality and consistency of available information is crucial. Several problems with data collection and management have been exposed, including limited funding for counties and localities to support data management; use of paper rather than electronic files that make retrieval difficult; nonstandardized race and ethnicity categories and offense definitions; and missing data caused by voluntary reporting, time pressures, and irregular work responsibilities.[37]

Time lags in state and jurisdictional compliance with data collection requirements should be phased out or eliminated. Consistent operational definitions of race, offense, arrest, and disposition can and should be implemented. Efforts to standardize data entry and calculations may assist states and localities.[38]

Reducing Racial Bias in Police, Probation, and Judicial Decision Making

Useful efforts to combat racial bias and covert racism have focused on increasing police and juvenile justice professionals' awareness of language and behavior patterns of minority youth, in order to redirect misconceptions of the danger they present, or the level of motivation they possess to cooperate with representatives of the juvenile justice system.[39] Cultural competency training can also be used to improve communication between professionals and individual youth and their families. Additional efforts have included training police officers to recognize the problem of DMC and its prevalence in the communities they police.[40]

Impacts of risk-assessment scales on decision making have been investigated.[41] Specific steps that have resulted from risk assessment reviews include statutory changes that restrict the criteria for detention; open options for placements that include extended family members, neighbors, and nonsecure community settings.[42]

Current conclusions from research indicate that the efficacy of various risk scales based on "actuarial" models or empirical correlates are roughly equal predictors of re-offending and community risk posed by an individual offender.[43] The predictive value of risk scales is enhanced when they include factors such as impulsivity, remorse, callousness-unemotional traits, inconsistent or lax discipline, and early-onset violence. Further longitudinal research, however, is necessary to hone and develop these scales and systematically investigate their unintended results in order to reduce racial bias. Constant review and revision of risk scales, such as that undertaken in Multnomah, Oregon,[44] is necessary to progressively develop "race-neutral" items that retain empirical validity.

An additional strategy to reduce DMC involves the construction of "racial impact statements" to inform legislators and other policy makers.[45] Using this approach, pending legislation is reviewed to identify potentially disparate effects on minorities prior to enactment. An extension could apply this strategy beyond statutes, to include other aspects of juvenile justice policy and administrative rules.

Employing Effective Treatment Interventions for Juvenile Offenders and Their Families to Reduce Delinquency

Treatment interventions for incorrigible, violent, and drug-involved youth have developed respectable evidence bases. Such treatments include functional family therapy, brief strategic family therapy, and multisystemic therapy.

Functional family therapy (FFT) is a clinical approach that integrates behavioral and family systems theory.[46] Evaluators have reported that FFT demonstrated statistically significant reductions in recidivism one year after treatment in felonies (35%), violent crimes (30%), and misdemeanors (21%), when compared to probation.[47]

Brief strategic family therapy (BSFT) adapts models of family therapy to increase cultural relevance for Hispanic families of youth who are engaged in high-risk behaviors, and seeks to change the patterns of family interactions that generate and/or maintain problematic adolescent behavior.[48] BSFT has been used most effectively with substance-abusing Hispanic youth.[49]

Multisystemic therapy (MST) is an intensive and comprehensive community based intervention with serious offenders that targets individual, family, and community factors.[50] In a 20-year follow-up study of serious and violent juvenile offenders receiving MST compared to those receiving individual therapy, felony recidivism rates were significantly lower for MST participants (34.8% vs. 54.8%).[51] A follow-up study of sexual offenders at eight years after intervention indicated that MST participants had lower recidivism rates than youth receiving regular community treatment, (8% vs. 46%) when considering sexual crimes and (29% vs. 58%) nonsexual crimes; MST participants also had 70 percent fewer arrests for all crimes, and spent 80 percent fewer days in detention than youth who received regular community treatment.[52]

Enhancing Community Capacity Building to Improve Youth
Development in Disadvantaged Communities

Community capacity building, in the form of community asset mapping, has been used to address many social ills over the past 20 years, but has not found its way into the mainstream of DMC literature. Community asset mapping specifies a procedure to systematically assess and literally map existing community resources that may be under-utilized, to effect change in an identified community problem.[53] DMC reduction efforts could employ this method to develop capacity for linking at-risk youth and families to community resources to prevent juvenile contact with the justice system, to expand interventions once it occurs, and as aftercare for youth released from placements.

Maximizing Multilevel Multisystem Coordination

The OJJDP has identified several "model programs" for DMC reduction.[54] These programs, however, consist predominantly of discrete efforts to impact the identified causes of DMC, rather than cross-cutting efforts to integrate them. Federal policy requires states to establish DMC boards and name a DMC coordinator, but recent reports indicate that only four states have completed statewide DMC assessments.[55]

Engagement of high-level policy makers in DMC reduction efforts has been recommended as a way to improve policy implementation.[56] An extension of these efforts, however, might include formation of DMC reduction cooperatives at the grassroots level, which could be linked statewide. Cooperative groups could include representatives from the units most affected by the problem, including local police, juvenile justice practitioners, community members, families, and delinquent youth themselves.[57]

CONCLUSION

The juvenile justice system stands as a structure intended to balance social control with social intervention, that is, to simultaneously protect society and dispense justice on individual, family, and community levels. The existence and persistence of DMC, however, calls the balance into question. The fact is that identified groups of people comprise numerical minorities in the general population, yet disproportionately exceed the majority group in the juvenile justice system. When these people have common racial characteristics and are systematically arrested, adjudicated, and incarcerated—whether by intention or ignorance—fundamental American ideals are jeopardized. The words of Martin Luther King Jr., written in the past, echo in the present, "Injustice anywhere is a threat to justice everywhere."[58] True protection of society is possible only when freedom for all citizens is valued as highly as security.

No matter how DMC is measured, it is a real and complex issue with significant personal and societal impacts. The complexity and intransigence of the problem may be daunting, but the need to address it should not be denied or ignored.

DISCUSSION QUESTIONS

1. When you hear the term "minority," what groups to you think of and why? Have your views on minority status changed over time?
2. Discuss some of the socioeconomic issues and problems that impact minority youth and what types of strategies do you think would effectively address their needs?
3. Does the introduction of staff and agency employees who come from minority groups enhance the viability of the criminal justice system? In what ways?
4. In what ways could treatments and interventions be improved by the introduction of culturally-sensitive correctional programming elements? Can you think of some examples of what some of the more promising measures would be?

ADDITIONAL RESOURCES

Andersen, Tia. "Race, Ethnicity, and Structural Variations in Youth Risk of Arrest: Evidence from a National Longitudinal Sample." *Criminal Justice and Behavior* (2015): 0093854815570963.

Cochran, Joshua and Daniel Mears. Race, Ethnic, and Gender Divides in Juvenile Court Sanctioning and Rehabilitative Intervention. *Journal of Research in Crime and Delinquency* 52, no. 2 (2015): 181–212.

Donnelly, Ellen A. "The Disproportionate Minority Contact Mandate an Examination of Its Impacts on Juvenile Justice Processing Outcomes (1997–2011)." *Criminal Justice Policy Review* (2015): 0887403415585139.

Fix, Rebecca L., and Barry R. Burkhart. "Relationships between Family and Community Factors on Delinquency and Violence among African American Adolescents a Critical Review." *Race and Justice* (2015): 2153368715583134.

Goshe, Sonya. "Moving Beyond the Punitive Legacy: Taking Stock of Persistent Problems in Juvenile Justice." *Youth Justice* 15, no. 1 (2015): 42–56.

Miller, Holly Ventura. "Juvenile Justice System Outcomes among Foreign-Born and Native-Born Latinos in the United States: An Exploratory Study." *Youth Violence and Juvenile Justice* (2014): 1541204014547592.

Peck, Jennifer, Micheal Lieber, and Sarah Jane Brubaker. "Gender, Race, and Juvenile Court Outcomes: An Examination of Status Offenders." *Youth Violence and Juvenile Justice* 12, no. 3 (2015): 250–267.

Stevens, Tia and Merry Morash. "Racial/Ethnic Disparities in Boys' Probability of Arrest and Court Actions in 1980 and 2000: The Disproportionate Impact of 'Getting Tough' on Crime." *Youth Violence and Juvenile Justice* 13, no. 1 (2015): 77–95.

Williams, Abigail B., Joseph P. Ryan, Pamela E. Davis-Kean, Vonnie C. McLoyd, and John E. Schulenberg. "The Discontinuity of Offending among African American Youth in the Juvenile Justice System." *Youth & Society* (2014): 0044118X14551322.

RELATED WEBSITES

American Civil Liberties Union, https://www.aclu.org/search/disproportionate%20minority

Kids Counsel.Org, http://www.kidscounsel.org/Out%20of%20Balance%20Failures%20in%20Addressing%20DMC%20in%20CT%20JJ%20system%202003.pdf

Models for Change: System Reform in Juvenile Justice, http://www.modelsforchange.net/about/Action-networks/Disproportionate-minority-contact.html

NCJRS: Justice in Indian Country Special Feature, https://www.ncjrs.gov/justiceinindiancountry/

Office of Juvenile Justice and Delinquency Prevention, http://www.ojjdp.gov/dmc/

SUPPORTING FILMS

American Gangster (2007)
Boyz n the Hood (1991)
Fruitvale Station (2013)
Malcolm X (1992)
"What I Learned as a Kid in Jail: Ismael Nazario" (2014) (TED Talks) https://www.ted.com/talks/ismael_nazario_what_i_learned_as_a_kid_in_jail

NOTES

1. Portions of this chapter were previously published in J. K. Mooradian, "You Can't Go Home Again: Disproportionate Confinement of African-American Juvenile Delinquents," in Marilyn Mcshane and Frank P. Williams (eds.), *Juvenile Violence and Delinquency Interventions: Monsters and Myths*, Vol. 2, pp. 99–118. West Port, CT: Praeger, 2007.

2. Office of Juvenile Justice and Delinquency Prevention (2004).

3. Pope, Lovell, and Hsia (2002).

4. Coleman.

5. Sentencing Project (2014).

6. Office of Juvenile Justice and Delinquency Prevention (2012).

7. Mooradian (2003).

8. Puzzanchera and Hockenberry (2015).

9. Pope, Lovell, and Hsia (2002).

10. "Disproportionate Minority Contact Technical Assistance Manual."

11. Michigan State University (2005).
12. Feyerherm and Butts (2002).
13. Ibid.
14. Piquero (2008).
15. Swift (2012).
16. Piquero (2008).
17. Office of Juvenile Justice and Delinquency Prevention (2012).
18. Juvenile Justice Evaluation Center (2005).
19. Blumstein (1995).
20. Farrington, Loeber, Stouthamer-Loeber, Van Kammen, and Schmidt (1996).
21. Hawkins, Laub, and Lauritson (1998).
22. Office of Juvenile Justice and Delinquency Prevention (2006)
23. Mooradian (2003).
24. Juvenile Justice Evaluation Center (2005).
25. "Youth Violence Data Sheet."
26. Cuevas, Finkelhor, Shattuck, Turner, and Hamby (2013).
27. McGee (2003).
28. Juvenile Justice Evaluation Center (2005).
29. Nellis (2011).
30. Office of Juvenile Justice and Delinquency Prevention (2004).
31. Alexander and Gyamerah (1997).
32. American Prosecutors Research Institute (2001).
33. Graham and Lowery (2006).
34. Bridges and Steen (1998).
35. Mooradian (2003).
36. National Conference of State Legislatures (2009).
37. Michigan State University (2005).
38. "Disproportionate Minority Contact Technical Assistance Manual."
39. Cabaniss, Frabutt, Kendrick, and Arbuckle (2007).
40. Annie E. Casey Foundation (2001).
41. Hoge, Vincent, and Guy (2013).
42. Cabaniss, Frabutt, Kendrick, and Arbuckle (2007).
43. Hoge, Vincent, and Guy (2013).
44. Annie E. Casey Foundation (2001).
45. Mauer (2008).
46. Sexton and Alexander (2002).
47. Sexton and Turner (2011).
48. Szapocznik and Williams (2000).
49. Szapocznik, Schwartz, Muir, and Brown (2012).
50. Henggeler and Borduin (1990).
51. Sawyer and Borduin (2011).
52. Borduin, Schaeffer, and Heiblum (2009).
53. Kretzmann and McKnight (1993).

54. "Model Programs Guide."
55. Office of Juvenile Justice and Delinquency Prevention (2012).
56. Cabaniss, Frabutt, Kendrick, and Arbuckle (2007).
57. Mooradian (2012).
58. King (1963).

REFERENCES

Alexander, Rudolph, and Jacquelyn Gyamerah. "Differential Punishing of African Americans and Whites Who Possess Drugs: A Just Policy or a Continuation of the Past?" *Journal of Black Studies* (1997): 97–111.

American Prosecutors Research Institute. *Disproportionate Minority Confinement: Practical Solutions for Juvenile Justice Professionals.* Alexandria, VA: American Prosecutors Research Institute, 2001.

Annie E. Casey Foundation. *Pathways to Juvenile Detention Reform: Reducing Racial Disparities in Juvenile Detention.* By Elenor Hinter Hoytt, Vincent Schiraldi, Brenda Smith, and Jason Ziedenberg. Baltimore, MD: Annie E. Casey Foundation, 2001.

Blumstein, Alfred. "Youth Violence, Guns, and the Illicit-Drug Industry." *Journal of Criminal Law and Criminology* 86, no. 1 (1995): 10–36.

Borduin, Charles M., Cindy M. Schaeffer, and Naamith Heiblum. "A Randomized Clinical Trial of Multisystemic Therapy with Juvenile Sexual Offenders: Effects on Youth Social Ecology and Criminal Activity." *Journal of Consulting and Clinical Psychology* 77, no. 1 (2009): 26–37.

Bridges, George S., and Sara Steen. "Racial Disparities in Official Assessments of Juvenile Offenders: Attributional Stereotypes as Mediating Mechanisms." *American Sociological Review* (1998): 554–570.

Cabaniss, Emily R., James M. Frabutt, Mary H. Kendrick, and Margaret B. Arbuckle. "Reducing Disproportionate Minority Contact in the Juvenile Justice System: Promising Practices." *Aggression and Violent Behavior* 12, no. 4 (2007): 393–401.

Coleman, Andrea. "A Disproportionate Minority Contact (DMC) Chronology: 1988 to Date." Office of Juvenile Justice and Delinquency Prevention. http://www.ojjdp.gov/dmc/chronology.html.

Cuevas, Carlos A., David Finkelhor, Anne Shattuck, Heather Turner, and Sherry Hamby. "Children's Exposure to Violence and the Intersection between Delinquency and Victimization." *Juvenile Justice Bulletin.* Washington, DC: Office of Juvenile Justice and Delinquency Prevention, 2013.

Disproportionate Minority Contact Technical Assistance Manual. Office of Juvenile Justice and Delinquency Prevention. https://www.ncjrs.gov/html/ojjdp/dmc_ta_manual/dmcfull.pdf.

Farrington, David P., Rolf Loeber, Magda Stouthamer-Loeber, Welmoet B. Kammen, and Laura Schmidt. "Self-Reported Delinquency and a Combined Delinquency Seriousness Scale for Boys, Mothers, and Teachers: Concurrent and Predictive Validity for African-Americans and Caucasians." *Criminology* 34, no. 4 (1996): 493–517.

Feyerherm, William, and Jeffrey Butts. "Recommended Methods for Measuring Disproportionate Minority Contact (DMC)." Presentation, Office of Juvenile Justice and Delinquency Prevention Training Sessions for Juvenile Justice Specialists and DMC Coordinators, 2002.

Graham, Sandra, and Brian S. Lowery. "Priming Unconscious Racial Stereotypes about Adolescent Offenders." *Law and Human Behavior* 28, no. 5 (2004): 483–504.

Hawkins, Darnell, John H. Laub, and Janet Lauritson. "Race, Ethnicity, and Serious Juvenile Offending." In *Serious Violent Juvenile Offenders: Risk Factors and Successful Interventions.* Edited by Rolf Loeber, and David P. Farrington, 30–46. Beverly Hills, CA: Sage, 1998.

Henggeler, Scott W., and Charles M. Borduin. *Family Therapy and Beyond: A Multisystemic Approach to Treating the Behavior Problems of Children and Adolescents.* Pacific Grove, CA: Brooks/Cole, 1990.

Hoge, Robert D., Gina Vincent, and Laura Guy. "Bulletin 4: Prediction and Risk/Needs Assessment." *National Institute of Justice.* July 2013. https://ncjrs.gov/pdffiles1/nij/grants/242934.pdf.

Juvenile Justice Evaluation Center. *Seven Steps to Develop and Evaluate Strategies to Reduce Disproportionate Minority Contact.* By Ashley M. Nellis. Washington, DC: Office of Juvenile Justice and Delinquency Prevention, 2005.

King, Martin Luther (1963). "Letter from Birmingham Jail." *The Atlantic Monthly,* April 16, 1963, 78–88.

Kretzmann, John P., and John L. McKnight. *Building Communities from the Inside Out: A Path toward Finding and Mobilizing a Community's Assets.* Chicago, IL: ACTA Publications, 1993.

Mauer, Marc. "Racial Impact Statements-Changing Policies to Address Disparities." *Criminal Justice.* 23, (2008): 16–21.

McGee, Zina T. "Community Violence and Adolescent Development an Examination of Risk and Protective Factors among African American Youth." *Journal of Contemporary Criminal Justice* 19, no. 3 (2003): 293–314.

Michigan State University. *Assessing DMC in Michigan: Youth Contact with the Justice System, 2003–2004 Report.* By Lori A. Post, Julie A. Hagstrom, Cedrick Heraux, Robin E. Christensen, and Vivek Joshi. East Lansing, MI: DMC Assessment Project, Michigan State University, 2005.

Model Programs Guide. Office of Juvenile Justice and Delinquency Prevention. http://www.ojjdp.gov/mpg/.

Mooradian, John K. *Disproportionate Confinement of African-American Juvenile Delinquents.* New York: LFB Scholarly Publishing, 2003.

Mooradian, John K. "Breaking the Lock: Addressing 'Disproportionate Minority Confinement' in the United States Using a Human Rights Approach." *Journal of Social Work* 12, no. 1 (2010): 37–50.

National Conference of State Legislatures. *Minority Youth in the Juvenile Justice System: Disproportionate Minority Contact.* By Jeff Armour and Sarah Hammond. Denver, CO: National Conference of State Legislatures, 2009.

Nellis, Ashley. "Policies and Practices That Contribute to Racial and Ethnic Disparity in Juvenile Justice." In *Disproportionate Minority Contact: Current Issues and Policies.* Edited by Nicolle Parsons-Pollard, 3–4. Durham, NC: Carolina Academic Press, 2011.

Office of Juvenile Justice and Delinquency Prevention. *Disproportionate Minority Confinement: 2002 Update.* By Heidi M. Hsia, George S. Bridges, and Rosalie McHale. Washington, DC: U.S. Department of Justice, Office of Justice Programs, Office of Juvenile Justice and Delinquency Prevention, 2004.

Office of Juvenile Justice and Delinquency Prevention. *Juvenile Offenders and Victims: 2006 National Report.* By Howard N. Snyder and Melissa Sickmund. Washington, DC: Office of Juvenile Justice and Delinquency Prevention, 2006. http://www.ojjdp.gov/ojstatbb/nr2006/downloads/NR2006.pdf.

Office of Juvenile Justice and Delinquency Prevention. *In Focus Fact Sheet: Disproportionate Minority Contact.* Washington, DC: Office of Juvenile Justice and Delinquency Prevention, 2012. http://www.ojjdp.gov/pubs/239457.pdf.

Piquero, Alex R. "Disproportionate Minority Contact." *The Future of Children* 18, no. 2 (2008): 59–79.

Pope, Carl E., Rick Lovell, and Heidi Hsia. "Disproportionate Minority Confinement: A Review of the Research Literature from 1989 through 2001." *Juvenile Justice Bulletin.* Washington, DC: Department of Justice, Office of Justice Programs, Office of Juvenile Justice and Delinquency Prevention, 2002.

Puzzanchera, Charles, and Sarah Hockenberry. "National Disproportionate Minority Contact Databook." *Office of Juvenile Justice and Delinquency Prevention.* June 15, 2015. http://www.ojjdp.gov/ojstatbb/dmcdb/.

Sawyer, Aaron M., and Charles M. Borduin. "Effects of Multisystemic Therapy through Midlife: A 21.9-Year Follow-Up to a Randomized Clinical Trial with Serious and Violent Juvenile Offenders." *Journal of Consulting and Clinical Psychology* 79, no. 5 (2011): 643–652.

Sentencing Project. *Disproportionate Minority Contact in the Juvenile Justice System.* By Joshua Rovner. Washington, DC: Sentencing Project, 2014.

Sexton, Thomas L., and James Alexander. "Functional Family Therapy: An Empirically Supported, Family-Based Intervention Model for At-Risk Adolescents and Their Families." In *Comprehensive Handbook of Psychotherapy Volume 2: Cognitive-behavioral Approaches.* Edited by Florence W. Kaslow, and Terrence Patterson, 140–177, Hoboken, NJ: Wiley, 2002.

Sexton, Thomas, and Charles W. Turner. "The Effectiveness of Functional Family Therapy for Youth with Behavioral Problems in a Community Practice Setting." *Journal of Family Psychology* 24, no. 3 (2010): 339–348.

Swift, James. "OJJDP Issues Update on Disproportionate Minority Contact." *Juvenile Justice Information Exchange.* December 10, 2012. http://jjie.org/ojjdp-issues-update-on-disproportionate-minority-contact/.

Szapocznik, José, and Robert A. Williams. "Brief Strategic Family Therapy: Twenty-Five Years of Interplay among Theory, Research and Practice in Adolescent Behavior Problems and Drug Abuse." *Clinical Child and Family Psychology Review* 3, no. 2 (2000): 117–134.

Szapocznik, José, Seth J. Schwartz, Joan A. Muir, and C. Hendricks Brown. "Brief Strategic Family Therapy: An Intervention to Reduce Adolescent Risk Behavior." *Couple and Family Psychology: Research and Practice* 1, no. 2 (2012): 134–145.

"Youth Violence Data Sheet." Centers for Disease Control. http://www.cdc.gov/violenceprevention/pdf/yv-datasheet-a.pdf.

Part V

Administering Justice: The Responsibility to Intervene and Treat

PREFACE TO PART V

The Juvenile Justice Imagination

The U.S. Census reports that the proportion of youth living in poverty has increased over the last decade and that poverty disproportionately affects children as a higher proportion of the population under 18 is living at or below the poverty level than the proportion of those 18 years of age or older.[1] More children are being brought up in single-parent homes; however, teen birth rates and high-school-dropout rates have both declined. Unfortunately, those who drop out are far more likely to be institutionalized than those who continue in school, and institutionalization mostly means incarceration in a correctional facility.[2] And, while the decrease in teen birth rates seems to be a positive trend, researchers are uncovering enough information about teen dating violence to label it a "critical health problem," as well as a precursor to domestic violence patterns in later life.[3]

The continuing growth of the at-risk population in communities across the country suggests that we must strive to create new, relevant strategies to address delinquency prevention. In his critique of existing research on juveniles, former commissioner of the Massachusetts' Department of Youth Services, Jerome Miller, commented that "as the theories have grown more realistic and the methodology more complicated, criminologists have grown more detached and disconnected from the stuff of their studies—offenders." He claims that this has resulted in juvenile institutions that are "filled with fabricated aliens made yet more alien by those who should know better, but who insufficiently understand the subjects of their research beyond narrow methodological parameters or highly controlled settings which demean and impoverish human experience."[4]

One of the radical approaches to bringing juveniles back to the community for treatment and reintegration is the idea of deinstitutionalization. When Dr. Miller closed the juvenile detention facilities across his state during his tenure releasing 95 percent of those held in secure confinement by 1972, he began a "great experiment" in youth corrections. In 2015 Nevada made a similar move, closing its only maximum security facility but the motivation was not a deep commitment to rehabilitation but the fact that the private company subcontracted to house and treat the youth had repeatedly been unable to meet the standards required to do so. As Nevada is reported to be one of the most expensive states in which to incarcerate juveniles, spending $195,406 per youth per year on incarceration, one wonders if there is not a better way to handle these youths.[5] For example, Miner-Romanoff[6] outlines a unique eight-week program that educates and sensitizes at-risk students to the workings of the juvenile justice system. Compared with control groups, the intervention group not only demonstrated increased understanding of the law, sentencing, and justice outcomes, but perceived the juvenile system to be fairer than their control counterparts.

As the program described previously demonstrates, to truly realize juvenile "corrections" we must invest in long-term education, prevention, intervention, and treatment. Imagine the innovative educational avenues we could pursue with the roughly $106 billion dollars spent on transferring youth through a punitive adult criminal court system.[7] Perhaps one of the areas that most needs research, discussion, and policy is that which considers the most recent advances in neurophysiology and neuropsychology. The extent to which culpability and even amenability to treatment can even be considered may be addressed by recent insights into brain development and its impact on behavior. As Laurence French explains,

> Generally speaking, hormonal infusion and rapid growth spurts during puberty, coupled with incomplete frontal lobe mylenation (neuronal insulation), creates a likelihood of both increased subcortical impulses and insufficient frontal lobe control over these impulses. And while the process of frontal lobe mylenation is usually complete at the time skeletal growth is completed (usually age 18 in Western societies) it takes another seven years for sufficient pathways to

be etched in the Basal Ganglia (neuronal super highway). This phenomenon accounts for the higher incidence of impulsive behaviors among youth and adults until age 25.[8]

Undoubtedly, the concern and resources we marshal today in order to address the problem of youth reflects our best hope for the future. More than reducing crime and creating healthier communities is the obligation not only to study but also to design, implement, and support the opportunities that will best allow children to thrive and to realize their potential. To do so, we must break the cycles: cycles of violence, cycles of abuse, and cycles of crime.

One of the critical elements of this journey to humane and productive corrections practices is to listen to the juveniles themselves and to invite them to be active participants in their own meaningful change processes. To do this we must listen to their own stories, detailed life chronicles that make them seem not as Miller's aliens, but normal. In the previous edition of this work, a number of books written by young offenders about their experiences both on the streets and in the justice system were profiled. Since then, three other essays have been published that provide what reviewers called "searingly honest," "alarming," "powerful" testimony about the warehousing and dehumanizing of American children locked up in public and private facilities. *Fish: A memoir of a Boy in a Man's Prison* by T. J. Parsell[9] and *I Cried, You Didn't Listen: A Survivor's Expose of the California Youth Authority* by Dwight E. Abbott[10] are both gripping accounts of the underbelly of the youthful incarceration experience. In another fascinating narrative, *My Lobotomy: A Memoir* by Howard Dully and Charles Fleming,[11] the reader is taken through an unbelievable journey of botched "treatment" and secret arrangements to "ice pick" the brain of a 12-year-old boy who had seemingly done nothing wrong.

As we gather personal and statistical information about the current status of youth corrections, we must begin to envision a more responsive and open system of justice, one that is capable of self-assessment and critique. The suggestions that appear in the chapters of this part give us much to think about in terms of prioritizing resources and designing options that are empirically tied to the best practices available today. For us to engage in effective youthful corrections requires an exercise of imagination. Imagine working in a system in which children are valued, one in which their needs are addressed in unique and individual ways. Imagine working with others who are optimistic and upbeat, encouraging, and caring, workers who take the time to mentor and teach, discipline, and listen and who work with families to repair and restructure themselves into healthy functioning units. Imagine healing lives and seeing progress and hopefulness, jobs and education come together as a reality despite the struggle and resistance, complications, and setbacks.

Imagine seeing it work. When someone asks, "What did you do today?" imagine what you would say.

The final part in this book provides a view of the present and future of juvenile justice and delinquency. The most serious treatment (or punishment if you are so inclined) for juveniles is placement in a juvenile correctional facility, and this confinement is documented in this section by Melanie Taylor. Clete Snell and Janet Eguzouwa examine some of the programs that have been proven to work in treating juvenile delinquency. The final chapter in this book, by Ronald Burns and Kendra Bowen, looks to the future of juvenile delinquency and juvenile justice. Where are we, where are we headed, and where should we be headed? This part tackles those questions in juvenile justice and provides an outlook that you can clearly see.

REFERENCES

Abbott, Dwight. *I Cried, You Didn't Listen: A Survivor's Expose of the California Youth Authority.* Oakland, CA: AK Press, 2006.

Dully, Howard, and Charles Fleming. *My Lobotomy: A Memoir.* New York: Random House, 2007.

French, Laurence. "Mental Retardation and the Death Penalty: The Clinical and Legal Legacy." *Federal Probation* 69, no. 1 (2005), 16–20.

Miller, Jerome. *Last One Over the Wall.* Columbus, OH: The Ohio State University Press, 1991.

Miner-Romanoff, Karen. "Juvenile Justice Education for At-Risk High School Youth: A Pilot Program." *Journal of Criminal Justice Education* 26, no. 1 (2015): 22–48.

"Misleading Juvenile Crime Report Reveals Bright Spot." *Reno Gazette Journal.* December 26, 2014, E1.

National Center for Juvenile Justice. *Juvenile Offenders and Victims: 2014 National Report.* By Melissa Sickmund and Charles Puzzanchera. Pittsburgh, PA: National Center for Juvenile Justice, 2014.

National Institute of Justice. *Life Course, Relationship, and Situational Contexts of Teen Dating Violence: A Final Summary Overview.* By Peggy C. Giordano, Monica A. Longmore, and Wendy D. Manning. Washington, DC: National Institute of Justice, 2015.

Parsell, T. J. *Fish: A Memoir of a Boy in a Man's Prison.* New York: Avalon, 2006.

Chapter 11

Juvenile Incarceration: Risks and Remedies

Melanie Taylor

Juvenile incarceration in the United States has long been aimed at rehabilitation, but the reality of the system has fluctuated between a punitive and rehabilitative orientation. The juvenile justice system was founded on the ideal that juveniles were inherently different from adults, thereby making them less culpable for their offenses. Their lack of maturity and self-control necessitated a system that was separate from adults where the focus of confinement was less on crime control and more on reforming behaviors. It was also believed that juveniles could be more easily rehabilitated, further justifying the informal and protective nature of the system. These goals came into question in the 1980s when the United States entered the "get-tough" era, resulting in more punitive treatment of juveniles and adults.[12] Then in the 1990s, perceptions of juveniles shifted following the declaration that an increased number of juveniles were growing more violent and required more formal and punitive responses.[13] The result was that an increased number of juveniles were housed in juvenile and adult correctional institutions.[14]

When responding to juvenile delinquents, criminal justice officials have typically been afforded higher levels of discretion than when dealing with adults. While police, judges, and probation officers tend to resolve cases more informally, once juveniles do enter into correctional institutions, they enter into facilities that strongly resemble prisons. This parallel has been recognized so frequently that juvenile justice advocates have shunned the typical language used to describe juvenile institutions (e.g., "safe schools," "reform schools"), instead opting to refer to them as "prisons."[15] Many institutions demonstrate these perceptions well, with barbed wire, strictly controlled movements, and secure cells. The current chapter explores what happens to juveniles once they enter into juvenile prisons. First, a brief history of juvenile institutions and their conditions will be examined. This is followed by a review of the current status of conditions in juvenile correctional facilities and an overview of how confinement practices of juveniles have changed since the 1970s. The chapter will conclude with model programs in juvenile corrections and potential solutions to the problems plaguing juvenile corrections for the last century.

HISTORY OF JUVENILE CORRECTIONS

The first juvenile institution, the New York House of Refuge, was established in 1825.[16] In the early days of the juvenile justice system, juveniles were institutionalized for committing offenses like stealing, running away, and vagrancy, all of which would now be considered nonserious offenses and would typically be dealt with informally. Rather than providing rehabilitative treatment for juveniles, the primary focus of the institution was hard labor. One examination of the New York House of Refuge from the 1850s to 1930s revealed there was a gap between the rhetoric espoused by administrators that the institution was reforming juveniles humanely and the reality of harsh conditions in the institution.[17] The practices carried out in the facility demonstrated that juveniles were being used for "cheap labor," not being treated from a parental perspective, deprived of basic necessities, and improperly classified, all of which were in contrast to the treatment the facility reportedly provided. Despite the apparent problems with the New York institution, the growing desire for formal controls of juvenile delinquents led to Houses of Refuge being adopted nationally.

In the mid-1850s, reformatories and training schools became more prevalent for the treatment and rehabilitation of juvenile offenders.[18] They focused less upon labor and more on education, an ideology that was more in line with the goal of juvenile reformation, which was the original intent of the juvenile justice system. Over time, juvenile institutions developed an increased focus on mental health treatment, programming, and job training in a variety of different programs including centralized training schools, forestry camps, and ranches.[19]

CURRENT STATUS OF JUVENILE
CORRECTIONAL CONDITIONS

In contrast to adult incarceration patterns, juvenile confinement rates have fairly accurately reflected offending trends over the past 30 years. In the adult system, both crime and incarceration rates increased significantly in the 1970s and 1980s, but as crime decreased in the 1990s, incarceration rates continued to rise. In the juvenile system, incarceration rates decreased in the 1990s, with a current confinement rate of approximately 225 juveniles per 100,000.[20] The decline in juvenile confinement has been due in part to the growing movement to seek alternatives to juvenile detention and treat juveniles in communities.[21] One aspect of juvenile corrections that remains unclear is the number of juveniles transferred from juvenile to adult courts annually. Trends in judicial and prosecutorial waivers to adult court suggest that fewer juveniles are now being transferred, but there is no accurate data on the number of juveniles being statutorily waived.[22] During the get-tough movement, states increasingly allowed for statutory waivers by waiving younger juveniles for less serious offenses, suggesting that fewer juveniles would now be transferred by judges or prosecutors.

Abuses of confined juveniles have decreased since the institutions of the 1800s, but modern-day facilities still experience turmoil (e.g., escapes, staff assaults, and suicides). One survey of nearly 1,000 juvenile facilities (i.e., detention centers, reception centers, training schools, and ranches) that housed over 60,000 youth reported that over a 30-day period, the escape rate was 1.22 per 100 juveniles.[23] The rate of juvenile-on-juvenile assaults was 3.12 per 100 and the juvenile-on-staff assault rate was 1.70 per 100 juveniles. Finally, suicides in juvenile facilities appear to be fairly common. One of the most extensive studies on juvenile suicide practices during confinement found that over a five-year period there were a reported 110 juvenile suicides by youth who were under some form of correctional supervision.[24] Of these 110 reported suicides, 37.9 percent occurred within the first 30 days of incarceration. Despite these issues of violence in juvenile facilities, staff reportedly do not fear assault and other types of victimization committed by the juveniles.[25]

In addition to physical violence, sexual violence is reportedly prevalent in juvenile facilities nationwide.[26] In 2002, nearly 10 percent of confined juveniles reported being sexually victimized by either a staff member or another juvenile. Of those victimized, the overwhelming majority of juveniles were sexually assaulted by a staff member (in 61% of cases no force was used), while only about one-fourth were victimized by another juvenile. In two facilities, over 30 percent of juveniles reported that they had experienced victimization while confined. The typical victims of sexual violence committed by staff were African American males, while victims of other juveniles were typically white females. Juveniles who identified as being homosexual were much more likely to be victimized than heterosexual youths. Eighty-six percent of victimized juveniles reported that they had engaged in more than one unlawful sexual encounter, with 20 percent saying they had experienced 11 or more encounters.

In 2011, the Annie E. Casey Foundation conducted a review of "systematic or recurring maltreatment" against juveniles in correctional facilities across the United States.[27] In order to qualify as having a pattern of abuse (e.g., sexual victimization, failing to protect juveniles from victimization, excessive use of isolation, and physical violence), a state had to have confirmed cases of institutional abuse in federal investigations, been the subject of a class action lawsuit, or had significant evidence of abuse through sources like newspaper articles or other types of exposes. It was found that 22 states had abusive conditions reported since 2000, 10 states had abusive conditions between 1990–2000, six states had abusive conditions reported between 1970 and 1990, and three states had evidence of abusive conditions since 2000. Based upon these reports, it is apparent that abuses against juveniles may be less consistent than in early juvenile institutions, but they persist nationwide to this day. One factor that may significantly contribute to abuses during confinement is facility overcrowding.

IMPACT OF OVERCROWDING

The Office of Juvenile Justice and Delinquency Prevention (OJJDP) publishes the Juvenile Residential Facility Census (JRFC), a biennial report focusing on characteristics of juvenile facilities, including a one-day count of the resident population and the rated capacity of the institution. In 2006, the JRFC reported that 32 percent of institutions were reportedly over the rated capacity.[28] Nine percent of public juvenile facilities were overcrowded and 27 percent of public and private facilities were at capacity, while larger facilities (i.e., 100 residents or more) were more likely to be overcrowded. Despite the decrease in overcrowding over the past decade, the JRFC shows that overcrowding is still concerning.

Numerous lawsuits have also been filed in response to overcrowded conditions in juvenile facilities. The Youth Law Center published a clearinghouse of 41 cases from 1971 to 1994 of documented cases where overcrowding was the basis for the case.[29] For example, a 1982 case in Tucson, Arizona, claimed that the facility was so overcrowded that youth slept on mattresses on the floor and had to "sleep with their feet and legs under the bottom bunk-bed" because the cell was so small. More recently, a lawsuit regarding conditions of California youth facilities led to increased monitoring of the institutions.[30] Similar reports as to the prevalence of overcrowding in juvenile facilities have been made across the United States.[31]

Overcrowding in juvenile institutions results in harms while incapacitated, but can also have long-term impacts on juveniles. One of the most extensive studies to date tested the relationship between institutional factors (e.g., crowding) and outcomes (e.g., suicide attempts, escapes, and juvenile on staff assaults).[32] The survey of 984 correctional institutions showed that crowding was a predictor of suicidal behavior in detention centers, as well as a predictor of juvenile on staff injuries and escapes from training schools. Staff in crowded facilities report feeling stressed out because they can only provide "structure and safety," rather than rehabilitation.[33] Crowding also results in increased violence, unsanitary conditions, decreased services, and a lack of staff attention. Changes in the degree of crowding, while partially the result of increased offending rates, has been due in part to policy reforms that draw more juveniles into the system.

CHANGES IN JUVENILE INCAPACITATION

Confinement practices of juveniles have changed significantly since the founding of the first juvenile institution in the 1800s. Although the juvenile system was founded on an ideal of rehabilitation, the treatment of incarcerated juveniles has varied, with some juveniles being treated like adult offenders and others being diverted from the system. Relatedly, the growth in juvenile diversion programs has led to a net-widening effect on juvenile sentences.[34] More specifically, juveniles who would have once been diverted out of the system have been increasingly pulled into it for the sake of reform. The current section will examine these policy shifts, first by examining how juveniles have been both removed from and placed into adult jails. It will then examine one aspect of net-widening that was seen in the 1980s with the rise of boot camps.

The Juvenile Justice and Delinquency Prevention Act

In 1974, the Juvenile Justice and Delinquency Prevention Act (JJDPA) was passed, requiring significant changes in the confinement practices of juveniles.[35] In order to receive full federal funding for juvenile justice programs, states were required to remove status offenders from secure facilities, remove juveniles under juvenile court jurisdiction from jails, separate juveniles from adults by both sight and sound in cases where juveniles had to be confined in adult facilities, and reduce disproportionate minority contact (DMC). These changes reinforced the foundation of the juvenile justice system that juveniles are different from adults and should be protected from exposure to the criminal justice system. However, one loophole has raised concerns of inappropriate placement of low-level juvenile delinquents. While status offenders are prohibited from confinement, status offenders can violate probation, resulting in a status offender being incapacitated for the probation violation.[36]

Another issue of concern is that juveniles under juvenile court jurisdiction are federally required to be sight and sound separated from adults while incapacitated, but juveniles under adult court jurisdiction do not have the same requirements.[37] Instead, individual states are left to make decisions on the incapacitation of juveniles in jails. As a result, it is estimated that 7,500 juveniles who are being prosecuted in adult court are housed in adult jails on any given day. Upon entering jail, juveniles face unique challenges that are significantly different from those housed in juvenile facilities. For example, juveniles in jail have increased risks of suicide and sexual assault. In order to ensure protection, many jails will keep juveniles completely separate from adults, but this practice results in juveniles having limited social contacts. This essentially equates to juveniles being housed in solitary confinement, further worsening mental health outcomes and the risk of suicide. In addition to incapacitation in adult jails, punitive treatment of juveniles in boot camps has been questioned following several high-profile reports of abuse by staff.

Rise of Juvenile Boot Camps

One of the most significant areas of change in the juvenile justice system and treatment of young offenders came in the 1980s with the advent of juvenile boot camps. Crowding in institutions during the 1980s and the growing ideology that the criminal justice system needed to be tougher on juveniles led to the expansion of boot camps.[38] Boot camps are used for first time and nonviolent offenders as a way to provide an alternative sentence that was both rehabilitative and punitive. They typically use military-style training, physical exercise, and a disciplinary style to treat juvenile offenders,[39] while at the same time boot camps also provide more counseling than other programs.[40]

The public popularity of boot camps led to the rapid expansion of programs nationwide. While boot camps were cheaper than traditional confinement options and decreased overcrowding in state facilities, cases of violence, abuse, and death led to questions over the inhumane treatment of juveniles. Dozens of juveniles have reportedly died in boot camps since the 1980s,[41] but one case in particular received extensive national media attention following the release of footage showing a 14-year-old being physically beaten by correctional officers.[42] In January 2006, Martin Lee Anderson was committed to a juvenile boot camp in Florida. One day after his arrival, he failed to comply with officers' orders to continue physical activity and was subsequently beaten, which resulted in his death. Although an initial autopsy found that he had died from sickle cell anemia, a second autopsy found that "the suffocation was caused by manual occlusion of the mouth, in concert with the forced inhalation of ammonia fumes that cause spasms of the vocal cords, resulting in internal blockage of the upper airway." While the officers were acquitted of any wrongdoing,[43] the public outcry led to the closure of Florida's juvenile boot camps, which were replaced with a new program that prohibited officers from most physical interactions with juveniles.[44]

Research on the effectiveness juvenile boot camps has been highly inconsistent, with some research finding that boot camps reduce recidivism while others find minimal to negative benefits. One of the first long-term follow up studies of boot camp effectiveness occurred at the California Division of Juvenile Justice (DJJ) (formerly California Youth Authority).[45] Juveniles were followed for an average of 7.5 years upon release from a boot camp/parole program titled Leadership, Esteem, Ability, and Discipline (LEAD) and compared with a control group of juveniles incarcerated at DJJ. Results indicated that there were no significant differences in long-term recidivism. While it is not surprising that the boot camp was not found to reduce recidivism, what was contrary to previous literature was the fact that the aftercare program, which is commonly believed to provide better rehabilitation, also showed no positive results. One key problem in the boot camp model is that "no clear theory is offered as to why the use of exercise may decrease criminal propensities."[46] In contrast to the benefits gained by individuals participating in military boot camps (e.g. career, salary), correctional boot camps do not provide such positive gains after incarceration. Boot camps have also been criticized because of their failure to modify environmental factors that initially contributed to delinquent behavior.[47] While boot camps may result in initial changes, the long-term benefits after an individual has returned to a crime producing environment remains to be seen.

REFORMING JUVENILE INSTITUTIONS

The persistence of harmful conditions in juvenile institutions since their inception makes the future of juvenile justice appear grim. While issues may remain in some facilities, model programs across the country show that meaningful changes are being made. These reforms are due, in large part, to increased protections of juveniles' civil rights and shifts in the structure of state institutions. The current section will discuss avenues for upholding the rights of confined juveniles, followed by an examination of structural reforms of juvenile facilities across the country.

Protecting the Civil Rights of Confined Juveniles

The recognition that juvenile facilities are detrimental to rehabilitation and can have abusive conditions has led to national initiatives to improve conditions of confinement, including the Juvenile Detention Alternatives Initiative (JDAI) and the Prison Rape Elimination Act (PREA).

One such avenue for reform is the Civil Rights of Institutionalized Persons Act (CRIPA). Juveniles and their families who sought to challenge treatment in institutions had little legal remedies until the passage of CRIPA in 1980.[48] CRIPA allows the Department of Justice (DOJ) to investigate correctional facilities when a pattern or practice of abuse is occurring in an institution. Following these investigations, most state and county institutions enter into a consent decree to reform institutional conditions in order to avoid costly lawsuits. This results in federal oversight of the agency until the changes required under the consent decree have been made. Since 1980, over 500 juvenile and adult facilities have been under investigation.[49]

One agency that was subject to a DOJ investigation was the Arizona Department of Juvenile Corrections (ADJC) in 2004.[50] Although the agency was under an earlier consent decree and investigation with the federal government as the result of a class action lawsuit in 1990, abuses persisted at the institution. Conditions at the institutions reportedly became so poor that county judges stopped committing juveniles.[51] Most notably, in 2003 and 2004, three juveniles committed suicide within a one-year period, resulting in the ADJC having one of the highest suicide rates in the country. A federal investigator at the time stated "over the explicit objections of mental health staff, one youth was confined in a Separation Unit for more than 18 days, again over the objections of mental health staff."[52] Issues that were noted under the second investigation included improper suicide prevention, abuse of juveniles by other juveniles and staff, a lack of education, and a general denial of rehabilitative services. Following a DOJ investigation, ADJC entered into a consent decree to make 136 reforms in the agency. To accomplish a long-term reform, a new director was hired who reformed the agency including firing staff who had prior allegations of abuse, establishing an investigations unit, retrofitting housing units to prevent future suicides, and implementing a juvenile grievance system. A subsequent examination of the agency nearly 10 years after the CRIPA reforms revealed that most of the changes had been sustained. One exception to this was a later investigation by the Arizona's auditor general (AAG) in 2009, which again found that suicidal juveniles at the ADJC were occasionally placed in separation.[53]

Reforming the Structure of Juvenile Corrections

The most significant change to the juvenile justice model in recent years has been a growing movement to decentralize treatment and custody in favor of small regionalized centers.[54] Historically juveniles have been housed in large institutions, which in many cases were very far from home. It has been argued that the treatment and rehabilitative services offered in these institutions have failed and conditions were poor because juveniles were only being warehoused, rather than having their individual needs met.[55] One of the first sweeping reforms in juvenile confinement occurred in the early 1970s when the commissioner of the Massachusetts Department of Youths Services (DYS), Jerome Miller, restructured the DYS.[56] Concerned that juveniles were being housed in abusive conditions that did not promote rehabilitation, Miller attempted to retrain the staff to be more treatment oriented. When he recognized that these efforts had failed because the ideals of crime control were fully embedded within the officer culture, he made the controversial decision to close most of the large centralized facilities in favor of smaller regional group homes. The new structure of DYS showed very favorable results, as the cost of confinement was significantly reduced and recidivism rates declined.

Arguably the most successful juvenile justice agency to date had similar origins as the ADJC. In 1975, Missouri's Division of Youth Services (MDYS) was under a consent decree because of abusive conditions, which resulted in the development of a statewide advisory board focused on rehabilitative treatment of juveniles.[57] Simultaneously, structural reforms were carried out by opening much smaller facilities that focused on rehabilitation.[58] Today, six distinctive features of the Missouri model include: (1) placement in small regional facilities close to home, (2) a focus on treatment instead of confinement, (3) fostering an environment free from physical and emotional abuse, (4) a focus on academic and vocational skill building, (5) involving families in rehabilitation, and (6) providing transitional aftercare. The result has been that juveniles have significantly lower recidivism rates when compared with those of juveniles leaving other state correctional programs across the country. Additionally, while the cost during treatment is high relative to other programs, in the long run MDYS is cheaper because the treatment duration is shorter than comparable programs and the prevention of future crime reduces other criminal justice expenses.

CONCLUSION

Since the foundation of the first juvenile institution in the early 1800s, confinement practices have changed significantly. While the juvenile justice system has always been oriented more toward rehabilitation than the adult system, treatment of confined juveniles has not always reflected this ideology. Abusive and harmful conditions have been reported in a variety of institutions, including deaths of juveniles sent to boot camps and victimization of juveniles housed in adult jails. Despite these issues, rehabilitation has always remained the focus of treating juveniles and is increasingly reflected in modern day institutions. Due to the recognition that certain types of programs, like boot camps and large correctional institutions, are harmful to the long-term outcomes of juveniles, changes have been made to improve the treatment of delinquents. Policy shifts now provide increased protections for confined juveniles and changes in organizational structures now foster more effective treatment of juveniles.

DISCUSSION QUESTIONS

1. After looking at juvenile incarceration from the early practices and reforms through current times, what elements would you retain and which policies and practices would you do away with?
2. Juvenile detention and incarceration are considered high-risk environments. Which risks do you see as the highest priority for addressing and how can these risks be reduced?
3. Should efforts to provide meaningful treatment programs and interventions be age-, race-, or gender-specific? Why or why not?
4. Given that preventing abuse by staff is an important facet of institutional safety, what characteristics would you look for in potential juvenile corrections employees and what screening mechanisms might you want to use?

ADDITIONAL RESOURCES

Annamma, Subini. "Disabling Juvenile Justice: Engaging the Stories of Incarcerated Young Women of Color with Disabilities." *Remedial and Special Education* 35, no. 5 (2014): 313–324.

Armstrong, Megan, Joyce Hartje, and William P. Evans. "Factors Affecting Juvenile Care Workers' Intent to Continue Working in Juvenile Corrections." *Criminal Justice Review* 39, no. 1 (2014): 5–18.

James, Chrissy, Jessica Asscher, Geert Stams, and Peter van der Laan. "The Effectiveness of Aftercare for Juvenile and Young Adult Offenders." *International Journal of Offender Therapy and Comparative Criminology* (2015): 0306624X15576884.

Melkman, Eran, Tehila Refaeli, Batya Bibi, and Rami Benbenishty. "Readiness for Independent Living among Youth on the Verge of Leaving Juvenile Correctional Facilities." *International Journal of Offender Therapy and Comparative Criminology* (2015): 0306624X15575117.

Peterson-Badali, Michele, Tracey Skilling, and Zohrah Haqanee. "Examining Implementation of Risk Assessment in Case Management for Youth in the Justice System." *Criminal Justice and Behavior* 42, no. 3 (2015): 304–320.

Sellers, Brian. "Community-Based Recovery and Youth Justice." *Criminal Justice and Behavior* 42, no. 1 (2015): 58–69.

Tapia, Mike, Henrika McCoy, and Lynsey Tucker. "Suicidal Ideation in Juvenile Arrestees Exploring Legal and Temporal Factors." *Youth Violence and Juvenile Justice* (2015): 1541204015579522.

Ulmer, Jeffery. "The Black Child-Savers, Criminal Justice Discretion, and the Ghost of George Stinney, Jr." *Contemporary Sociology: A Journal of Reviews* 44, no. 3 (2015): 322–325.

Weaver, Robert, and Derek Campbell. "Fresh Start: A Meta-Analysis of Aftercare Programs for Juvenile Offenders." *Research on Social Work Practice* 25, no. 2 (2015): 201–212.

Wexler, Jade, Nicole Pyle, Andrea Flower, Jacob Williams and Heather Cole. "A Synthesis of Academic Interventions for Incarcerated Adolescents." *Review of Educational Research* 84, no. 1 (2014): 3–46.

RELATED WEBSITES

American Correctional Association, http://www.aca.org/

American Probation and Parole Association, http://www.appa-net.org/eweb/

The Dangers of Detention—Justice Policy Institute, http://www.justicepolicy.org/research/1978

National Center for Youth In Custody, http://npjs.org/ncyc/

National Institute of Corrections (NIC), http://nicic.gov/

SUPPORTING FILMS

Books Not Bars (2008) http://www.snagfilms.com/films/title/books_not_bars

Lock em Up! Juvenile Injustice at Rikers Island Prison (short, 2011)

Minor Differences (2012)

Stealing Time (2011)

Tattooed Tears (California Youth Authority, 1979)

NOTES

1. National Center for Juvenile Justice (2014), 8.
2. Ibid., 15.
3. National Institute of Justice (2015).
4. Miller (1991), 243.
5. "Misleading Juvenile Crime Report Reveals Bright Spot" (2014).
6. Miner-Romanoff (2015).
7. Ibid., 22.
8. French (2005), 16.
9. Parsell (2006).
10. Abbott (2006).
11. Dully and Fleming (2007).
12. Butts and Mears (2001).
13. Feld (1999).
14. Sickmund, Sladky, Kang, Puzzanchera.
15. Pisciotta (1996); Taylor (2013).
16. Bernard (1992).
17. Pisciotta (1996).

18. Feld (1999).

19. Bernard (1992).

20. Sickmund, Sladky, Kang, Puzzanchera.

21. Annie E. Casey Foundation (2011).

22. Butts and Mears (2001).

23. Office of Juvenile Justice and Delinquency Prevention (1994).

24. Office of Juvenile Justice and Delinquency Prevention (2009).

25. Gordon, Moriarty, and Grant (2003).

26. Bureau of Justice Statistics (2013).

27. Annie E. Casey Foundation (2011).

28. Hockenberry, Sickmund, and Sladky (2009).

29. Youth Law Center (1996).

30. Rothfeld (2008).

31. "Crowding in Juvenile Detention: A Problem Solving Approach"; Wang (2003).

32. Office of Juvenile Justice and Delinquency Prevention (1994).

33. Burrell (1998).

34. Decker (1985).

35. Hsia (2004).

36. Taylor (2013).

37. Campaign for Youth Justice (2007).

38. National Institute of Justice (1996).

39. MacKenzie, Brame, McDowall, and Souryal (1995).

40. MacKenzie, Wilson, and Kider (2001).

41. Janofsky (2001)

42. Sexton (2006).

43. Merzer (2010).

44. Cooper (2006).

45. Bottcher and Ezell (2005).

46. Correia (1997).

47. Henggeler and Schoenwald (1994).

48. Dinerstein (1989).

49. Department of Justice (2011); "The Civil Rights of Institutionalized Persons Act: Has It Fulfilled Its Promise?" (2005).

50. Taylor (2013).

51. Taylor, Decker, and Katz (2013).

52. Department of Justice (2004).

53. Office of the Auditor General (2009).

54. Research and Evaluation Center (2011).

55. Annie E. Casey Foundation (2010).

56. Miller (1991).

57. Huebner (2012).

58. Annie E. Casey Foundation (2010).

REFERENCES

Annie E. Casey Foundation. *The Missouri Model: Reinventing the Practice of Rehabilitating Youthful Offenders.* By Richard Mendel. Baltimore, MD: Annie E. Casey Foundation, 2010.

Annie E. Casey Foundation. *No Place for Kids: The Case for Reducing Juvenile Incarceration.* By Richard Mendel. Baltimore, MD: Annie E. Casey Foundation, 2011.

Bernard, Thomas. *The Cycle of Juvenile Justice.* New York: Oxford University Press, 1992.

Bottcher, Jean and Michael E. Ezell. "Examining the Effectiveness of Boot Camps: A Randomized Experiment with a Long-Term Follow Up." *Journal of Research in Crime and Delinquency* 42, no. 3 (2005): 309–332.

Bureau of Justice Statistics. *Sexual Victimization in Juvenile Facilities Reported by Youth, 2012.* By Allen Beck, David Cantor, John Hartge, and Tim Smith. Washington, DC: Bureau of Justice Statistics, 2013.

Burrell, Sue. "The Human Impact of Crowding in Juvenile Detention." *Journal for Juvenile Justice Detention Services* 13, no. 1 (1998): 42–48.

Butts, Jeffrey A., and Daniel P. Mears. "Reviving Juvenile Justice in a Get-Tough Era." *Youth & Society* 33, no. 2 (2001): 169–198.

Campaign for Youth Justice. *Jailing Juveniles: The Dangers of Incarcerating Youth in Adult Jails in America.* By Arya Neelum. Washington, DC: Campaign for Youth Justice, 2007.

"The Civil Rights of Institutionalized Persons Act: Has It Fulfilled Its Promise?" *National Council on Disability.* August 8, 2005. http://www.ncd.gov/publications/2005/08082005.

"Crowding in Juvenile Detention: A Problem Solving Approach." *Office of Juvenile Justice and Delinquency Prevention.* April 27, 2000. http://www.juvenilenet.org/jjtap/archives/crowding/partcpnt.pdf.

Cooper, Robert. "Florida Boot Camps to Close." *USA Today,* April 26, 2006. http://usatoday30.usatoday.com/news/nation/2006-04-26-boot-camps_x.htm.

Correia, Mark. "Boot Camps, Exercise, and Delinquency: An Analytical Critique of the Use of Physical Exercise to Facilitate Decreases in Delinquent Behavior." *Journal of Contemporary Criminal Justice* 13, no. 2 (1997): 94–113.

Decker, Scott. "A Systematic Analysis of Diversion: Net Widening and Beyond." *Journal of Criminal Justice* 13, no. 3 (1985): 207–216.

Department of Justice. *CRIPA Investigation of Adobe Mountain School and Black Canyon School in Phoenix, Arizona; and Catalina Mountain School in Tucson, Arizona.* Washington, DC: U.S. Department of Justice, Civil Rights Division, 2004.

Department of Justice. *Department of Justice Activities under the Civil Rights of Institutionalized Persons Act.* Washington, DC: U.S. Department of Justice, Office of Legislative Affairs, 2011.

Dinerstein, Robert. "Rights of Institutionalized Disabled Persons." In *One Nation, Indivisible: The Civil Rights Challenge for the 1990s.* Edited by Reginald C. Govan and William L. Taylor, 388–413. Washington, DC: Citizens' Commission on Civil Rights, 1989.

Feld, Barry. *Bad Kids: Race and the Transformation of the Juvenile Court. Studies in Crime and Public Policy.* New York: Oxford University Press, 1999.

Gordon, Jill, Laura Moriarty and Patricia H. Grant. "Juvenile Correctional Officers' Perceived Fear and Risk of Victimization Examining Individual and Collective Levels of Victimization in Two Juvenile Correctional Centers in Virginia." *Criminal Justice and Behavior* 30, no. 1 (2003): 62–84.

Henggeler, Scott and Sonja K. Schoenwald. "Boot Camps for Juvenile Offenders: Just Say No." *Journal of Child and Family Studies* 3, no. 3 (1994): 243–248.

Hockenberry, Sarah, Melissa Sickmund, and Anthony Sladky. "Juvenile Residential Facility Census, 2006: Selected Findings." *Juvenile Offenders and Victims: National Report Series.* Washington, DC: Office of Juvenile Justice and Delinquency Prevention, 2009.

Hsia, Heidi. "OJJDP Formula Grants Program Overview." *OJJDP Fact Sheet.* Washington, DC: Office of Juvenile Justice and Delinquency Prevention, 2004.

Huebner, Beth M. "The Missouri Model: A Critical State of Knowledge." In *Reforming Juvenile Justice: A Developmental Approach.* Edited by Richard J. Bonnie, Robert L. Johnson, Betty M. Chemers, and Julie A. Schuck, 411–429. Washington, DC: The National Academies Press, 2012.

Janofsky, Michael. "States Pressed as 3 Boys Die at Boot Camps." *The New York Times,* July 15, 2001. http://www.nytimes.com/2001/07/15/us/states-pressed-as-3-boys-die-at-boot-camps.html.

MacKenzie, Doris, David Wilson, and Suzanne B. Kider. "Effects of Correctional Boot Camps on Offending." *The Annals of the American Academy of Political and Social Science* 578, no. 1 (2001): 126–143.

MacKenzie, Doris, Robert Brame, David McDowall, and Claire Souryal. "Boot Camp Prisons and Recidivism in Eight States." *Criminology* 33, no. 3 (1995): 327–357.

Merzer, Martin. "U.S.: No Charges in Florida Boot Camp Death." *NBC News,* April 16, 2010. http://www.nbcnews.com/id/36599286/ns/us_news-crime_and_courts/t/us-no-charges-florida-boot-camp-death/#.VPI4ai79wSk.

Miller, Jerome. *Last One Over the Wall: The Massachusetts Experiment in Closing Reform Schools.* Columbus: Ohio State University Press, 1991.

National Institute of Justice. *Boot Camps for Juvenile Offenders.* By Blair B. Bourque, Mei Han, and Sarah M. Hill. Washington, DC: National Institute of Justice, 1996.

Office of Juvenile Justice and Delinquency Prevention. *Conditions of Confinement: Juvenile Detention and Corrections Facilities.* By Dale G. Parent, Valerie Lietner, Stephen Kennedy, Lisa Livens, Daniel Wentworth, and Sarah Wilcox. Washington, DC: Office of Juvenile Justice and Delinquency Prevention, 1994.

Office of Juvenile Justice and Delinquency Prevention. *Juvenile Suicide in Confinement: A National Survey.* By Lindsay Hayes. Washington, DC: Office of Juvenile Justice and Delinquency Prevention, 2009.

Office of the Auditor General. *Arizona Department of Juvenile Corrections: Suicide Prevention and Violence and Abuse Reduction Efforts.* Phoenix, AZ: State of Arizona, Office of the Auditor General, 2009.

Pisciotta, Alexander. *Benevolent Repression: Social Control and the American Reformatory-Prison Movement.* New York: NYU Press, 1996.

Research and Evaluation Center. *Resolution, Reinvestment, and Realignment: Three Strategies for Changing Juvenile Justice.* By Jeffrey Butts and Douglas Evans. New York: John Jay College of Criminal Justice, City University of New York, 2011.

Rothfeld, Michael. "Judge Acts on Juvenile Hall Conditions." *Los Angeles Times,* March 13, 2008. http://articles.latimes.com/2008/mar/13/local/me-monitor13.

Sexton, Christine. "Autopsy Ties Boy's Death to Boot Camp." *The New York Times,* May 6, 2006. http://www.nytimes.com/2006/05/06/us/06bootcamp .html?_r=2&.

Sickmund, Melissa, T. J. Sladky, Wei Kang, and Charles Puzzanchera. "Easy Access to the Census of Juveniles in Residential Placement: 1997–2013." *Office of Juvenile Justice and Delinquency Prevention.* http://www.ojjdp.gov/ ojstatbb/ezacjrp/.

Taylor, Melanie. *A Case Study of the Civil Rights of Institutionalized Persons Act: Reforming the Arizona Department of Juvenile Corrections.* PhD diss., Arizona State University, 2013.

Taylor, Melanie, Scott Decker, and Charles Katz. "Consent Decrees and Juvenile Corrections in Arizona: What Happens When Oversight Ends." *Justice Research and Statistics Association Forum* 3, no. 31 (2013): 1–5.

Wang, Justina. "Invisible Offenders: Juvenile Detention Centers Struggle to Meet the Unique Needs of Their Fastest-Growing Population." *The Chicago Reporter,* December 1, 2003. http://www.thefreelibrary.com/Invisible+ offenders%3A+juvenile+detention+centers+struggle+to+meet+the . . . -a01 12355531.

Youth Law Center. *Juvenile Detention and Training School Overcrowding: A Clearinghouse for Court Cases.* San Francisco, CA: Youth Law Center, 1996.

Chapter 12

What Works with
Juvenile Offenders?

Clete Snell and Janet Eguzouwa

For much of the history of the field of criminology, delinquency prevention or intervention strategies often developed as a common-sense adaptation to the popular theory of the time. Few were ever evaluated for their effectiveness in reducing delinquency. Both theory and evaluation research have come a long way since that time. However, there continue to be challenges in evaluating what works. Most program evaluations have serious design flaws. Few use the "gold standard" of experimental designs with random assignment to treatment groups and alternative interventions.[1] Most program evaluations utilize a quasi-experimental design comparing outcomes for the treatment group with a nonrandom comparison group. At least one study has found that design flaws actually have a systematic effect on findings such that weaker designs are more likely to report positive effects.[2]

There are also inconsistencies in the reviews of delinquency programs.[3] There are different top 10 lists depending on the screening criteria and the type of outcomes. Many reviews summarize evaluation studies and come to a general conclusion about effectiveness.[4] These reviews are inherently subjective. One modern trend to reduce the subjectivity of reviews is to use meta-analysis. The results of small localized individual studies are often insufficient to provide us with confident answers to questions of general importance.[5] Meta-analysis allows us to compare or combine results across a set of similar studies. In the individual study, the units of analysis are the individual observations. In meta-analysis the units of analysis are the results of individual studies. While meta-analysis does include the problem of researcher subjectivity in determining the criteria for study inclusion, it is a much more accepted technique for examining the effectiveness of programs.[6] In fact, in criminal justice too few studies have used randomized designs, making it unrealistic to restrict program reviews by those criteria.[7]

Because of the lack of true experiments in criminal justice, it is important for readers and reviewers to understand the measurements and methods in these studies. Knowing that something works is often not enough; researchers want to know why it works. Not all components from a program will be equally effective. Knowing which parts of a program are effective and knowing which ones are not can allow the program to be fine-tuned in such a way as to increase effectiveness, decrease cost, and ultimately extend the life of the program. In a similar vein, researchers can define success in a number of different ways. One study's definition of success may be a failure in another study. Take a typical drug court for example. How is recidivism defined? Is it getting probation revoked, getting convicted on a different charge, being charged with a new crime, being arrested, or using drugs or alcohol? The varying definitions of success necessitate a discussion of the methods and measurements used in the studies. Therefore, when reading through this chapter, one may notice a methods heavy, measurement heavy discussion. However, these measurements and methods provide a context for what works and why it works.

The Blueprints for Violence Prevention initiative actually uses an even stricter standard in certifying program effectiveness.[8] To make it to the Blueprint list a program must demonstrate effects on problem behaviors using a rigorous experimental design, its effects must persist after participants are no longer involved in the program, and it must be successfully replicated in another site.[9] This strict criterion has resulted in the promotion of only 11 Blueprint programs.[10]

IMPLEMENTATION OF THE BLUEPRINTS FOR VIOLENCE PREVENTION PROGRAMS

Eleven model juvenile delinquency programs have been identified by the Center for the Study and Prevention of Violence's Blueprints for Violence Prevention initiative.[11] The project was developed with the goals of identifying effective, evidence-based violence prevention programs and replicating those programs nationally.[12] Mihalic and Irwin conducted a two-year evaluation of the implementation of eight of the 11 model programs in 42 replication sites, specifically examining adherence to program goals, percentage of the core program components achieved, dosage (the amount of treatment), and sustainability.[13] Most of the sites faced serious challenges when implementing the programs in the real world.[14] The quality of technical assistance, consistent staffing, and community support were all related to successful program implementation.[15] Additionally, the quality of program materials, time required for implementation, and complexity of the program were related to successful implementation.[16]

The Study Group on Very Young Offenders

The Office of Juvenile Justice and Delinquency Prevention (OJJDP) developed a Study Group on Very Young Offenders.[17] The study group focused on persistent delinquency between the ages of 7 to 12 and disruptive and aggressive behavior during the toddler years.[18] The study group consisted of 23 criminologists with expertise in delinquency. They reviewed hundreds of studies, conducted analysis of existing data, and surveyed more than one hundred practitioners in the field.[19] Among the most important findings was that the majority of serious, violent, and chronic offenders have a history of conduct problems and the antisocial careers of male juvenile offenders begin, on average, at age seven.[20]

It was the study group's recommendation that interventions must be developed at a much younger age than the current practice of intervention in adolescence.[21] They advocated prevention and intervention programs that target multiple domains of risk.[22] The study group cited four programs developed specifically for young delinquent offenders. The Michigan Early Offender Program provides specialized, intensive, in-home interventions to youth who are aged 13 or younger at the first time of adjudication and have two or more prior police contacts.[23] The Toronto Under 12 Outreach Project emphasizes a multisystemic approach combining interventions for children, parents, schools, and communities.[24] Finally, the Sacramento County Community Intervention Program provides services coordinated by a community intervention specialist. This specialist conducts a family assessment in the areas of mental health, substance abuse, finances, family functioning, and social functioning and coordinates service delivery.[25]

Principles of Effective Prevention and Intervention Programs

In a review-of-reviews approach, Nation and colleagues[26] sought to identify general principles of effective prevention strategies in the areas of substance abuse, risky sexual behavior, school failure, and juvenile delinquency and violence. They identified nine principles within the three areas; program characteristics, matching programs to the target population, and implementing and evaluating prevention programs.[27]

In terms of program characteristics, effective programs are comprehensive. They include multiple interventions targeting the same problem.[28] They also include multiple settings such as the community, family, school, and peer groups.[29] Additionally, effective programs use varied teaching methods that include interactive instruction and skill development such as role-playing peer pressure resistance.[30] Effective programs have sufficient dosage. This aspect refers to exposure to the intervention in enough intensity or over long enough time to have the desired impact. Some prevention programs increase the intensity of the treatment to counter the specific risk of individuals and provide follow-up services when needed.[31] Effective programs are theory driven.[32] Many delinquency prevention programs are not based upon theories, or theories that have empirical support. Theory-based interventions that focus on the known causes of delinquency and include research on the best methods for targeting risk factors were also related to positive outcomes.[33] Fourth, most reviews emphasized the importance of positive relationships. Some emphasized improving parent–child relationships,[34] while others suggested positive peer relationships,[35] or adult mentors.[36]

In terms of matching the program with a target population effective prevention programs intervene at the right time to have the greatest impact.[37] Many programs are implemented after youth are already displaying the problem behavior. Many agree that the transition from elementary to middle school is an important time for prevention of problem behaviors.[38] Prevention programs also need to be culturally relevant to the participants. They should take into account local community norms and cultural beliefs and practices.[39]

In terms of implementation and evaluation, effective programs include staff that are competent, well-trained, supported, and effectively supervised.[40] Outcome evaluations are critical in determining program impact, providing feedback to practitioners, and avoiding the replication of ineffective and expensive programs.[41]

Lipsey also examined the characteristics of effective interventions in a meta-analysis of juvenile delinquency programs.[42] He found that programs that emphasized a therapeutic approach were most successful and discipline-oriented programs were least effective in reducing delinquency.[43] Additionally, the interventions examined were equally effective regardless of the level of supervision (e.g., custodial facility, community supervision, or no official supervision).[44] The greatest reductions in recidivism occurred among the highest risk youth.[45] Finally, the largest effects on reducing delinquency came from cognitive-behavioral programs but other interventions (i.e., restorative justice, counseling, and multiple coordinated services) were nearly as effective.[46]

Early Childhood Development and Parenting Programs

Anderson and colleagues conducted a meta-analysis of early childhood development programs that were publicly funded and systematic in nature.[47] The review team assessed program effectiveness in the areas of cognitive, social, health, and family outcomes among at-risk youth.[48] The meta-analysis found strong support for the impact of early childhood development programs on cognitive development and increasing readiness to learn.[49] There were fewer studies that examined the impact of early development programs on social risk behaviors such as teen pregnancy and delinquency. These studies found significant improvements in high-school graduation and employment.[50] They found significant decreases in teen pregnancies and delinquency.[51]

Farrington and Welsh conducted a meta-analysis of family-based crime prevention programs.[52] They included evaluations where the family was the focus of the intervention, a measure of delinquency or anti-social behavior was included, a randomized or well-controlled design was used, and the sample size was 50 participants or more.[53] There were 40 different evaluations included in the analysis in the general areas of home visiting, preschool, parent training, school-based, home/community, and multisystemic therapy programs.[54] Over half of the evaluations found a significant decrease in delinquency that persisted long term. The mean effect size was 0.321.[55] Behavioral parent training programs were most effective and school-based programs were least effective.[56] All other types of family-based programs were effective in reducing delinquency.[57] The authors note that research is needed to identify the particular components of family-based programs that are effective in reducing delinquency.[58]

Another meta-analysis examined the impact of early parenting training programs for families with children up to age five years in preventing antisocial behavior and delinquency.[59] Parent training programs are designed to provide parents tools to engage in effective child rearing with the ultimate goal of reducing antisocial behavior. The analysis included 55 studies using randomized and controlled experimental designs with pre-post evaluations of family programs.[60] The results indicated that family and parent training programs can have a small to moderate effect (ES = 0.35) in reducing antisocial behavior and delinquency.[61] There was not a significant difference in the effectiveness of parent training versus home visit programs.[62]

Kaminski, Valle, Filene, and Boyle conducted a meta-analysis of parenting programs designed for children ages 0–7 with the purpose to identify whether specific components of the program (i.e., content covered, delivery method) were related to better outcomes.[63] Consistent with other reviews parent behavioral training programs have a significant impact on changing parenting behavior and preventing early childhood behavior problems.[64] The results suggest that the parenting programs included in the analysis had a larger impact on parenting knowledge and attitudes then behaviors and skills.[65] The programs had a greater impact on internalizing behaviors then externalizing behaviors and for developing cognitive and educational skills more than social skills or prosocial behavior.[66] Programs that required parents to practice skills with their own children had larger effects on parenting behaviors.[67] Programs that taught emotional communication were also more effective.[68] Emotional communication includes active listening, teaching parents to help identify and deal with emotions, and teaching parents to reduce negative communication. Positive interaction between parents and children and consistency in discipline reduced negative external behaviors such as aggression.[69]

Cognitive-Behavioral Therapy

Cognitive behavioral therapy (CBT) attempts to discover and understand the nature of dysfunctional thoughts in order for them to be modified.[70] It assumes that cognitive deficits and distortions are learned and can be changed by emphasizing individual accountability and teaching offenders to understand how their thinking processes are related to their criminal behavior.[71]

Landenberger and Lipsey[72] conducted a meta-analysis of programs that were either well-known cognitive-behavioral therapy programs, such as Moral Reconation Therapy[73] and Thinking for a Change,[74] or programs that were substantially similar in purpose and methods. The analysis included juvenile and adult offenders and the outcome variable was criminal offending after treatment. Overall, there was a 25 percent decrease in recidivism among those who received CBT as compared to a control group.[75] The most effective CBT programs reduced recidivism by 50 percent compared to control groups.[76] The CBT programs that had the largest impact on recidivism included components on anger control and interpersonal problem solving.[77] None of the major CBT brand name programs produced significantly lower recidivism rates than non-brand name programs.[78]

Wilson, Bouffard, and Mackenzie conducted a meta-analysis of cognitive-behavioral programs delivered solely in group settings to adult and juvenile offenders.[79] In the 20 studies examined 18 found that cognitive-behavioral treatments have a moderate effect in reducing criminal behaviors among convicted adult and juvenile offenders.[80] The two studies that reported no effect were considered weak in their methodology.[81]

The sample of studies included six evaluations of Moral Reconation Therapy (MRT), seven evaluations of Reasoning and Rehabilitation (R&R), and seven other less-known cognitive-behavioral programs. The results found the largest positive effects with the less-known programs followed closely by MRT.[82] An important limitation of this meta-analysis was that about half of the studies included were methodologically weak.

Lipsey, Landenberger, and Wilson improved upon the Wilson et al. meta-analysis by only including CBT evaluations that used randomized designs or quasi-experimental designs where the treatment and control groups were matched, statistically controlled, or compared on risk-related variables.[83] A total of 58 CBT evaluations met their eligibility criteria.[84] Among all studies, they found a 25 percent reduction in recidivism among offenders who received CBT therapy in comparison to those who did not receive it.[85] Interestingly, studies using randomized designs did not have significantly different effect sizes than those without random assignment.[86] There was no difference in program effectiveness between adult and juvenile offenders.[87] Dosage, measured as number of program hours, was related to the effectiveness of CBT in that more program dosage led to lower recidivism rates.[88] Additionally, CBT is more effective when combined with other services such as mental health counseling, employment and vocational training, and educational programs.[89] Finally, major named types of CBT programs were not more effective than a generic category of programs.[90] Among program elements that were related to lower recidivism were individual attention (one-on-one treatment that supplements CBT group sessions), anger control (identifying triggers and cues that provoke anger), and cognitive restructuring (activities and exercises aimed at recognizing and modifying the distortions and errors that characterize criminogenic thinking).[91]

McCart, Priester, Davies, and Azen conducted a meta-analysis comparing behavioral parent-training (BPT) with CBT on reducing antisocial behavior (measured as aggression or delinquency) among youth.[92] There were 30 BPT and 41 CBT studies included in the analysis.[93] Overall, BPT had a larger effect (0.47) than CBT (0.35) on reducing antisocial behavior.[94] BPT was significantly more effective for youth aged 6–12 years than CBT.[95] Youth in this age range are more likely more influenced by their parents and are less developed in their abstract cognitive skills.[96] Adolescents aged 13–18 were much more likely to benefit from CBT.[97]

School-Based Intervention Programs

School-based programs typically focus on fighting, verbal conflict, and disruptive behavior within schools. Schools that do not effectively control disruptive behavior may inadvertently create an environment where violence is normative. Wilson, Lipsey, and Derzon conducted a meta-analysis of school-based programs.[98] Criteria for the analysis included programs designed for preschool through 12th graders, an outcome variable that represented aggressive behavior, and experimental or quasi-experimental designs that included control conditions and pre-test and post-tests.[99] The analysis found a 0.25 mean effect size on aggressive behavior among the 172 evaluations.[100] Programs were more effective in schools with a higher baseline of disruptive behavior.[101] Behavioral and counseling approaches were more effective than multimodel and peer mediation programs.[102] Interventions were more effective when they were relatively intense, used one-on-one formats, and were administered by teachers.[103] The vast majority of programs included in this analysis were demonstration programs; only 26 programs were routinely used in schools.[104]

Wilson and Lipsey updated their analysis of school-based programs to include more recent programs created to control aggressive and disruptive behavior. They used the same inclusion criteria as in the original meta-analysis.[105] The 249 eligible studies were divided into four categories: (1) universal programs delivered to all students in a classroom setting; (2) selected/indicated programs designed for students selected because of their behavior problems; (3) special school or classes developed away from mainstream classrooms such as alternative schools and schools-within-schools; and (4) comprehensive/multimodel programs that include several distinct intervention elements.[106] Overall, school-based programs have a positive effect on reducing aggressive and disruptive behavior (decrease of 25–33%).[107] Universal programs and selected/indicated programs were the most effective approaches.[108]

In a narrower examination of school-based programs, Merrell, Gueldner, Ross, and Isava conducted a meta-analysis of bullying intervention programs.[109] Because there are a relatively small number of evaluations of antibullying programs the criteria for inclusion in the meta-analysis were somewhat broad and resulted in only 16 studies.[110] The analysis found that the school bullying interventions included in the analysis had a modest positive effect.[111] The interventions were more likely to positively impact knowledge, attitudes, and self-perceptions than bullying behavior.[112]

A more recent meta-analysis of antibullying program evaluations included more rigorous research designs and resulted in 44 program evaluations.[113] Overall, the analysis found the interventions were successful in reducing bullying. Bullying behavior decreased by 20–23 percent and victimization decreased by 17–20 percent.[114] Programs that were more intensive in approach, included meetings with parents, firm disciplinary methods, and improved playground supervision were most effective in reducing bullying.[115] Peer-based programs actually led to an increase in bullying behavior.[116]

CONCLUSION

This review relied primarily on meta-analyses and systematic reviews of existing programs. Meta-analysis permits us to develop general conclusions from the rather large number of evaluations that have been conducted since the What Works? movement gained momentum. It has moved beyond finding model programs to finding model practices. One conclusion that can be drawn from this review of best practices is that practitioners do not need to implement a model program. In fact, many of the programs reviewed performed better than Blueprint model programs in reducing delinquency. Additionally, there does not appear to be a specific type of intervention that is far more effective than other interventions. All of the different types of programs were effective in preventing or reducing delinquency. However, it appears that specific interventions are more effective at different stages of development. Finally, it has become increasingly clear that intervention programs are most effective when they target juvenile offenders that pose the greatest risk of recidivism.

DISCUSSION QUESTIONS

1. What are some of the challenges in trying to determine what an effective delinquency program is? What would be your criteria for considering a program or intervention a success?
2. Explain what we have learned from the Blueprints for Violence Prevention Programs and how relevant that might be to other types of less serious delinquency?
3. When conducting research on program effectiveness, we often compare those in the treatment to a "control group". What would you consider a meaningful control group and how would you go about obtaining the participation of such a control group?
4. According to research results, what appear to be the most effective programs or program components and which offenders appear to get the most out of treatment?

ADDITIONAL RESOURCES

Burke, Jeffrey, and Rolf Loeber. "The Effectiveness of the Stop Now and Plan (SNAP) Program for Boys at Risk for Violence and Delinquency." *Prevention Science* 16, no. 2 (2015): 242–253.

deVries, Sanne, Machteld Hoeve, Mark Assink, Geert Jan J. M. Stams and Jessica Asscher. "Practitioner Review: Effective Ingredients of Prevention Programs for Youth at Risk of Persistent Juvenile Delinquency-Recommendations for Clinical Practice." *Journal of Child Psychology and Psychiatry* 56, no. 2 (2015): 108–121.

Fagan, Abigail, and Andrea Lindsey. "Gender Differences in the Effectiveness of Delinquency Prevention Programs: What Can Be Learned from Experimental Research?" *Criminal Justice and Behavior* 41, no. 9 (2014): 1057–1078.

Kuhn, Emily and Robert Laird. "Family Support Programs and Adolescent Mental Health: Review of Evidence." *Adolescent Health, Medicine & Therapeutics* 5 (2014): 127–142.

Land, Kenneth. "Delinquency Referrals; Predictive and Protective Factors for Serious, Violent, and Chronic Offenders; and Juvenile Justice Interventions." *Criminology & Public Policy* 13, no. 1 (2014): 79–82.

May, Jessica, Kristina Osmond, and Stephen Billick. "Juvenile Delinquency Treatment and Prevention: A Literature Review." *Psychiatric Quarterly* 85, no. 3 (2014): 295–301.

Nissen, Laura Burney. "Alcohol and Drug Prevention, Intervention, and Treatment Literature; A Bibliography for Best Practices." *Best Practices in Mental Health* 10, no. 1 (2014): 59–98.

Rubin, Ted. "Community-Based Interventions and Collaborations Further and Sustain Juvenile Justice Progress." *Juvenile Justice Update* 20, no. 6 (2015): 1–8.

Sellers, Brian. "Community-Based Recovery and Youth Justice." *Criminal Justice and Behavior* 42, no. 1 (2014): 58–69.

Solomon, David, Brittni Morgan, Kia Asberg, and David McCord. "Treatment Implications Based on Measures of Child Abuse Potential and Parent Mental Health: Are We Missing and Intervention Opportunity?" *Children and Youth Services Review* 43, (2014): 153–159.

RELATED WEBSITES

Big Brothers Big Sisters of America, http://www.bbbs.org

Crime Solutions, www.CrimeSolutions.gov

Delinquency and Juvenile Justice, http://www.sheldensays.com/juvenile_justice_page.htm

Girls and Juvenile Justice, http://www.sheldensays.com/girlsjuvjustice.htm

Peter Greenwood: Prevention and Intervention Programs for Juvenile Offenders, http://www.princeton.edu/futureofchildren/publications/docs/18_02_09.pdf

Social Programs That Work, http://evidencebasedprograms.org/1366-2/multisystemic-therapy-for-juvenile-offenders

SUPPORTING FILMS

Video Series: Through Our Eyes: Children, Violence and Trauma (2014), http://www.ovc.gov/pubs/ThroughOurEyes/

White Squall (1996)

NOTES

1. Sherman et al. (1998), 6.
2. Weisburd, Lum, and Petrosino (2001), 64.

3. Greenwood (2008), 187.
4. Ibid.
5. Ibid., 188.
6. Ibid., 189.
7. Farrington and Petrosino (2001), 36.
8. Elliott (1998), 2.
9. Ibid.
10. Ibid.
11. Mihalic and Irwin (2003), 313.
12. Ibid.
13. Ibid., 313–314.
14. Ibid., 323.
15. Ibid.
16. Ibid.
17. Loeber, Farrington, and Petechuk (2003), 3.
18. Ibid.
19. Ibid.
20. Ibid., 4.
21. Ibid., 9.
22. Ibid., 10.
23. Howitt and Moore (1991), 28.
24. Hyrnkiw-Augimeri, Pepler, and Goldberg (1991), 8.
25. Child Welfare League of America (1997), 5.
26. Nation et al. (2003), 450.
27. Ibid.
28. Ibid., 451.
29. Sagrestano and Paikoff (1997), 8.
30. "Preventing Drug Use among Children and Adolescents" (2003), 10.
31. Carnahan (1994), 105.
32. Nation et al. (2003), 450.
33. Kumpfer (1997), 12.
34. Kumpfer, and Alvarado (1995), 260.
35. Mulvey, Arthur, and Reppucci (1993), 162.
36. Grossman, Baldwin, and Tierney (1998), 420.
37. Nation et al. (2003), 453.
38. "Preventing Drug Use among Children and Adolescents" (2003), 5.
39. Ramey, Landesman and Ramey (1992), 137.
40. Lewis, Battistich, and Schaps (1990), 50.
41. Hansen (2002), 430.
42. Lipsey (2009), 128.
43. Ibid., 137.
44. Ibid., 138.
45. Ibid.
46. Ibid., 144.

47. Anderson et al. (2003), 35.
48. Ibid., 34.
49. Ibid., 39.
50. Ibid.
51. Ibid.
52. Farrington and Welsh (2003), 127.
53. Ibid., 129.
54. Ibid.
55. Ibid., 143.
56. Ibid.
57. Ibid., 145.
58. Ibid.
59. Piquero, Farrington, Welsch, Tremblay, and Jennings (2009), 85.
60. Ibid., 46.
61. Ibid., 78.
62. Ibid., 85.
63. Kaminski, Valle, Filene, and Boyle (2008), 570.
64. Ibid., 580.
65. Ibid.
66. Ibid.
67. Ibid.
68. Ibid.
69. Ibid.
70. Lipsey, Landenberger, and Wilson (2007), 4.
71. Ibid.
72. Landenberger and Lipsey (2005), 453–454.
73. Little and Robinson (1989), 85.
74. Bush, Glick, and Taymans (1997).
75. Landenberger and Lipsey (2005), 460.
76. Ibid., 469.
77. Ibid., 468.
78. Ibid., 469.
79. Wilson, Bouffard, and Mackenzie (2005), 175.
80. Ibid., 198.
81. Ibid.
82. Ibid.
83. Lipsey, Landenberger, and Wilson (2007), 7.
84. Ibid., 10.
85. Ibid., 21.
86. Ibid., 22.
87. Ibid.
88. Ibid.
89. Ibid., 20.
90. Ibid., 22.

91. Ibid., 21.
92. McCart, Priester, Davies, and Azen (2006), 530.
93. Ibid., 534.
94. Ibid., 538.
95. Ibid.
96. Ibid.
97. Ibid.
98. Wilson, Lipsey, and Derzon (2003), 137–138.
99. Ibid.
100. Ibid., 145.
101. Ibid., 147.
102. Ibid.
103. Ibid.
104. Ibid.
105. Wilson and Lipsey (2007), 130.
106. Ibid., 135–136.
107. Ibid., 141.
108. Ibid.
109. Merrell, Gueldner, Ross, and Isava (2002), 28.
110. Ibid., 29.
111. Ibid., 38.
112. Ibid.
113. Ttofi and Farrington (2011), 30.
114. Ibid., 43.
115. Ibid.
116. Ibid., 44.

REFERENCES

Anderson, Laurie M., Carolynne Shinn, Mindy T. Fullilove, Susan C. Scrimshaw, Jonathan E. Fielding, Jacques Normand, Vilma G. Carande-Kulis, and Task Force on Community Preventive Services. "The Effectiveness of Early Childhood Development Programs: A Systematic Review." *American Journal of Preventive Medicine* 24, no. 3 (2003): 32–46.

Bush, Jack, Barry Glick, and Juliana Taymans. *Thinking for a Change.* Washington, DC: National Institute of Corrections, United States Department of Justice, 1997.

Campbell Collaboration. *Effects of Cognitive-Behavioral Programs for Criminal Offenders: A Systematic Review.* By Mark Lipsey, Nana A. Landenberger, and Sandra Jo Wilson. Oslo, Norway: Campbell Systemic Reviews, 2007.

Carnahan, Sharon. "Preventing School Failure and Dropout." In *Risk Resilience and Prevention: Promoting the Well-being of All Children.* Edited by Rune J. Simionsson, 103–123. Baltimore, MD: Paul H. Brookes Publishing, 1994.

Child Welfare League of America. *Early Intervention: Crafting a Community Response to Child Abuse and Violence.* By T. R. Brooks and M. Petit. Washington, D.C.: Child Welfare League of America, 1997.

Elliott, Delbert S. *Blueprints for Violence Prevention.* Boulder, CO: University of Colorado, Center for the Study and Prevention of Violence, 1998.

Farrington, David P., and Anthony Petrosino. "The Campbell Collaboration Crime and Justice Group." *The Annals of the American Academy of Political and Social Sciences* (578) 1 (2001): 35–49.

Farrington, David P., and Brandon C. Welsh. "Family-Based Prevention of Offending: A Meta-Analysis." *Australian & New Zealand Journal of Criminology* 36, no. 2 (2003): 127–151.

Greenwood, Peter. "Prevention and Intervention Programs for Juvenile Offenders." *The Future of Children* 18, no. 2 (2008): 185–2010.

Grossman, Jean Baldwin, and Joseph P. Tierney. "Does Mentoring Work? An Impact Study of the Big Brothers Big Sisters Program." *Evaluation Review* 22, no. 3 (1998): 403–426.

Hansen, William B. "Program Evaluation Strategies for Substance Abuse Prevention." *Journal of Primary Prevention* 22, no. 4 (2002): 409–436.

Howitt, Pamela S., and Eugene Arthur Moore. "The Efficacy of Intensive Early Intervention an Avaluation of the Oakland County Probate Court Early Offender Program." *Juvenile and Family Court Journal* 42, no. 3 (1991): 25–36.

Hrynkiw-Augimeri, Leena, Debra Pepler, and Kenneth Goldberg. "An Outreach Program for Children Having Police Contact." *Canada's Mental Health* 41, no. 2 (1993): 7–12.

Kaminski, Jennifer Wyatt, Linda Anne Valle, Jill H. Filene, and Cynthia L. Boyle. "A Meta-Analytic Review of Components Associated with Parent Training Program Effectiveness." *Journal of Abnormal Child Psychology* 36, no. 4 (2008): 567–589.

Kumpfer, Kimberley L. "What Works in the Prevention of Drug Abuse: Individual, School and Family Approaches." *Youth Substance Abuse Prevention Initiative: Resource Papers* (1997): 69–106.

Kumpfer, Karol L., and Rose Alvarado. "Strengthening Families to Prevent Drug Use in Multi-Ethnic Youth." In *Drug Abuse Prevention with Multiethnic Youth.* Edited by Gilbert L. Botvin, Steven P. Schinke, and Mario A. Orlandi, 255–294. Thousand Oaks: CA: Sage, 1995.

Landenberger, Nana A., and Mark W. Lipsey. "The Positive Effects of Cognitive–Behavioral Programs for Offenders: A Meta-Analysis of Factors Associated with Effective Treatment." *Journal of Experimental Criminology* 1, no. 4 (2005): 451–476.

Lewis, Catherine, Vic Battistich, and Eric Schaps. "School-Based Primary Prevention: What Is an Effective Program?" *New Directions for Child and Adolescent Development* 1990, no. 50 (1990): 35–59.

Lipsey, Mark W. "The Primary Factors That Characterize Effective Interventions with Juvenile Offenders: A Meta-Analytic Overview." *Victims and Offenders* 4, no. 2 (2009): 124–147.

Lipsey, Mark, Nana A. Landenberger, and Sandra Jo Wilson. "Effects of Cognitive-Behavioral Programs for Criminal Offenders: A Systematic Review." *Campbell Systematic Reviews* 3, no. 6 (2007): 1–27.

Little, Gregory L., and Kenneth D. Robinson. "Effects of Moral Reconation Therapy upon Moral Reasoning, Life Purpose, and Recidivism among Drug and Alcohol Offenders." *Psychological Reports* 64, no. 1 (1989): 83–90.

Loeber, Rolf, David P. Farrington, and David Petechuk. "Child Delinquency: Early Intervention and Prevention." *Child Delinquency Bulletin Series.* Washington, DC: Office of Juvenile Justice and Delinquency Prevention, 2003.

McCart, Michael R., Paul E. Priester, W. Hobart Davies, and Razia Azen. "Differential Effectiveness of Behavioral Parent-Training and Cognitive-Behavioral Therapy for Antisocial Youth: A Meta-Analysis." *Journal of Abnormal Child Psychology* 34, no. 4 (2006): 525–541.

Merrell, Kenneth W., Barbara A. Gueldner, Scott W. Ross, and Duane M. Isava. "How Effective Are School Bullying Intervention Programs? A Meta-Analysis of Intervention Research." *School Psychology Quarterly* 23, no. 1 (2008): 26–42.

Mihalic, Sharon F., and Katherine Irwin. "Blueprints for Violence Prevention, from Research to Real-World Settings: Factors Influencing the Successful Replication of Model Programs." *Youth Violence and Juvenile Justice* 1, no. 4 (2003): 307–329.

Mulvey, Edward P., Michael W. Arthur, and N. Dickon Reppucci. "The Prevention and Treatment of Juvenile Delinquency: A Review of the Research." *Clinical Psychology Review* 13, no. 2 (1993): 133–167.

Nation, Maury, Cindy Crusto, Abraham Wandersman, Karol L. Kumpfer, Diana Seybolt, Erin Morrissey-Kane, and Katrina Davino. "What Works in Prevention: Principles of Effective Prevention Programs." *American Psychologist* 58, no. 6 (2003): 449–456.

Piquero, Alex R., David P. Farrington, Brandon C. Welsh, Richard Tremblay, and Wesley G. Jennings. "Effects of Early Family/Parent Training Programs on Antisocial Behavior and Delinquency." *Journal of Experimental Criminology* 5, no. 2 (2009): 83–120.

"Preventing Drug Use among Children and Adolescents." National Institute of Drug Abuse. October, 2003. http://www.drugabuse.gov/publications/preventing-drug-abuse-among-children-adolescents/introduction.

Ramey, Sharon Landesman, and Craig T. Ramey. "Early Educational Intervention with Disadvantaged Children—To What Effect?" *Applied and Preventive Psychology* 1, no. 3 (1992): 131–140.

Sagrestano, Lynda M., and Roberta L. Paikoff. "Preventing High-Risk Sexual Behavior, Sexually Transmitted Diseases, and Pregnancy among Adolescents." In *Enhancing Children's Wellness.* Edited by Roger P. Weissberg, Thomas P. Gullotta, Robert L. Hampton, Bruce A. Ryan, and Gerald R. Adams, 76–104. Thousand Oaks, CA: Sage, 1997.

Sherman, Lawrence W., Denise C. Gottfredson, Doris L. MacKenzie, John Eck, Peter Reuter, and Shawn D. Bushway. "Preventing Crime: What Works, What Doesn't, What's Promising." National Institute of Justice: Research in Brief. Washington, DC: National Institute of Justice, 1998.

Ttofi, Maria M., and David P. Farrington. "Effectiveness of School-Based Programs to Reduce Bullying: A Systematic and Meta-Analytic Review." *Journal of Experimental Criminology* 7, no. 1 (2011): 27–56.

Weisburd, David, Cynthia M. Lum, and Anthony Petrosino. "Does Research Design Affect Study Outcomes in Criminal Justice?" *The Annals of the American Academy of Political and Social Science* 578, no. 1 (2001): 50–70.

Wilson, David B., Leana Allen Bouffard, and Doris L. Mackenzie. "A Quantitative Review of Structured, Group-Oriented, Cognitive-Behavioral Programs for Offenders." *Criminal Justice and Behavior* 32, no. 2 (2005): 172–204.

Wilson, Sandra Jo, and Mark W. Lipsey. "School-Based Interventions for Aggressive and Disruptive Behavior: Update of a Meta-Analysis." *American Journal of Preventive Medicine* 33, no. 2 (2007): 130–143.

Wilson, Sandra Jo, Mark W. Lipsey, and James H. Derzon. "The Effects of School-Based Intervention Programs on Aggressive Behavior: A Meta-Analysis." *Journal of Consulting and Clinical Psychology* 71, no. 1 (2003): 136–149.

Chapter 13

The Future of Delinquency Prevention and Treatment

Ronald Burns and Kendra Bowen

Client RC-183 please step forward. Please place your body into the scanner and look into the screen. Thank you. Now, observe the consequences of your actions as they appear on the screen. Pay particular attention to the impact you've had on the victim and their family. Your physiological responses to the victims' reactions are being measured and appropriate treatment will be rendered. Now, please step away from the scanner and proceed to Floor 29 where Dr. Carlson will administer your treatment in the form of electromagnetic radiation and implant adjustment. Thank you.

The preceding scenario may seem far-fetched to some; however, consider the societal changes we've experienced in the past 30 years, particularly with regard to our responses to crime, delinquency, and justice. The use of high-technology, biometrics, and DNA evidence in the criminal and juvenile justice systems may have seemed far-fetched to earlier generations, however, they are becoming increasingly ingrained in our systems of justice, and, along with similar developments, are expected to become part of standard operating procedures.

To comment on the future of delinquency prevention and treatment requires diligent consideration of numerous issues, not the least of which is the methods by which we forecast the future. In looking toward the future, researchers often use quantitative and qualitative research methods. Greater confidence in forecasting the future is attained through using multiple approaches, similar to the manner in which criminologists have greater confidence in discussing crime trends using quantitative data from the Uniform Crime Reports and National Crime Victimization Surveys, along with other data.

Forecasting the future also requires consideration of temporal and spatial issues. Futurists may comment on issues expected to occur 5, 10, 50, or any number of years from now. To be sure, there are no restrictions on how far into the future one can look, however, the confidence level generally decreases as one looks further ahead. For instance, we have greater confidence in the weather forecast for tomorrow than we do in the forecast for five days from now. Spatial factors generally concern the scope of the issue under observation. For instance, one could comment on future events and developments at the international, national, state, county, local, neighborhood, and/or individual levels. Forecasting the future is a vital, although challenging task, that incorporates much uncertainty.

Contributing largely to the challenges of forecasting the future is the unpredictability of human behavior. Although futurists apply scientific approaches, one can never be certain how, why, or when particular behaviors will impact society. Consider the impacts of the terrorist attacks against the United States on September 11, 2001. Now, consider how futurists have had to revise their earlier projections in light of those events. While some may have projected the vulnerability of the United States to such attacks, it is unlikely that many forecasted such drastic changes, particularly in relation to air travel and the restructuring of our federal law enforcement agencies.

This chapter addresses the future of delinquency prevention and treatment. Comments are offered in light of qualitative changes that have occurred, those taking place, and the changes anticipated to occur. Quantitative analyses are dispersed throughout the projections, as are qualitative considerations, including comments by leading forecasters who have considered what we can expect with regard to these issues. Our look to the future is preceded by an overview of historical developments and current trends pertaining to delinquency prevention and treatment.

HISTORICAL DEVELOPMENTS AND CURRENT TRENDS

The history of delinquency and responses to it are well documented, although a brief discussion is warranted to offer a look to the future.[1] Bartollas and Schmalleger highlighted the historical periods regarding juvenile justice within the United States, beginning with the colonial period (1636–1823) and its emphasis on families being responsible for correcting the actions of their children. The house of refuge period (1824–1898) emphasized the institutionalization of juveniles, while the juvenile court period (1899–1966) provided youthful offenders access to a court system designed to meet the specific needs of wayward juveniles. The juvenile rights period (1967–1975) provided juveniles greater due process rights in the courts, while the reform agenda period of the mid-to-late 1970s stressed diversion from the juvenile justice system for status offenders and nonserious delinquents. The social control and juvenile crime period of juvenile justice emerged in the 1980s, and brought increased social control over juveniles.[2] It was a move away from the reform efforts of the 1970s, a trend that continued into the 21st century. Gang crime, crimes associated with crack cocaine, gun crime, and media sensationalism of juvenile offending contributed to the radical shift in philosophy with regard to juvenile justice.

Recently, there is evidence of a shift away from the more punitive approach to delinquency that began in the 1980s, toward a more rehabilitative focus. Though many states drifted toward a more punitive stance at the latter part of the 20th century, most retained some semblance of their original rehabilitative approaches. In the time of large budget cuts due to economic recession, policy makers began questioning the high confinement rates that the punitive approach left in its wake and began seeking less costly alternatives.[3] In doing so, funding initiatives focused more on evidence-based practices that proved to be successful, which has contributed to an enhanced focus on rehabilitation.

The decreased emphasis on punishing youthful offenders has been supported by a wave of psychological, biological, and developmental studies exploring the structural development of the adolescent brain. This work conclusively found that the human brain is not fully developed until early adulthood.[4] These studies influenced recent court rulings that eased the punitive stance on juveniles waived to adult courts for serious felony convictions, and they offer many important implications for the future of delinquency prevention and treatment.

CONTEXTUALIZING DELINQUENCY PREVENTION AND TREATMENT

Examination of the future of delinquency treatment and prevention requires consideration of what constitutes delinquency prevention and treatment. The two are similar, yet distinct in various ways. For instance, prevention and treatment are similar in the sense that they both seek to promote an orderly society. They differ, though, as prevention seeks to thwart delinquency before it occurs (and is thus proactive), while treatment efforts target the cessation of delinquency after it has occurred, and is thus a reactive approach.

Delinquency Prevention

Prevention has been, and continues to be, a vital component of most efforts to confront delinquency. The long-standing belief that young people are more impressionable than adults has resulted in greater prevention efforts directed toward youth. It is felt by many that preventing delinquency is more effective than "correcting" or "fixing" misguided youths. There are three types of prevention: primary, secondary, and tertiary. Primary prevention attempts to prevent delinquent acts from occurring. It largely includes preschool education, parent education, school-based prevention programs, and community–school partnerships. Secondary prevention attempts to provide additional support when primary prevention efforts are ineffective, and targets at-risk youth who are showing early signs of aggressive or violent behaviors. It includes programs such as mentoring and non–conflict resolution. Tertiary prevention efforts are the most intensive, and attempt to limit recidivism after delinquency has taken place. Tertiary prevention strategies include treatment and rehabilitation interventions targeting delinquent youth.

The future holds much promise for evidence-based prevention programs for youth. For example, the Center for the Study and Prevention of Violence (CSPV) hosts the Blueprints for Healthy Youth Development, one of the most comprehensive and strict registries of evidence-based programs designed for youth that target all levels of risk.[5] Researchers from the center reviewed over 1,300 programs targeting different levels of prevention for juveniles, and found that less than 5 percent were model or promising programs.[6]

Delinquency Treatment

Delinquency treatment efforts are concerned with rehabilitating young offenders, primarily through identifying the underlying causes of delinquency and implementing appropriate methods of correction. Treatment programs are typically based on "the assumption that delinquent behavior is a manifestation or symptom of some other deeper problem" in which symptoms are identified, diagnoses are made, and treatment is pursued.[7] Treatment programs typically follow psychiatric or psychological approaches, although the medical model is evident in some treatment programs, particularly those involving alcohol and/or drug abuse.[8] Such programs are found in both community and institutional settings, and can be used in conjunction with punitive approaches.

FACTORS INFLUENCING DELINQUENCY TREATMENT AND PREVENTION

Many factors will influence the future of delinquency treatment and prevention, including societal changes. Historically, the United States initially was an agrarian society, thus there were no programs or institutions for juveniles, as there was little government involvement in family life. Accordingly, families were expected to confront problem children internally. As industry evolved and large cities emerged, wayward juveniles became more visible in society, which ultimately encouraged government involvement in the form of institutionalization. From a futurist's perspective, one could have anticipated such changes given historical developments in society in general.

Other periods of juvenile justice developments reflect events that shaped society as a whole. For instance, the juvenile rights period occurred at a time in U.S. history when many groups were fighting for civil rights (e.g., Native Americans, prisoners, African Americans), while the reform agenda period occurred during a time when the criminal (adult) justice systems were promoting community corrections. The shift toward punishing and getting tough on juveniles that began in the 1980s was reflective of, among other things, a more conservative U.S. population, the enhanced use of incarceration for adult offenders, and greater emphasis on retribution and deterrence in the adult justice system. The relatively recent movement away from a punitive approach is reflective of budgetary crises and evidence that institutionalizing juveniles is limited in its ability to prevent further involvement in crime and delinquency.[9] With regard to the latter, Bartollas and Miller noted that: "Every study that has ever been done on juveniles released from institutions has found extremely high rates of recidivism," ranging from 50 to 70 percent.[10]

In addition to the broad factors that influence delinquency prevention and treatment, futurists often observe particular social forces, or what are considered drivers of the future. Among the prominent drivers of crime, delinquency, and justice-based futures research are demographics, economics, crime factors, technology, and public opinion. Regarding delinquency treatment and prevention, demographic projections help justice officials and policy makers anticipate population fluctuations and the characteristics of the anticipated changes. In turn, for instance, planners can speculate whether or not there will be available treatment slots for the forecasted number of juveniles in need. The U.S. Census forecasted increased percentages of minority groups in society in the immediate and long-term future, thus there appears to be a notable need to further emphasize multiculturalism in all aspects of justice, and for recognition of and response to the disproportionate percentage of minority youth involved in the juvenile justice system. The disproportionate confinement of minority juveniles has been particularly problematic in the juvenile justice system, leading to intervention by the Office of Juvenile Justice and Delinquency Prevention to address the concern.

Economic factors play a significant role in crime and justice. Forecasters regularly consider economic indicators to effectively anticipate future trends and changes. Put simply, a strong economy typically decreases the likelihood of crime and delinquency. A weak economy generally has the opposite effect. Economic trends could be used to anticipate an increased presence of juveniles in the justice system, in turn commanding an increased need for rehabilitation opportunities and prevention efforts if indeed they are the approaches to be taken. Poverty is a strong predictor of involvement in our justice systems, and involvement in the juvenile justice systems is a strong predictor of involvement in the criminal justice system. Understanding that crime and delinquency are often financially motivated provides guidance for treatment and prevention efforts, and highlights the need for directed and continued programming regarding education, job skills, and financial management. Economic factors also notably impact funding for juvenile justice in general, which could influence the extent to which opportunities for prevention and rehabilitation are available.

The qualitative nature of illegal behaviors is notably important when discussing the future of delinquency prevention and treatment. Understanding what to expect with regard to the qualitative nature of delinquency inherently affects the quantity and quality of treatment and prevention opportunities needed and provided. One merely needs to observe recent, punitive societal reactions to gang crime, gun crime, and drug-related crimes to understand how the nature of crime impacts societal response.

With an eye on the future, one must consider the increased opportunities for high technology–facilitated crime and delinquency, and the usefulness of technology in justice-based practices. The technology age is upon us and with it comes increased opportunities for delinquency and corresponding treatment and prevention needs. Young children and young adults alike are growing up in a society that relies heavily on technology, and are becoming increasingly adept with automation. As society changes, so do forms of crime and delinquency and the need for innovative forms of prevention and treatment. As suggested in the opening scenario, technology is expected to become increasingly ingrained in responses to crime and delinquency. The use of electronic monitoring, global positioning system (GPS) tracking, biometrics, digital interfacing, and online counseling and training are but a few examples of how technology has been integrated in our justice systems.

Shifts in public opinion undoubtedly influence future events. Societal concern about crime, delinquency, and justice beginning in the 1980s largely contributed to more punitive responses to unlawful behavior. Public concern for juvenile violence led to policy shifts directed away from the historical rehabilitative ideals of juvenile justice toward a more punitive approach. Juvenile boot camps as a form of punishment and rehabilitation became increasingly popular with politicians and the public alike beginning in the 1980s. Boot camp programs seemed an ideal option as they offered a noticeably obvious form of punishment (e.g., the drill instruction) tempered with rehabilitation (e.g., instilling discipline). Their introduction and use were symbolic of the transition from a focus on juvenile rehabilitation toward an emphasis on punishment.

Several scholars earlier offered their views of what lies ahead for tomorrow's youth, and their comments remain relevant. For instance, futurist Gene Stephens noted a series of issues impacting efforts to properly guide at-risk youth, including the increasing gap between the wealthy and the poor, a growing number of single-parent households, less accountability for children as more families require both parents to work, and an expanding gun culture.[11] These and related issues impacted delinquency prevention and treatment around the turn of the 21st century and generally continue to do so. Recent suggestions that we are returning to a more rehabilitative approach may symbolize our recognition of the importance of the input offered by Stephens and others who have looked to the future of juvenile justice.[12]

THE FUTURE OF DELINQUENCY
TREATMENT AND PREVENTION

In their account of the future of juvenile justice, Bartollas and Miller identify several problems in modern society that affect youths at risk. Particularly, they note the challenges associated with dysfunctional families, and families in which there is limited accountability of children as both parents may be forced to work; the socioeconomic structure of society in which there is a rapidly expanding underclass in the United States; deteriorating urban neighborhoods, which are conducive to delinquency and other forms of misbehavior; dangerous inner-city schools that may prohibit learning and encourage delinquency; the negative influences of gangs; and the attitudes of high-risk youth who may feel a sense of hopelessness.[13]

Given the impact of the aforementioned drivers, the problems faced by youths, and the fluctuations in the approaches taken to address delinquency, it is difficult to clearly understand what lies ahead for delinquency prevention and treatment. Nevertheless, it remains important to project what is believed will likely happen in the future. The following discussion of the anticipated future of delinquency prevention and treatment is organized into short-, mid-range, and long-term projections of the future of delinquency treatment and prevention. An examination of the future of the juvenile court system precedes this discussion, simply because the courts are particularly powerful in determining the sanctions juveniles receive and the outcomes of their cases in general.

The Future of Juvenile Courts

The future of delinquency prevention and treatment will undoubtedly be influenced by the future of the juvenile courts. In light of the recent shift away from the punitive ideals initiated in the last couple of decades, juvenile courts appear to be refocusing on the rehabilitative and protective ideals upon which they were founded. For instance, the percentage of youths transferred into the jurisdiction of the adult court is an important indicator of the orientations and approaches taken by juvenile courts. The number of delinquency cases waived to adult court peaked at 13,600 cases in 1994, which was twice the number of cases waived in 1985. Juvenile courts waived an estimated 5,400 cases in 2011, which was 61 percent fewer cases than in 1994.[14] Support for a more rehabilitative approach to delinquency is noted by a National Institute of Justice–supported survey of juvenile justice practitioners and professionals, including many who work in juvenile courts, which found that respondents were strongly in favor of a rehabilitative, as opposed to punitive, response to delinquency. Respondents most strongly agreed that finding alternatives to secure detention and policymaker support for rehabilitation were the highest priorities in their jurisdictions.[15]

The trend toward rehabilitation and community-based alternatives has prompted the increased use of juvenile specialty courts. These courts, also referred to as "problem-solving" courts, focus on the problems underlying delinquency and treat these problems with therapeutic interventions.[16] Specialty courts focus on the rehabilitation of juveniles, and are largely modeled after the adult specialty courts that gained popularity in the 1980s and 1990s.[17] There are numerous types of specialty courts, which may focus on mental health, substance abuse, and gang involvement. Juvenile and adult specialty courts exist in every state in the United States.[18]

The U.S. Supreme Court recently offered three important decisions affecting the future of the juvenile justice system. In *Roper v. Simmons* (2005), the Court ruled that the Eighth and Fourteenth amendments prohibit the imposition of the death penalty on offenders who were under the age of 18 when their crimes were committed. In *Graham v. Florida* (2010), the Court ruled that a sentence of life imprisonment without the possibility of parole, imposed on a minor for a nonhomicidal offense, is unconstitutional. The Court later expanded on the *Graham* decision, in *Miller v. Alabama*, 2012, and ruled that mandatory penalties of life imprisonment without the possibility of parole for juveniles are unconstitutional. Through their decisions in these cases, the Court recognized the fundamental differences between juveniles and adults: juveniles are less culpable than adults and therefore deserve less retributive punishment.[19] These Court decisions will have important implications for juveniles in the future, as states are required to take a less punitive stance on serious juvenile offenders, and the rulings recognized the developmental differences between juveniles and adults.

Legislation will further impact juvenile court practices, as analyses of proposed and enacted juvenile justice legislation between 2005 and 2007 found that over one thousand juvenile justice measures were introduced in state legislatures, resulting in over three hundred new laws and policies. Analyses of the content of these acts suggest an emphasis on rehabilitative approaches to delinquency. Among the more prominent themes in the bills enacted during the years of study were restoring the jurisdiction of the juvenile court, limiting the transfer of juveniles to the adult system to the most violent offenses, and abolishing or restricting the most severe punishments, such as capital punishment and life in prison without the possibility of parole.[20] The following chronologically based sets of expectations provide more general outlooks on what we can expect with regard to delinquency prevention and treatment.

Short-Range Expectations

Recent public opinion polls show that the general public and juvenile justice practitioners are in favor of rehabilitation as a means to reduce delinquency. These polls suggest the public is willing to pay extra taxes for rehabilitative services towards youth and even support rehabilitation for youth who commit violent crimes.[21] The Center for Children's Law and Policy (CCLP) conducted eight focus groups in four cities combined with a national phone survey and found that 89 percent of respondents agreed that juveniles have the potential to change, and 70 percent agreed that incarcerating youth without utilizing rehabilitative services is akin to giving up on them.[22]

Current trends in juvenile justice indicate a continued shift away from enhanced punitiveness toward an increased emphasis on rehabilitation and prevention. In their examination of juvenile justice in the twenty-first century, Bartollas and Miller noted: "The deinstitutionalization movement is likely to continue and even expand, given the high costs of institutionalization and the successful outcomes of many community-based correctional programs."[23] To be sure, punishment will continue to be used to address delinquency, although it is expected that it will not be used to the extent it has beginning in the 1980s until relatively recently. Among the primary factors contributing to the shift are economic and related budgetary concerns of governments, evidence demonstrating the effectiveness of better incorporating the community into justice-based efforts, and evidence and beliefs that getting tough on juveniles has limited, and sometimes detrimental long-term effects.

Getting tough on crime and delinquency brings a corresponding lack of funding for prevention and treatment. Similar to major corporations, municipalities must work within the confines of financial budgets, and more generally, limited resources. Getting tough is expensive. In light of decreasing budgets, government officials are tasked with determining where limited resources will be best allocated.

It is anticipated that we will continue to recognize juveniles as "correctable" and impressionable in the sense that we can prevent their involvement in delinquency and "fix" those who have ventured down the wrong paths. In discussing the future of juvenile justice, Jackson and Knepper earlier noted: "Despite the overall emphasis on accountability, prevention will continue to be a theme" in years to come.[24] They also identify community involvement as a "pervasive theme" in future juvenile court practices. Their statement is echoed by Benekos and Merlo who commented: "Even through 'get-tough' political rhetoric and adultification legislation has characterized juvenile justice (beginning in the 1980s), the juvenile justice system will continue with its mission to help youthful offenders and reduce delinquency."[25]

It is anticipated that the short-term future of delinquency prevention and treatment will largely involve the contributions of various community resources, assisted by technological developments. With regard to the former, for instance, many police departments have adopted a community-oriented philosophy, which relies heavily on police interaction with communities, particularly with regard to crime prevention. One of the more positive contributions of community policing efforts is the involvement of law enforcement in crime and delinquency prevention. Efforts to prevent delinquency are apparent in various community policing programs, including the U.S. Department of Justice's Youth-Focused Community Policing initiative, which focuses on establishing and strengthening police–community relationships to address delinquency prevention, intervention, and enforcement.

Clear and Cadora discussed community justice as an alternative approach to addressing crime and delinquency in which areas with a high concentration of crime are targeted for attempts to strengthen informal systems of social control. They cite the emphasis on informal social control, proactive approaches to crime and delinquency, problem solving, and partnership development with residents, businesses, and various social services as key components of community justice.[26] Restorative justice, with its "focus on crime as harm, and justice as repairing the harm, offers a vision that elevates the role of crime victim, yet views victim, offender, and community as equal customers of juvenile justice services and as important, active co-participants in responding to juvenile crime."[27] Both community justice and restorative justice require substantial input and accountability from the general public. To be sure, efforts to involve the community in delinquency prevention and treatment exist today. It is projected, however, that in the future we can expect greater community involvement in delinquency prevention and treatment.

It is expected that notable grassroots efforts will be made toward community delinquency prevention and rehabilitation. Dawson earlier aptly noted that: "An integral part of any juvenile justice system is a network of private, charitable, or religious institutions, facilities, and programs."[28] The community has much to directly offer with regard to delinquency prevention and treatment. Among the community-based options available to respond to delinquency are diversion from the system, probation, intensive supervision probation, restorative justice efforts, restitution, community service, work programs, aftercare, family group conferencing, teen court, and electronic monitoring. To be sure, this is not a comprehensive list of available options to confront delinquency in the community, and innovative approaches are certainly in the works or will emerge in the future.

In discussing the integration of technology into corrections, Fabelo noted: "A correctional establishment that takes advantage of all the potential offered by the new technologies to reduce the costs of supervising criminal offenders and minimize the risk they pose to society will define the field of technocorrections."[29] The future undoubtedly will bring about a series of technology-based alternatives and helpful scientific advancements that are expected to contribute much to the future of delinquency prevention and treatment. We can expect the continued introduction and integration of technological advancements on an initially limited, but increasing, scale in the short-range future of delinquency prevention and treatment.

Mid-Range Expectations

The above-noted short-term expectations regarding the future of delinquency prevention and treatment are anticipated to, at some point in the future, come under criticism. Emphases on correctional practices are cyclical, as one merely needs to examine the shifts in correctional focuses throughout history with regard to both juveniles and adults. Primarily, the shifts involve fluctuations between getting tough and rehabilitation. The primary reasons for the fluctuations often include societal developments, limited positive results, and public outcry to alter correctional practices.

Treatment and prevention practices currently involve many uncertainties, meaning that we can't be certain that efforts directed toward the prevention of youth violence and attempts to rehabilitate offenders are being put to good use. Further treatment and rehabilitation are often seen as being soft on crime, which is not always popular with much of society. Delinquency prevention and treatment efforts will need to be more effective than they currently are in order for them to remain popular options for addressing youthful misbehavior. Recent developments in the hard sciences and technology, and their increased and potential use in our justice systems, appear to offer much promise with regard to prevention and treatment efforts.

Mid-range expectations for the future of delinquency and treatment practices involve a period of transition as scientific advancements and emerging technologies facilitate better understanding human behavior and how to control it, and generate a host of related challenges and concerns. This period is anticipated to include advanced medicines, more in-depth analyses and understanding of the human brain, and technology-assisted training, rehabilitation, and controls that facilitate prevention and treatment efforts.

The fictitious opening scenario of this chapter, which involves a technological application of behavior modification with a dose of technology-based reality therapy, seems far-fetched by today's standards for correctional practices. However, today's science fiction may be tomorrow's reality. One merely needs to compare today's world with society as it existed thirty-five years ago to appreciate the forcefulness of technological advances. It is shortsighted to believe that we've "maxed out" with regard to technological development. Recall the earliest computers, or the early, text-based version of the Internet. Now, consider the evolution of both the computer and the Internet. We should we remain optimistic that similar, major developments will occur as technology continuously evolves and we direct our efforts to issues such as delinquency prevention and treatment.

The mid-range future may include implants as an accepted practice in delinquency prevention and treatment. Stephens noted that implants, the use of which generates controversy, could be applied as a form of birth control, to control behavior, to monitor one's health, to ensure proper functioning of one's brain, and to assist individuals with learning deficiencies.[30] While the development of implants continues, society must come to terms with the ethical considerations inherently associated with their use and the use of related advancements.

In light of the entrepreneurship and creativity apparent in society's recent technological transformation, it is projected that the energies and resources that have thus far been put into developing marketable, recreational and material goods and services will eventually be recognized in technological approaches to delinquency prevention and treatment. In other words, society will increasingly seek, and develop, technology-based programs, simulators, virtual realities, assessment centers, correctional facilities, and the like to reduce the burden on human efforts to prevent and confront delinquency, and provide overall more effective responses to wayward youth.

Researchers continuously stress the need to identify specific programs to meet the needs of particular youths. It is possible that in the future, full-body scans and measured physiological and mental responses could facilitate the identification of appropriate technology-based prevention programs or rehabilitative efforts. Or, perhaps technological advances could be used to address some of the larger social issues that contribute to delinquency (e.g., poverty, broken homes, etc.).

These and related advancements in both science and technology, along with many other factors such as economics, globalism, and general societal changes, will provide the foundation for, and potential to disrupt, effective long-term delinquency prevention and treatment practices. This anticipated transformation toward a more advanced society will generate a host of potentially unanticipated concerns such as those pertaining to ethics, legal issues, and privacy issues. For instance, consider a society in which individuals with particular brain characteristics are identified as potentially dangerous. Would it be ethical, legal, or fair to alter one's brain simply due to their potential to be dangerous? Or, should we wait until they misbehave before we perform brain alterations? Further, the initial integration of such science is likely to generate many unanticipated side effects and related issues (e.g., legal issues, privacy, etc.) that will need to be addressed.

These and a host of related issues will have to be addressed as society moves from personal evaluations, diagnoses, and plans toward more scientific and technology-based ones. This period is anticipated to generate much controversy as the altering of human behavior becomes reality and the many associated kinks must be worked out, including the potential for the "over-control" of human behavior, net widening in the justice system, and privacy issues. Human behavior is complex by nature, although scientific developments have the potential to reduce the complexities in a positive manner. Altering human behavior, however, has much potential to generate a series of important issues that will need to be thoroughly addressed. Consider, for example, the potential harms associated with terrorist groups identifying a means to alter brains in a manner to support their negative causes.

This period of transition will likely encourage much societal reflection on the usefulness of scientific and technological advancements. There is also the concern that legal protections may be unable to keep pace with the rapid pace of technology, particularly with regard to corrections.[31]

Ultimately, the obstacles associated with the anticipated scientific and technology-based developments will ultimately be overcome, leading to long-range expectation of the large-scale indoctrination of scientific and technological developments in delinquency prevention and treatment.

Long-Range Expectations

As mentioned, the confidence levels in forecasts of the future diminish as one projects further into the future. Nevertheless, a conservative forecast of the future suggests advanced scientific and technology developments will play a significant role in delinquency treatment and prevention. The aforementioned period of transition will experience turbulence, however legislators, scientists, justice professionals, and the general public are expected to ultimately identify the means to best utilize the developments and overcome the challenges. Long-range expectations for the future of delinquency prevention and treatment involve the large-scale implementation of scientific and technological advancements that will be able to far more effectively understand and alter human behavior in a humane, ethical, and effective manner.

Pharmacological developments, including drugs designed to control human behavior both within and outside of institutions, will impact the future of delinquency prevention and treatment. Some of these drugs are currently used with mentally ill and other offenders, and continued development in the area could result in benefits with regard to controlling the behaviors of all in society. Fabelo suggested that "It is only a matter of time before research findings in this area lead to the development of drugs to control neurobiologic processes," and ultimately help manage offenders and prevent misbehavior. He further cites the development of genetic "management" technologies as potential contributors.[32]

Adding to this optimistic projection of delinquency prevention and treatments in the future is the impact of globalism. Scientists and researchers in general from around the world can more easily collaborate and share research findings today than at any period of time in history. Advancements in technology, in particular, facilitate the global sharing of information, which has much potential to relatively rapidly increase the likelihood of altering human behavior in a positive manner, and the general sharing of information that could largely benefit the future of delinquency prevention and treatment.

It is anticipated that there will be a shift in the provision of juvenile correctional services following this projected large-scale indoctrination of advanced scientific and technological advances into delinquency and treatment practices. Particularly, it is anticipated that prevention and treatment efforts will become more aligned with and provided by medical practitioners as opposed to justice-based practitioners, as is currently largely the case. Certainly, medical practitioners, counselors, psychologists, and related professionals are currently involved in prevention and, particularly, treatment efforts, however it is anticipated that doctors and scientists will be the primary professionals responsible for preventing and treating delinquency.

There will, of course, remain the need for a juvenile justice system, as it is hard to currently fathom any scientific development that prevents all misbehavior. As optimistic as we are in our forecast of the future, we are somewhat uncomfortable describing a society in which there is no misbehavior. Juvenile justice practices, however, will likely not be primarily focused on punishment as a means for altering misbehavior. Instead, juvenile justice—based practices will likely adopt more of a behavior-modification or social services–oriented approach designed to promote job skills training, education, financial management, and the like. The violence and related negative aspects currently associated with too many juvenile facilities are expected to disappear, as better screening, classification, and control devices will promote more productive environments.

ONWARD

To be sure, this account of the future of delinquency prevention and treatment is particularly optimistic. As noted, projecting the future is filled with uncertainties, and we recognize that our vision of the future in these areas is far from certain. Our projection is based on historical, current, and anticipated developments, and we have identified areas of potential successes and challenges. The onus is on each of us to help create a society in which we wish to live and leave for future generations.

Forecasters sometimes create scenarios, akin to the one presented at the opening of this chapter, of what the future may look like, which could and/or should provide guidance for current and future practices.[33] Based on the scenarios, efforts are made to work backward, and realize the means to get there from the present. One merely needs to observe the evolution of computers and the Internet to understand the importance of having a vision and remaining optimistic.

Stojkovic and Klofas earlier noted that futurists must confront three substantial issues in looking to the future. First, they must give due consideration to the past and the present. Second, they must scientifically project from the past toward the future. Finally, futurists must question their "own role in creating (the) future rather than passively accepting it."[34]

The success of future efforts to prevent or treat delinquency depends largely on our level of optimism. Successful visionaries typically consider how they can make things happen, not why they can't. We must remain vigilant in our efforts to incorporate scientific, technological, and other advancements into our efforts to address delinquency, with strong consideration of all potential implications. Among other things, remaining optimistic and recognizing that the future is not predetermined should encourage us to assume a more proactive role in efforts directed toward the future of delinquency prevention and treatment.

DISCUSSION QUESTIONS

1. Explain how it can be said that our current system of juvenile justice contains elements of all of the previous eras. Specifically, indicate which philosophies, practices or emphases seem to be continued from the past.
2. What do you see for the future of delinquency treatment and prevention and how would emerging technologies be incorporated?
3. Will the delinquent of the future be different characteristically from those we work with today? In what ways?
4. In terms of professional employment, what new skills and talents will the juvenile justice worker of the future need to possess?
5. In what unique ways can the community be more active in the prevention and treatment of delinquency in the future?

ADDITIONAL RESOURCES

Arya, Neelum. "Family-Driven Justice." *Arizona Law Review* 56, no. 3 (2014): 623–706.

Cohn, Alvin. "Juvenile Focus." *Federal Probation* 78, no. 3 (2014): 1–15.

Committee on a Prioritized Plan to Implement a Developmental Approach in Juvenile Justice Reform; Committee on Law and Justice; Division of Behavioral and Social Sciences and Education. *Implementing Juvenile Justice Reform: The Federal Role.* Washington, DC: National Research Council of the National Academies, 2014.

Cramer Brooks, Carol and David Roush. "Transformation in the Justice System." *Reclaiming Children & Youth* 23, no. 1 (2014): 42–46.

DeGue, Sarah, Linda Valle, Melissa Holt, Greta Massetti, Jennifer Matjasko, and Andra Tharp. "A Systematic Review of Primary Prevention Strategies for Sexual Violence Perpetration." *Aggression and Violent Behavior* 19, no. 4 (2014): 346–362.

Fagan, Abigail, and David Hawkins. "Enacting Preventive Interventions at the Community Level: The Communities That Care Prevention System." In *Handbook of Adolescent Drug Use Prevention: Research, Intervention Strategies and Practice.* Edited by Lawrence Scheir, 343–360. Washington, DC: American Psychological Association, 2015.

Klevens, Joanne, Sarah Barnett, Curtis Florence, and DeWayne Moore. "Exploring Policies for the Reduction of Child Physical Abuse and Neglect." *Child Abuse & Neglect* 40 (2015): 1–11.

Scheir, Lawrence. "Concluding Remarks: The Future Is Here Now." In *Handbook of Adolescent Drug Use Prevention: Research, Intervention Strategies and Practice.* Edited by Lawrence Scheir, 541–553. Washington, DC: American Psychological Association, 2015.

Schreibersdorf, Lisa. "Bringing the Best of Both Worlds: Recommendations for Criminal Justice Reform for Older Adolescents." *Cardozo Law Review* 35, no. 3 (2014): 1143–1166.

Skeem, Jennifer, Elizabeth Scott, and Edward Mulvey. "Justice Policy Reform for High-Risk Juveniles: Using Science to achieve Large-Scale Crime Reduction." *Annual Review of Clinical Psychology* 10 (2014): 709–739.

Van Horn, M. Lee, Abigail Fagan, David Hawkins and Sabrina Oesterle. "Research Article: Effects of Communities That Care System on Cross-Sectional Profiles of Adolescent Substance Use and Delinquency." *American Journal of Preventive Medicine* 47, no. 2 (2014): 188–197.

Walters, Glenn. "Continuous versus Categorical Models of Delinquency Risk." *American Journal of Criminal Justice* 39, no. 3 (2014): 395–410.

RELATED WEBSITES

Abuse in Detention Centers, http://www.sheldensays.com/abuseindetentioncenters.html

Committee for Children, http://www.cfchildren.org

I Have a Dream Foundation, http://www.ihaveadreamfoundation.org/html/

International Association of Chiefs of Police (IACP): Youth Focused Policing Resource Center, http://www.iacpyouth.org/

National Council of Juvenile and Family Court Judges, http://www.ncjfcj.org/

National Dropout Prevention Center/Network, http://www.dropoutprevention.org

SUPPORTING FILMS: DELINQUENCY: PAST AND PRESENT

Bad Boy (1949)
Blackboard Jungle (1955)
A Clockwork Orange (1971)
Gridiron Gang (2006)
Havoc (2005)
Rebel without a Cause (1955)
Riot on Sunset Strip (1967)
River's Edge (1987)
West Side Story (1961

NOTES

1. Rosenheim, Zimring, Tanenhaus, and Dohrn (2002); Wolcott (2001).
2. Bartollas and Schmalleger (2014), 12–15.
3. Center for Juvenile Justice Reform (2010).

4. Bernstein (2014).
5. Greenwood and Turner (2010).
6. "Find What Works."
7. Bynum and Thompson (2005), 440.
8. Ibid.
9. Ibid.; Slobogin and Fondacaro (2014).
10. Bartollas and Miller (2014), 338.
11. Stephens (2010).
12. Ohlin (1998).
13. Ibid.
14. Hockenberry and Puzzanchera (2014).
15. Urban Institute (2009).
16. Meekins (2006).
17. Children at Risk (2014).
18. Ibid.
19. Fondacaro (2014).
20. Children at Risk (2014).
21. "Polling on Public Attitudes: Treatment of Youth in Trouble with the Law" 2013.
22. Ibid.
23. Bartollas and Miller (2014), 344.
24. Jackson and Knepper (2003), 387.
25. Benekos and Merlo (2005), 37.
26. Clear and Cadora (2003).
27. Bilchik (1997), ii.
28. Dawson (1990), 148.
29. Fabelo (2000), 1.
30. Stephens (1997).
31. Ibid.
32. Ibid., 2.
33. Burns (1998); Cole (1995).
34. Stojkovic and Klofas (1995), 282–284.

REFERENCES

Bartollas, Clemens, and Frank J. Schmalleger. *Juvenile Delinquency*, 9th edition. Upper Saddle River, NJ: Pearson, 2014.

Bartollas, Clemens, and Stuart J Miller. *Juvenile Justice in America*, 7th edition. Upper Saddle River, NJ: Pearson, 2014.

Benekos, Peter J., and Alida V. Merlo. "Reaffirming Juvenile Justice: Strategies for the Future." In *Visions for Change: Crime and Justice in the Twenty-First Century*, 4th edition. Edited by Roslyn Muraskin and Albert R. Roberts, 17–42. Upper Saddle River, NJ: Prentice Hall, 2005.

Bernstein, Nell. *Burning Down the House: The End of Juvenile Prison*. New York: The New Press, 2014.

Bilchik, Shay. "Forward." In *Balanced and Restorative Justice for Juveniles: A Framework for Juvenile Justice in the 21st Century*, ii. Washington, DC: Office of Juvenile Justice and Delinquency Prevention, 1997.

Burns, Ronald. "Forecasting Bollinger: Methods for Projecting the Future of Jails." *American Jails*, November 1998: 55–56.

Bynum, Jack E., and William E. Thompson. *Juvenile Delinquency: A Sociological Approach*, 6th edition. New York: Pearson, 2005.

Center for Juvenile Justice Reform. *Improving the Effectiveness of Juvenile Justice Programs: A New Perspective on Evidence-Based Practice*. By Mark W. Lipsey, James C. Howell, Marion R. Kelly, Gabrielle Chapman, and Darin Carver. Washington, DC: Center for Juvenile Justice Reform, 2010.

Children at Risk. *Juvenile Specialty Courts: An Examination of Rehabilitative Justice in Texas and Across the Nation*. By Robert Sanborn, Mandi Sheridan Kimball, Dawn Lew, Kavita C. Desai, Todd J. Latiolais, Lauren Hislop, Jasmine Reed, Emma Sholl, Caleb Thornton, Cynthia Akatugba, Farrah Lang, and Elizabeth Miguez. Houston, TX: Children at Risk, 2014.

Clear, Todd R., and Eric Cadora. *Community Justice*. Belmont, CA: Wadsworth, 2003.

Cole, George F. "Criminal Justice in the Twenty-First Century." In *Crime and Justice in the Year 2010*. Edited by John Klofas and Stan Stojkovic, 4–17. Belmont, CA: Wadsworth, 1995.

Dawson, Robert A. "The Future of Juvenile Justice: Is It Time to Abolish the System?" *Journal of Criminal Law & Criminology* 81, no. 1 (1990): 136–155.

Fabelo, Tony. "'Technocorrections': The Promises, the Uncertain Threats." *Sentencing & Corrections: Issues for the 21st Century*. Washington, DC: National Institute of Justice, 2000.

"Find What Works." *Blueprints for Healthy Youth Development*. http://www.blue printsprograms.com/.

Fondacaro, Mark R. "Rethinking the Scientific and Legal Implications of Developmental Differences Research in Juvenile Justice." *New Criminal Law Review* 17, no. 3 (2014): 407–441.

Greenwood, Peter W., and Susan Turner. "Juvenile Crime and Juvenile Justice." In *Crime and Public Policy*. Edited by James Q. Wilson and Joan Petersilia, 88–129. New York: Oxford University Press, 2010.

Hockenberry, Sarah, and Charles Puzzanchera. "Delinquency Cases Waived to Criminal Court, 2011." *Juvenile Offenders and Victims: National Report Series*. Washington, DC: Office of Juvenile Justice and Delinquency Prevention, 2014.

Jackson, Mary S., and Paul Knepper. *Delinquency and Justice*. Boston, MA: Allyn and Bacon, 2003.

Meekins, Tamar M. "Specialized Justice: The Over-Emergence of Specialty Courts and the Threat of a New Criminal Defense Paradigm." *Suffolk University Law Review* 40, no. 1 (2006): 1–55.

Ohlin, Lloyd E. "The Future of Juvenile Justice Policy and Research." *Crime & Delinquency* 44, no. 1 (1998): 143–153.

"Polling on Public Attitudes: Treatment of Youth in Trouble with the Law." National Juvenile Justice Network. November, 2013. http://www.njjn.org/uploads/digital-library/Update-Polling-Attitudes_Jan2014.pdf.

Rosenheim, Margaret K., Franklin E., David S. Tanenhaus, and Bernadine Dohrn, eds. *A Century of Juvenile Justice.* Chicago, IL: University of Chicago Press, 2002.

Slobogin, Christopher, and Mark R. Fondacaro. *Juveniles at Risk: A Plea for Preventive Justice.* New York, NY: Oxford University Press, 2014.

Stephens, Gene. "Youth at Risk: Saving the World's Most Precious Resource." *The Futurist* 31, no. 2 (1997): 31–37.

Stephens, Gene. "Youth at Risk: A New Plan for Saving the World's Most Precious Resource." *The Futurist* 44, no. 4 (2010): 16–21.

Stojkovic, Stan, and John M. Klofas. "Preparing for the Year 2010." In *Crime and Justice in the Year 2010.* Edited by John Klofas and Stan Stojkovic, 281–296. Belmont, CA: Wadsworth, 1995.

Urban Institute. *Past, Present, and Future of Juvenile Justice: Assessing the Policy Options (APO).* By Janeen Buck-Willison, Daniel P. Mears, Tracey Shollenberger, Colleen Owens, and Jeffrey A. Butts. Washington, DC: The Urban Institute, 2009.

Wolcott, David. "The Cop Will Get You: The Police and Discretionary Juvenile Justice, 1890–1940." *Journal of Social History* 35, no. 2 (2001): 349–371.

Epilogue

While the chapters you have just read cover a broad range of topics related to delinquency, it is possible to conclude that there are two layers of delinquency—one is composed of the rare but high-profile media events that shock audiences and ignite controversy over the circumstances leading up to, and the resolution of, these crimes. For example, not long ago, members of a high-school football team drugged a 13-year-old girl and gang-raped her over a period of hours before dumping her unconscious body on her family's doorstep. In another state, a 17-year-old senior-class president stood outside his apartment as an acquaintance he had hired stabbed his mother to death.

Unfortunately, these types of news stories seem to form the basis of our perceptions about youthful offenders and their offenses, which are distorted images and statistically unlikely occurrences. One exacerbating factor is that unlike the past, where reporters had to be strictly factual and neutral, today's news personalities use terms like "horrendous," "devastating," and "brutal" when describing an alleged crime. The "colorized" versions of events that we are exposed to are subjective and emotional versions of actions that bias listeners and perhaps frighten them as well. The second factor that distorts the context of our view of delinquency is the exposure that we get to not only every sensational criminal event from 24-hour news stations and websites but also to the discussion surrounding it, and responses to it, via social media. Thus, angry, vengeful, and ill-informed opinions are circulated as truths and consumers of social media are likely to read disproportionate amounts of reactions to events rather than factual coverage of the events themselves.

Post-test: Factors Possibly Related to Delinquency

Factors	Amount and Nature of Influence on Delinquency
Poverty	
Mental Illness	
Low Education Level	
Drug/Alcohol Abuse	
Family Problems (fighting, divorce, criminal history)	
Personality/Self-Esteem	
Anger or Revenge	
Peer Pressure	
Bad Neighborhoods	
Poor Parenting	
Low Self-Control	
Other	

In contrast to these rare but sensational juvenile crimes, the second layer of offenses contains the routine but most common delinquent activities: truancy, shoplifting, drug abuse, simple assault, and disorderly conduct. These daily misdemeanors constitute the crimes that define majority of juvenile arrests every year. This is not material generally associated with "must-see" reality television but it best exemplifies the normal range of juvenile delinquency much like it has for decades in America.

So, now that we have completed the readings, it is time to revisit the original checklist we constructed at the beginning of this book. At this time, consider again each of the following factors and before looking at your previous answers, write down how influential, in the context of delinquency, you believe each variable to be.

It might be instructive to compare your comments from before and after you have processed the readings in this collection. Discuss these concepts with fellow classmates, family members, and associates at work. How different do your views seem from others and to what extent does knowing someone who was involved in delinquent activity shape your own perceptions?

About the Editors and Contributors

EDITORS

MICHAEL CAVANAUGH, Ph.D., is currently an assistant professor in the Department of Criminal Justice at the University of Houston-Downtown. Michael R. Cavanaugh received a Ph.D. in Criminal Justice from Sam Houston State University. He has published articles in a few notable journals including the *Journal of Quantitative Criminology, American Journal of Public Health, Journal of Offender Rehabilitation,* and the *Journal of Interpersonal Violence.* Additionally, he is the co-author of the book, *The Legal Rights of the Convicted,* 2nd edition (LFB Publishing, 2015).

MARILYN D. McSHANE, Ph.D., is currently professor of criminal justice at the University of Houston-Downtown. She and Frank Williams edited the previous Praeger series on juvenile justice, *Youth Violence and Delinquency* as well as the Sage *Encyclopedia of Juvenile Justice.* She and Dr. Williams are the authors of six editions of the text *Criminological Theory* as well as *A Thesis Resource Guide for Criminology and Criminal Justice* (Prentice Hall, 2008). She has published a number of articles about incarcerated juveniles as well as youth in community corrections. In addition, Dr. McShane has taught for the U.S. State Department's International Law Enforcement Academy in Roswell, New Mexico, and she has served on the Executive Board of the Academy of Criminal Justice Sciences several times.

CONTRIBUTORS

PETER J. BENEKOS, Ph.D., is professor of criminal justice at Mercyhurst University. He has conducted research and published in the areas of juvenile justice, corrections, and public policy. He is the coauthor with Alida V. Merlo and Dean John Champion of *The Juvenile Justice System: Delinquency, Processing, and the Law*, 8th edition (Pearson) and coauthor with Alida V. Merlo of *Crime Control, Politics, and Policy*, 2nd edition (Anderson), and the coeditor with Alida V. Merlo of *Controversies in Juvenile Justice and Delinquency*, 2nd edition (Anderson). Professor Benekos is a past president of the Northeastern Association of Criminal Justice Sciences.

BARBARA E. BLOOM, Ph.D., is a professor in the Department of Criminology and Criminal Justice Studies at Sonoma State University. Among her publications are several state and national studies: Modeling Gender-Specific Services in Juvenile Justice: Policy and Program Recommendations, Why Punish the Children? A Reappraisal of the Children of Incarcerated Mothers in America, and a National Institute of Corrections sponsored study, Female Offenders in the Community: An Analysis of Innovative Strategies and Programs. Recent publications include Gendered Justice: Addressing Female Offenders and Gender-Responsive Strategies: Research, Practice and Guiding Principles for Women Offenders. She is a past president of the Western Society of Criminology (WSC) and a recipient of the 2003 WSC Fellow Award for important contributions to the field of criminology. She is a recipient of the American Probation and Parole Association 2003 University of Cincinnati Award for the publication *Gender-Responsive Strategies: Research, Practice and Guiding Principles for Women Offenders.*

KENDRA BOWEN, Ph.D., is an assistant professor in the Department of Criminal Justice at Texas Christian University. She obtained her doctoral degree from the Indiana University of Pennsylvania in 2011. Her current research focuses on clergy sexual abuse and offender reentry. Additional research interests include SORN law compliance and unintended consequences, as well as decision making in violent situations. Her most recent publications appear in the *Western Criminology Review* and the *Criminal Justice Policy Review*.

RONALD BURNS, Ph.D., is professor of criminal justice, and chair of the Department of Criminal Justice at Texas Christian University. He is the author of eight books and various research manuscripts on topics including policing, white collar crime, and multiculturalism.

JANET EGUZOUWA graduated with an undergraduate degree in criminal justice from Sam Houston State University, in Huntsville, Texas. While studying at Sam Houston, she volunteered with the Walker County

Courthouse, as well as, a safe house for abused and battered women and children. The time spent with the women reignited her passion for criminal justice and social fairness. Janet went on to study at the University of Houston-Downtown, and sought a graduate degree in criminal justice. Her exiting project focused on Juvenile Justice Intervention Programs within the United States, with an emphasis on some of the more effective programs evaluated within the last 10 years. Her interests include past and present research on juvenile justice; specifically the implementation and enforcement of juvenile law and other notable programs. Janet plans to further her education in the near future if the opportunity presents itself. Currently, she is not working in the criminal justice field but hopes to start a career in the near future.

TRAQINA EMEKA, Ph.D., is associate professor of criminal justice at the University of Houston-Downtown. Her research interests include victimology, crime prevention, delinquency, and community corrections. She has published a number of articles in the areas of child abuse, victimology, juvenile recidivism, and community corrections and is the coauthor of *American Victimology* (LFB Scholarly) with Marilyn McShane.

STEPHANIE FAHY is a criminal justice research manager at ICF International in Fairfax, Virginia. Ms. Fahy has a decade of experience conducting research and evaluation on a variety of criminal justice research topics, including racial profiling and gangs; however, her primary area of research interest and expertise is human trafficking. She is currently co–principal investigator for a project that examines the child welfare responses to domestic minor sex trafficking victims. She has also managed several human trafficking projects and managed a national database of human trafficking investigations called the Human Trafficking Reporting System (HTRS). In addition to her professional work experience, Ms. Fahy is a Ph.D. candidate at Northeastern University. Her dissertation is focused on understanding how criminal justice officials in Massachusetts are responding to commercially sexually exploited children, specifically minors who are involved in prostitution, following the passage of a safe harbor law that is designed to shield prostituted youth from prosecution.

JUDITH HARRIS, Ph.D., is an assistant professor in the Department of Criminal Justice at the University of Houston Downtown (UHD). Dr. Judith A. Harris, received her Ph.D. from Texas Southern University in the Administration of Justice. Her research interests include jail reentry, the integration of service learning into established courses, and women on death row.

ANTONIO HERNANDEZ completed his master's degree in criminal justice at the University of Houston-Downtown (UH-D). He currently teaches as an adjunct professor with UH-D and is also a sergeant with the Harris County Constables' Office Precinct 1.

MING LI HSIEH is a doctoral candidate in criminal justice and criminology at Washington State University and is a senior research associate of the Washington State Institute for Criminal Justice. Her research includes an examination of gender gap trends, risk assessment instruments, crime control polices, and comparative policing. Ming-Li recently won the award for the outstanding student paper of the International Section of the ACJS and second place for the student paper for the Division of International Criminology of the ASC. She has articles published in *Criminal Justice Policy Review* and *International Criminal Justice Review*. She coauthored the book *Women in Criminal Justice* with Marilyn D. McShane.

ALIDA V. MERLO, Ph.D., is professor of criminology at Indiana University of Pennsylvania. Previously, she was a professor of criminal justice at Westfield State University in Massachusetts. Her research is in the areas of juvenile justice, women and law, and criminal justice policy. She is the coauthor (with Peter J. Benekos and Dean John Champion) of *The Juvenile Justice System: Delinquency, Processing, and the Law*, 8th edition, coauthor (with Peter J. Benekos) of *Crime Control, Politics & Policy*, 2nd edition, coeditor (with Peter J. Benekos) of *Controversies in Juvenile Justice and Delinquency*, 2nd edition; and coeditor (with Joycelyn M. Pollock) of *Women, Law & Social Control*, 2nd edition. She is a past president of the Academy of Criminal Justice Sciences. In 2014, she received the Outstanding Teacher Award from the College of Health and Human Services. In 2012, she was presented with the Academy of Criminal Justice Sciences Minority Mentor Award. Previously, she received the Academy's Fellow Award and Founder Award.

MARCOS MISIS, Ph.D., is an assistant professor of criminal justice at Northern Kentucky University. His research interests include criminological theory, drug addiction, and issues in policing, homeland security, and terrorism.

JOHN K. MOORADIAN, Ph.D., is associate professor and associate director of the School of Social Work at Michigan State University. He is a licensed master social worker and licensed marriage and family therapist. His research focuses on issues that affect oppressed and marginalized people, and on family relationships. He is author of *When Minority Exceeds Majority: Understanding and Addressing Disproportionate Minority Contact*.

ALEXANDRIA PECH did her undergraduate work at Sonoma State University in Psychology and Human Development and is currently a doctoral student in Family Studies and Human Development at the University of Arizona. Her research analyzes risk and protective factors in children of incarcerated parents to predict child developmental outcomes. Her research interests stem from her 21 years of personal experience as the daughter of an incarcerated father.

REBECCA PFEFFER, Ph.D., is an assistant professor in the Department of Criminal Justice at the University of Houston-Downtown. Dr. Pfeffer's research focuses generally on the victimization of vulnerable populations, including victims with special needs and victims of both human trafficking and hate crimes. Her current areas of interest includes public policies addressing prostitution, both in terms of the buying and selling of sex, and specifically investigates effective law enforcement responses to the problem of prostitution. As a research associate at Northeastern University's Center for Criminal Justice Policy Research, she managed two National Institute of Justice–funded studies about human trafficking: one about the barriers to the successful identification and prosecution of human trafficking cases in the United States, and one about the experiences of labor trafficking victims in this country.

CLETE SNELL, Ph.D., is currently professor of criminal justice at the University of Houston Downtown and obtained his Ph.D. from Sam Houston State University. He is the author of *Peddling Poison: The Tobacco Industry and Kids* (Praeger) and *Neighborhood Structure, Crime and Fear of Crime* (LFB Scholarly). Dr. Snell has been conducting program evaluations for the Harris County Courts over the past few years. He is a shameless Dallas Cowboys' fan.

MELANIE TAYLOR, Ph.D., is an assistant professor in the Department of Criminal Justice at the University of Nevada, Reno. She received a master's degree in criminal justice from the University of Nevada, Las Vegas and a doctorate in criminology and criminal justice from Arizona State University. Her current research interests are: abuses in correctional facilities, civil rights of inmates, juvenile detention, juvenile delinquency, victimology, and gender.

FRANK P. WILLIAMS III, Ph.D., is professor emeritus at the California State University-San Bernardino where he was chair for seven years. He has published a number of articles, research monographs, encyclopaedias, and books in areas ranging from criminological theory to correctional management. His recent works include *Statistical Concepts for Criminal Justice* *and Criminology* (Prentice Hall, 2008) and *Imagining Criminology* (Taylor & Francis, 1999), and he is coauthor of *Criminological Theory*, 5th edition (Prentice Hall, 2009), *A Thesis Resource Guide for Criminology and Criminal Justice* (Prentice Hall, 2008), and the three-volume edited set *Youth Violence and Delinquency: Monsters and Myths* (Praeger, 2008).

Index